Brancusi

Edward Steichen: **Brancusi in his studio,** 1925

Brancusi

A Study of the Sculpture
by Sidney Geist

Grossman Publishers New York 1968

for Daniel

Contents

Preface	iii
The life	1
The sculpture	11
Reflections	139
Appendixes	183
Notes	207
List of the sculptures	213
Bibliography	233
Index	237

Preface

Our understanding of the art of Brancusi up to the present has been based on impressionistic, biographically oriented criticism on the one hand, and fragmentary knowledge of the sculpture on the other; it has been prey to metaphysical interpretation from without and to all manner of doubt and imprecision from within. The disarray in which the œuvre is customarily presented has tended, besides, to disturb its clear design and to dissolve the relations between the whole and its parts.

This study aims to redress the lack of formal analysis which has been accorded Brancusi and to make more complete and exact the information which is indispensable to an understanding of the sculpture. Its principal feature is the examination of Brancusi's œuvre in temporal sequence.

In the case of Brancusi the establishment of such sequence is almost automatically revelatory. It reveals an artist of imposing intellectuality—a fact which has been suspected, hinted at, but not demonstrated; it reveals a body of work whose inner relations make it appear a tightly reasoned essay in the problems and problematics of sculpture. Temporal order here lays bare a series of intentions which is unique in sculptural history and a process of creation which is one of the monuments of the mind.

A logical Brancusi is introduced not to supplant the poet, but to illuminate a long effort in which a craft or science of sculpture was always intimately bound to the larger purposes of his art. Nor is it meant to efface the man. Although this study is essentially formal, I shall suggest a number of biographical relations between the artist and the sculpture which are new to the literature of this subject, and shall adduce biographical information whenever it is known to me and appears to influence the creation or the understanding of the sculpture. The sculptor's own words will be used whenever possible; the record here is not voluminous though perhaps greater than is generally known. I regret that there are a number of sources of information which I am not permitted to designate.

The central portion of this study is, then, a sequential examination of the sculpture of Constantin Brancusi. It is preceded by a biographical sketch and followed by a more general discussion of the works than a piece-by-piece scrutiny seemed to permit. There is here only a limited discussion of the drawings, and no mention of the stools, tables, doorway, tools, and other artifacts which Brancusi made in some number. The famous bases and pedestals are not examined and are discussed only enough to explain my neglect of them.

Only rarely have I permitted the surface of the exposition here to be broken by the scholarly cruxes that lie beneath it. These can be discerned in all their abundance in the "List of the sculptures." But their existence has made it impossible in many cases to extract significance from the sequence of the œuvre. I have been able to do so only to the degree that the present state of information seemed to permit.

This volume is intended for any interested reader. For scholars I have recorded my sources in the section, "Notes," where they are listed by page number. The notes in their turn refer for the most part to materials listed in the "Bibliography," which contains only works dealing with Brancusi to which this volume makes reference. Certain graphic and documentary materials are gathered in the "Appendixes," and these are noted in the text. Finally, there is a "List of the sculptures."

At the head of this list is a key to abbreviations used in this volume. The sculptures in the list are given the same numbers as the text illustrations, the object illustrated being the first work listed whenever there is more than one example. I designate as a *work* (a) any object of which there is a photograph, if the work is lost, (b) any state of a work if it differs radically from another state, (c) any plaster which exists in no other state, and (d) any unique work in stone, wood, or bronze. When there are several bronzes from a marble, and these are of the same form and size, I list them as one *work*. When similar bronzes vary significantly in size or form they are listed separately. My decisions as to significant variation for the purpose of this list are, necessarily, arbitrary. In any case I have tried to record all the *objects* in the sculptural œuvre, and their number in this volume is 248.

Brancusi made many plaster casts of his sculpture and in rare instances changed them slightly from the originals. While he listed a price for plaster casts in the Armory Show, it seems that eventually he did not sell any but used them for his own purposes, often as gifts. These casts are grouped after the list of the sculptures, as are a number of "lost" objects and objects concerning which there is some question.

The illustrations of the sculpture are in the scale of an inch to the foot, except for the monumental works at Tirgu Jiu, a few other works too large or too small to be presented at this scale, and works which are lost and exist only in photographs; the exceptions are marked in the captions with a plus or minus sign to indicate deviations from the scale, or with a question mark when the size is unknown. The four versions of the monumental plaster *Cock* are all in the same scale. The captions have been kept as brief as possible, fuller information being available under the same number in the list of the sculptures.

Precise knowledge of the works—of their actual number and variety—and reliable information concerning their dates (and hence their order) and their sizes has long been lacking; and the widespread scattering of the œuvre—from Oregon eastward to India—has made it difficult for students to examine it at first hand. To remedy this situation I have undertaken to see as many of the sculptures as possible, and have studied all but a few—between Chicago, Illinois, and Buzau, Rumania; of the 207 objects that are recorded in my list of the sculptures and that are in existence, I have seen eighty percent. I have read a great many Rumanian documents dealing with Brancusi, and have met and corresponded with a number of persons who were intimately associated with him. Though this is not primarily a scholarly work, it is based on a considerable amount of research; for in spite of the existence of other studies of Brancusi the dating of the works had to be investigated anew. But many questions remain, and where they exist I have placed a "?" beside the date; a smaller degree of doubt is expressed by a question mark in parentheses.

The most certain criterion of the date of a sculpture is the fact that a date is inscribed on it, and even in two or three such cases there is a margin of doubt. After this there are criteria of varying validity: inclusion in an exhibition, inclusion in a dated photograph, mention in a review or article, the testimony of the sculptor or other knowledgeable persons, and, in the absence of these, stylistic considerations. The last are the most untrustworthy; besides, it is unreasonable to start with a premise of "style" when it is the artist's style that we are trying to discover. When the date is not inscribed on a work and is not thoroughly doubtful to me. I have tried to make clear my reasons for the dating in the list of the sculptures. My intention is to treat the matter as demonstrable or not, rather than as a realm of undocumented "authority."

Although this list is longer and more exact and intelligible than any that has been published, it is nevertheless indebted to the previous work of Ionel Jianou, and I hope it will be of use to the future author of a *catalogue raisonné*.

Despite the claim of great inclusiveness, both in its data and illustrations, which this small volume makes, it is in many respects a first rather than a last word on its subject.

The placement of the sculptures in their chronological order, or what, in doubtful cases, I think this to be, opens issues which are not exhausted in this study.

The thoroughness of the presentation here of works prior to 1914 is most immediately indebted to the researches of Barbu Brezianu, an associate of the Institutul de Istoria Artei in Bucharest. Mr. Brezianu's exploration of Brancusi's early years and his discovery of any number of crucial documents have made it possible to reconstruct a period in Brancusi's life heretofore mysterious; it is a duty to point to his enterprising scholarship and a pleasure to acknowledge his generosity and cooperation. I wish to acknowledge, too, the usefulness of the studies of Mrs. Athena Tacha Spear of the Allen Memorial Art Museum, Oberlin College, and of her list of the Brancusi holdings of the Musée National d'Art Moderne, Paris.

In Bucharest I had the personal and scholarly assistance of Prof. George Oprescu and of the critic and art historian Petru Comarnescu. But my Rumanian friends and helpers in my research are many—Mircea Popescu, director of the Institutul de Istoria Artei; M. Maxy, director of the Muzeul de Arta R.S.R., Bucharest; Miss Nicol Bortes, director of the Muzeul de Arta of Craiova; Miss Elena Udriste, director of the Muzeul Raional of Tirgu Jiu; Dr. Balintescu, director of the State Archives in Craiova; Mrs. Cecilia Cutzescu-Storck; Mrs. Amelia Pavel; Florea Florescu; Vasile Dragutz; Mrs. Militza Patrascu; Adrian Petringenaru; Mrs. Tzuculescu and Miss Ciornea of the print room of the Biblioteca Academiei; Stefan Georgescu-Gorjan; Miss Irina Fortunescu; Peter Pandrea; Nicolae Sandulescu—and I thank them all. I wish to pay special homage to the writings and person of V. G. Paleolog, a great spirit and a great Brancusian.

I have had the kind assistance of Mme. M.-N. Pradel-de Grandry, formerly of the Musée National d'Art Moderne in Paris. Christian Zervos has given permission to publish many photographs. Mme. Denise Roché of Sèvres, was most generous with her time and precious documents. Andrew Forgas of Melbourne, Barnet Hodes of Chicago, Mrs. Jeanne Robert Foster of Schenectady, and Ben L. Reid of Mount Holyoke College were very helpful to me. Baroness Renée Frachon, who is at home on three continents, has been an informative and charming correspondent.

In New York I have benefited often from the assistance and knowledge of Dr. Louise Averill Svendsen of the Solomōn R. Guggenheim Museum. Miss Dorothy Miller, Alfred H. Barr, Jr., their assistants and the librarians of the Museum of Modern Art have been most kind and helpful. I wish to thank the following for their aid and forbearance: Mrs. Ernest Brummer, Miss Georgia O'Keeffe, Miss Jody Bradley, Miss Jane Wade, Marcel Duchamp, Meyer Schapiro, Mrs. Margarete Bieber, Bruce Barton, Mrs. Margaret Cucci, Mrs. Calvert Coggeshall, Harold Diamond, Miss Judith Irby, Thomas Dawson, Hans Noë and Norman Wiener. Seymour Hacker's bookshop was an invaluable library; Ralph and Hortense Carpentier put me up and put up with me during much of the writing of this book. I am most grateful to Hilton Kramer, who urged me to write about Brancusi, for reading the manuscript and making helpful suggestions. Edward Steichen generously gave permission to use his beautiful photograph as the frontispiece here.

In the end this book would have been impossible without the interest and patience of the art dealers and private persons who, like the many museum directors and curators in the United States and Europe, answered my questions and gave me access to their collections and permission to publish photographs of works in their possession. I thank them all for their help; their many names will be found in the list of the sculptures.

New York, 1967   SIDNEY GEIST

viii

Brancusi

The life

"My life," said Brancusi, "has been a succession of marvelous events."

Constantin Brancusi was born on February 19, 1876, in Rumania in the hamlet of Hobitza near Pestisani, district of Gorj, in the foothills of the Transylvanian Alps. His parents were peasants, small landholders; he had three half-brothers older than himself, besides two brothers and a sister. In this large family he felt an attachment only to his mother and sister, whose love alleviated the poverty and harshness of a back-country existence. Yet woodland and stream and flock had charms which were to have a lasting effect on his imagination, while the region's rigorous social code and ironic humor left their mark on his character.

Having run away from home twice before, Constantin left his family definitively when he was eleven years old. By this time he had manifested traits which were to be permanent: a strong will, a tendency to be alone, independence of action, intellectual curiosity, and the ability to learn quickly. In Tirgu Jiu he worked at menial tasks till in 1892 he went to Craiova.

Three years later he entered the School of Arts and Crafts, from which he was graduated with honors in 1898. He had excelled in woodworking and specialized in sculpture, receiving high grades in all subjects; his seriousness and application had been noteworthy too. At twenty-two, the oldest in his class, he wore a neat small beard, the only one in the class, and was short and compactly built. He had supported himself by working and with the help of a small grant that was locally administered; additional grants now enabled

1

him to go to Bucharest and enter the School of Fine Arts. Here he quickly distinguished himself, won several prizes, and, after completing three years of study, closed his career in Bucharest with a life-sized anatomy figure and a commissioned portrait of a pioneer of Rumanian medicine, having managed in the meanwhile to take a brief trip to Vienna. In spite of his seriousness he was a good companion. He had an excellent voice and was interested in native music, folklore, and arts, as well as in mathematics, biology, and physics.

In the middle of 1904, after a journey of over a year across Europe, most of it on foot, he arrived in Paris and the next year enrolled at the Ecole des Beaux-Arts in the studio of Antonin Mercié. He survived a period of financial difficulty by washing dishes, and by working and singing in a Rumanian church. He had, besides, a small grant that came from Rumania and the help of Rumanian friends in Paris; his skill at portraiture brought him a number of commissions. Then in 1906 he exhibited at the Salon d'Automne, earning the praise of Rodin. He eventually worked in Rodin's studio, but left after a short time, uttering his famous, "Nothing can grow in the shadow of the great trees."

A commission in 1907 to do a monument for a grave in Rumania led him to make *The Prayer*, a pivotal work which marked his rupture with Rodin's influence at the same time that it acknowledged his debt to the Master.

From then on he was on his own path. His person was impressive from the start, and his work was immediately appreciated. Encomiums from Paris appeared in the Rumanian press, and Clive Bell mentioned him in an early article. He exhibited outside of Paris at the phalanstery of the Abbaye de Créteil* in the summer of 1907. In Paris he was in con-

* A commune of artists, writers and a printer—A. Gleizes, R. Arcos, G. Duhamel, C. Vildrac, A. Mercereau, H.-M. Barzun, and L. Linard—who intended to offer the fruits of their labors directly to the masses without the intervention of the bourgeoisie. The Abbaye, 20 kilometers from Paris, existed from the fall of 1906 to early in 1908.

stant touch with a circle of Rumanian artists and writers. His relations with his native country were continuous; before the war he made two trips to Bucharest and was represented in nine exhibitions in Rumania* where his sculpture soon became a matter of contention and entered a number of collections, notably that of Victor N. Popp. Five works by Brancusi were displayed in the Armory Show in New York in 1913; several months later he showed three sculptures in London. In February 1914 he had five pieces in an important Cubist exhibition in Prague organized by Alexandre Mercereau. In March he showed eight works—in marble, wood and bronze—at Alfred Stieglitz's Gallery of the Photo-Secession in New York; this was his first one-man exhibition, and an early bond in a long relationship with American admirers and collectors.

Brancusi was a friend of Rousseau, Modigliani, Matisse, Léger, Apollinaire, Jacob, Picasso, González, Cocteau, Cendrars, Lipchitz, Pach, and many other of the artists and writers of the crowded period before the First World War. Late in 1912, when the Paris police covered up Epstein's carving on the Oscar Wilde memorial, Brancusi was part of a small band that accompanied Epstein on daily trips to the Père Lachaise cemetery to pull the tarpaulin off. With Ortiz de Zarate he carved a poem of Apollinaire's on Rousseau's gravestone.

In 1914 John Quinn† began collecting his sculpture, thus easing his financial situation considerably. He continued to work during the war, not having been accepted for military

* In 1907, 1908, 1909 (twice), 1910 (twice), 1912, 1913, and 1914. After the war, in 1920, 1924, 1927, 1928 (twice), and 1929.

† John Quinn (1870–1924), lawyer and student of modern Irish literature, amassed a great collection of modern art. He acquired 27 sculptures by Brancusi, two being gifts of the sculptor; in the years 1914–23 he spent almost $21,000 for these works.

service. For a time he lived outside of Paris; in 1918 he was in a hospital with a broken leg.

At the Salon des Artistes Indépendants of 1920 Brancusi's entry, *Princess X*, was withdrawn because of its alleged phallicism. A small scandal ensued; Brancusi vowed he would never exhibit his work in Paris again. But critical attention came to him in the form of an ever-growing number of articles on his work, both in Europe and the United States: *The Little Review* issued a Brancusi number in 1921, with many reproductions and an appreciation by Ezra Pound; in July 1924 *the transatlantic review* reproduced five drawings; and *This Quarter*, published in Paris, had a Brancusi number in 1925 that included forty-six illustrations, a group of Brancusi's aphorisms, and an Aesopian fable written by the sculptor.

Brancusi liked to sit at the cafés of Montparnasse, frequented the music halls and movie houses of the *quartier*, enjoyed parties, and kept abreast of events. In 1921 he impetuously went off to Corsica for two weeks with Raymond Radiguet, and in 1922 he took a young woman with him on a trip to Rumania. In 1923 he played a well-photographed game of golf with Henri Pierre Roché* and John Quinn while Erik Satie and Jeanne Foster, an American poet, gave advice. During a Fourteenth of July celebration he and Braque roamed the streets, their faces painted red, white, and blue in cubist patterns. By 1923 "the great little Brancusi seems in danger . . . of becoming part of the Paris stunt." When he relaxes on the Côte d'Azur he builds a "temple" out of driftwood.

At the "Festival Dada" in May 1920, Brancusi was in the audience, and his name was included in a tract called "Contre

* H. P. Roché (1879–1959) devoted an active life to painting, literature, and travel, and on occasion to journalism and government service. He arranged the first meeting between Picasso and Gertrude Stein, and was the author of *Jules et Jim*, 1953, the novel from which a film of the same name was made.

Cubisme, Contre Dadaisme," distributed in March 1922. He was at a famous meeting, the "Congrès de Paris," held at the Closerie des Lilas on February 17, 1922, to protest André Breton's actions against Tristan Tzara; he signed the resolution and wrote, besides, "In art there are no outsiders." In spite of this apparent generosity there is little record of his praise for other artists apart from the ancients, the long-deceased Rodin, and some Rumanian friends. Brancusi was named to the jury of the Prix Helena Rubinstein, created in 1937; the prize was given that year to Henri Laurens. For the announcement of an exhibition of paintings by an American artist, Anne Harvey, he wrote a few lines recommending the painter to the public.*

Early in 1926 Brancusi went to New York on the occasion of a small one-man show at the Wildenstein Galleries; a gala party in his honor was given by artists of the Penguin Club at an Italian restaurant on Union Square. He visited the city again later that year to attend his third one-man show, of 26 pieces, at the Brummer Gallery. His bronze *Bird in Space* involved him in a lengthy litigation with the U.S. Customs Office which claimed it was not a work of art but an object of manufacture. William Zorach and Jacob Epstein among others testified on his behalf, and toward the end of 1928 a decision was handed down in his favor. The affair was much reported in the press and made a public figure of the quiet and contemplative sculptor.

Brancusi seems to participate less in the artistic life of Paris from this point on. His supporter Quinn had died in 1924, his close friend Satie in 1925. The trips to America may have had a sobering effect, and he had passed his fiftieth birthday. When in Paris he stayed close to his studio, and his funda-

* "Annie[1] is a girl who asked no one's advice to do her painting. I entrust it to you just as it is, and assure you, my hand in the fire, that she will continue. Go and see, on my word. BRANCUSI.
"[1]I call her Annie for short, because when I first met her she was only about two feet high."

5

mental seriousness made an impression on all who knew him. In 1927 a critic wrote, "Brancusi leads the life of a sage (not of an ascetic)."

By the next year he had moved from no. 8 to no. 11 Impasse Ronsin, *"mes trois baraques,"* to which he later added two studios and where he was to live for thirty years (appendix 27).

His sculpture continued to enter American collections. Katherine S. Dreier, the founder of the Société Anonyme, acquired a number of works; the Arensbergs* bought nine pieces that had belonged to Quinn and six others from the artist, besides drawings, an arch and a bench.

In 1933 Brancusi met the dashing Maharajah of Indore, who bought three of his *Birds in Space* and discussed with him the design of a mausoleum and temple for meditation to be built in India. Later that year he sent a group of sculptures to New York for his second exhibition at the Brummer Gallery; the catalogue listed fifty-eight items and the shipment was reported to weigh twenty-four tons.

The next year Brancusi was commissioned to do an ensemble of works for the public park of Tirgu Jiu in Rumania, to commemorate the heroic resistance to the Germans there in the First World War. In the summer of 1937 he went to Tirgu Jiu to see to the execution of his designs, and in November, after witnessing the beginning of the assembly of the almost hundred-foot-high *Endless Column*, he left for India to visit the Maharajah of Indore.

Brancusi stayed at Indore for about a month without seeing the Maharajah, who was indisposed, and left without discussing the temple, which was never built. But he was enchanted by India, made friends with an elephant, and pol-

---

* Louise (d. 1953) and Walter Conrad (1879–1954) Arensberg gave their collection of over a thousand items to the Philadelphia Museum of Art in 1950. Mr. Arensberg was a poet and an active figure in the Bacon-Shakespeare controversy.

ished his two marble *Birds*. By the turn of the year he was in Egypt, making his way eventually to Holland and Rumania.

Before the Second World War he made a last trip to New York on the occasion of the tenth anniversary of the Museum of Modern Art, and paid a visit to the Art Institute of Chicago. Brancusi stayed in Paris during the difficult years of the war, creating only two new motifs, the *Turtles*, his last; in the following years he worked on a monumental version of *The Cock* of 1924 and on other plans for the public use of his sculpture. He received many visitors and entertained his friends, hardly ever leaving the Impasse Ronsin. In 1955 the Solomon R. Guggenheim Museum in New York mounted his largest one-man exhibition, which his infirmities prevented him from visiting. On the occasion of his eightieth birthday, the Muzeul de Arta in Bucharest held an exhibition of works of Brancusi from Rumanian collections.

He died on March 16, 1957, aged eighty-one, having willed his studio and its contents to the French nation; he had become a French citizen shortly before his death. He is buried in the Cimetière Montparnasse.

Brancusi's great public fame came after the Second World War, when he was working very little. In 1947 his friend V. G. Paleolog published, in Bucharest, a monograph on the sculpture which, unfortunately, did not achieve circulation; it might have turned the discussion of Brancusi away from a number of myths that grew up around him, of the peasant in Paris, of the solitary artist always in his studio, of the devotee of Milarepa, the Tibetan saint.

He lived in cities for seventy years, and moved in the world with grace and sophistication. He knew almost every famous figure in the arts of his day, and many of them had passed through his studio. Public personage though he was, he was a member of no artistic group, and his private life was a mystery even to his friends. Captivated by women and girls, he was also attractive to them. His conversation was witty and worldly; by turns he could be sweet and saintlike or sharply cutting. His ideas on politics and social relations were conservative, in contrast to the generosity of his real relations with people. He loved flowers in his studio; his cooking, often of Rumanian dishes, was famous. Once he had the means to do so, he indulged a taste for wine which, as time went on, became excessive; he smoked ceaselessly.* Though physically strong, he did not have a hardy constitution and was always liable to sickness. He read widely and curiously, and made a hobby of photography, taking excellent pictures of his works.

His last years, when his fame was greatest and his sculpture coveted on all sides, were personally difficult. Ill, a captive in the Impasse, unable to work, he suffered greatly. But visitors were impressed to the end by his sculpture and his studio, his presence, his speech and his silence.

Brancusi's was a long, interesting and productive life, but it does not appear to be a "succession of marvelous events." The changes of condition or fortune in Brancusi's life, the pattern of success, dissappointment, struggle, and achievement, do not seem markedly different from those of many another artist.

But there is an occasion which may hold the clue to Brancusi's language. Like other artists he had undertaken sculpture thinking that Art was a certain thing—a devotion, a skill, perhaps a magical kind of mimesis—and with the making of *The Prayer* it became what Picasso has called "something else." Later, speaking to H. P. Roché, he said that *The Kiss* (of Cimetière Montparnasse) was his "road to Damascus." On that road a revelation took place, and a revelation is surely a marvelous event in the mind.

Anyone with a poetic sense of existence might see his life as constantly marvelous, and Brancusi had such a sense. But it operated not in a mystic's passive reading of the world,

* And eventually had to be treated for nicotine poisoning.

but in an active transformation of the given, by art and thought. It was the habit of his imagination to lift the mundane events of his life to the level of the marvelous, to transform these events by the work of art, and to carry even this work to a further state in pursuit of its purest form and meaning.

The work of art and the occasions of illumination that accompanied it supplied Brancusi with the essential *"merveilles"* of his life.

The sculpture

The earliest works of Brancusi belong to legend, they disappear in time or dissolve into thin air: a snowman made by the boy; a violin, now lost, fashioned by the youth of wood from a crate, an instrument marvelously resonant.

A portrait made in Craiova is also lost, and none of Brancusi's studies at the Craiova School of Arts and Crafts seem to have survived; but a handful of faded photographs and four sculptures record his progress at the School of Fine Arts, Bucharest, and in the short period before his departure for Paris.

The first work of Brancusi which we can examine is a copy, preserved in a photograph, of a cast of the head of the *Laokoön;* the photograph itself was preserved by the sculptor.

1. Laokoön Study
(?)lost; clay; 1898

The *Laokoön Study* was executed as part of the entrance examination for the School of Fine Arts, and was an auspicious beginning: it is skillfully modeled in clay in a resourceful impressionist manner that loses none of the expressiveness and force of the original. This is no first effort; its manifest excellence supposes a certain experience. At the time, Brancusi was twenty-two and a half years old, an advanced age for a new student.

Several months later, again submitting to the plaster cast (appendix 1), Brancusi did a head of the Emperor Vitellius, "a bust after the antique" which was awarded an honorable mention. It is the earliest existing work by Brancusi, an admirable academic study that quietly commands attention.

2.

5.

3.

4.

The full form of the head and neck, rendered in a continuous skin of elevations and depressions, captures the character and easy articulation of the original. In the bronze, which was cast in 1964, we seem to see a Roman portrait whose modernity is betrayed only by a gentleness of approach or perhaps a sympathy for the subject. Less dramatic than the *Laokoön Study*, this head too is turned to its left in a gesture not without pathos.

The photographs of Brancusi's other school studies show a copy in relief of a *Mars Borghese* in the Louvre, an *Anatomy Study*, also in relief, of a nude man seen three-quarters from the rear, and a third relief, seen three-quarters from the front, of a nude man with his hands crossed on his chest that Brancusi submitted as part of his examination for the diploma. These works attest to the studiousness and skill of the young sculptor, to his absorption of an academic training that was excellent, and to the suppression of whatever temperament he may have had. The examination relief exhibits a realism that is expert and convincing; all, we note, are high reliefs.

Probably of this period, and done soon after he received his diploma—in 1902, when he was twenty-six—is the head of a young woman, *Character Study*, of which we have only the photograph. Here for the first time Brancusi goes beyond the academic confines: the head projects the somber inner life of the sitter, the face firmly modeled in spare curving surfaces, with a looser handling in the hair and the bosom. In this work we sense psychological truth and a penetration into character which the earlier studies had not led us to expect.

Of 1902 is a *Portrait of Ion Gorjan* which exists in plaster, never having been cast in bronze. The

7.

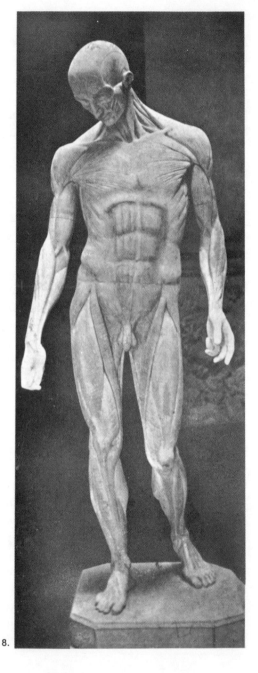

8.

model was a young businessman of Craiova and friend of the sculptor, and the portrait so resembles a contemporary photograph of the sitter as to suggest that Brancusi worked from it (appendix 2). The portrait was done, however, from nature with the help of calipers; if it gives the impression of being a little smaller than life-size, this is the result of Brancusi's proficiency in the use of the measuring instruments and a too great dependence on them.

7. Portrait of Ion Gorjan
20⅜"; plaster; 1902

Except for the finely executed mustache, the sculpture shows not the slightest stylistic quirk or flair. Brancusi's whole effort is in the service of truthfulness, although he misses the virile cast of the model. But he has avoided the pompous and the insipid—common dangers of this sculptural genre. The portrait seems to rest on a point of balance between respect for the sitter and respect for the sculptor. Like the *Vitelius* it holds the attention by the gentlest of means—quietness, self-containment, frankness and a grace of drawing and adjustment.

Pursuing researches undertaken at the academy, and after numerous dissections, Brancusi and his anatomy instructor, Prof. Dimitrie Gerota, make a life-size flayed figure, the *Ecorché*. Graceful, classic, instructive, it combines Brancusi's art and skill and science (though the first least), and this work is still studied in Rumania. Unusual in an *écorché* is the slight smile, a reminder of the classical *Antinous* (Museo Capitolino) on which is was based.

8. Écorché
69½"; plaster; 1902

Before leaving for Paris Brancusi was commissioned early in 1903 to do a bust of Gen. Dr. Carol Davila, one of the founders of modern medicine in Rumania. Working from a death mask, Brancusi modeled a head that suggests a rich interior life. It is something of an anomaly to see the fine face,

9.

10.

11.

12.

13.

14.

with its expression of gentle melancholy, caught between the sharply defined ornaments of a kepi and the medals on the chest, but Brancusi is not responsible for these. He apparently rendered them summarily; the authorities, dissatisfied, had them pointed up and Brancusi disowned the portrait, not acknowledging it as his till many years later. He never worked on the bronze, cast in 1912, which is probably why the surface is uncertain in places. A panache that adorned the kepi was broken off in the course of time.

Brancusi's journey to Paris and his initial period of hardship and adjustment prevented him from making sculpture for almost a year and a half. But by the end of 1905 he has a sizable production which shows a normal, unexceptional development of the talent he had manifested in Bucharest. His gift for portraiture leads him to embark on a series of busts of acquaintances done from life, and earns him several commissions which he executes from photographs, all fresher and easier in manner than his previous work. *Portrait of a Concierge, Portrait of Dr. Zaharie Samfirescu, Portrait of a Waiter, Portrait of a Restaurant Owner* and the *Portrait of Mrs. Victoria Vaschide* survive only in photographs. Here, as in other examples, it is not possible to guess, on stylistic grounds, which heads were done from nature; in fact, the *Portrait of Dr. Samfirescu* was done from a photograph. All impress us as truthful; each has a distinct personal inflection. These portrayals are devoid of histrionics or sculptural flamboyance. Nevertheless the volume of the bosom, often only a vague mass below the neck, is given great importance: a device intended to mitigate the head's appearance of having been severed from the body,

17

Brancusi's studio, 10 Place de la Bourse, 1905

and to suggest something of the nature of that body.

A photograph taken in Brancusi's first studio in Paris, at 10 Place de la Bourse, shows five portraits in relief and in the round, and a group of small studies. The ensemble is so curious and unexpected, especially what can be seen of the studies, that it would be impossible to identify it as from the hand of Brancusi if it did not include the first state of *Pride*, and if the photograph did not have his writing on the back. We note that like his studies in Bucharest, these are high reliefs, and they may well be Brancusi's first works in Paris. We see the sculptor still struggling with the problem of how to terminate the portrait.

The simplest solution is achieved in the head of a girl in bronze, entitled *Pride*, made while Bran-

15. Head of a Young
    Woman **relief**
    (?)lost; plaster; 1905(?)

16. Head of a Woman **relief**
    (?)lost; plaster; 1905(?)

17. Portrait of a Woman
    (?)lost; plaster; 1905

18. Portrait of a Man with
    a Goatee
    (?)lost; plaster; 1905

19. Study for Pride
    (?)lost; plaster; 1905

cusi was a student at the Ecole des Beaux-Arts, where he enrolled in the summer of 1905. The work includes only a small area below the throat, the fuller shoulders and bosom of the early state of the work having been diminished considerably; it is, then, Brancusi's most compact sculpture to date. *Pride* is exquisitely fashioned and exhibits a roundness and fullness of form new in Brancusi's work. He must have thought highly of it: it is the earliest of his Parisian pieces to be cast in bronze.

20. Pride
12"; bronze; 1905

It is also the first of his works to be named significantly; the title contributes a dimension to the sculpture that, in the case of the portrait, mere identification with a model did not supply. But what does this title signify? The image here is, after all, a pretty girl, quite frankly portrayed, who does not appear especially proud.

An explanation may be found in the photograph of Brancusi's studio at 10 Place de la Bourse. Directly in front of the *Study for Pride* we discern a small sculpture that shows a girl turning her head away from the embrace of a rather beastly man. The girl closely resembles the one in the larger sculpture, and we are led to suppose an episode of a repulsed kiss as the origin of the title *Pride*. For Brancusi the balm of art takes the sting out of personal pain.

At the Ecole des Beaux-Arts, Brancusi worked assiduously from the model, doing a new figure almost daily and destroying everything he made. Of these studies there remains only a photograph of a nude male figure in a sketchy state. The pose is that of Houdon's *Ecorché* (appendix 3); Brancusi has no trouble in capturing it. But it is curious that no photograph of any original figure study survives.

21. Study after Houdon
(?)lost; clay; 1905

19

22. Bust of a Boy
13¾"; bronze; 1906

23. Head of a Boy
8⅛"; plaster, black patina;
1906

24. Portrait of G. Lupescu
(?)lost; plaster; 1906

In *Bust of a Boy* Brancusi goes beyond his usual skill as a modeler. The veiled glance is a new kind of achievement, and a genuine mystery is generated by the inclination and gentle turning of the head. Brancusi, now impatient of symmetry, and as though to jar the mildness of the total image, cuts off the right shoulder; in the context of the naturalism of *Bust of a Boy*, this is the most daring gesture Brancusi has made up to this time.

For the first time he takes a cast of the head alone. It is in plaster, patinated black and mounted upright, and in this new position seems to wear a new expression. It is the most compact object Brancusi has made. It and the *Bust* are signs of an effort to go beyond the reportorial, to register the truth by new means or give the truth a special emphasis.

Portrait of G. Lupescu, a commission done from a photograph and apparently intended as a cemetery monument, is known only from a photograph. The amorphous chest is here larger than in any previous work, yet manages to be more than merely rhetorical.

Portrait of Nicolae Darascu is a work of great vivacity and immediacy; it has a marked unity of touch, the usual free handling of the chest having been communicated to the head and features of the face. The young painter (1883–1959), a friend of Brancusi's, is portrayed nude to the waist. Emboldened by his handling of *Bust of a Boy,* Brancusi cuts the right (painting) arm off near the bottom of the shoulder muscle.* The violence to anatomic

* Darascu: "With what am I going to paint, Costache?"
Brancusi: "With your eyes."

20

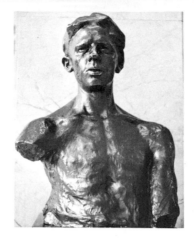

25. Portrait of Nicolae
Darascu
25¼"; bronze; 1906

wholeness imparts a charge of energy to the piece, and disturbs the profile in a way echoed by the treatment of the head: the projecting stub of the arm is on the same side as the free ear. The right and left halves of this portrait are strikingly different: the one agitated and open, the other calm and closed. This double character, together with the look of concentration, the parted lips, the intentionally unstructured modeling of the surface, creates a lifelikeness that seems to leap from the metal. The impression of this portrait shifts constantly as the light upon it or the spectator's point of view changes. Counter to the general naturalism are some daring flat planes on the right shoulder and on the nose. But this work is Rodinesque, all but expressionist, and Brancusi's most thoroughgoing essay in this manner.

Photographs of Brancusi's studio reveal a male portrait which has not been found and a study of the nude upper torso of a boy. The latter seems to be life-size; the head is upright; the right arm is cut off below the shoulder, the left arm is complete, the forearm crossing the body and resting on an indeterminate shape. The piece was probably destroyed; it is painfully, even banally, naturalistic. The truncation of the arm, a device so effective in the *Darascu*, serves no noteworthy purpose here.

Two works afford an unexpected glimpse of an emotional, even romantic, Brancusi. A small sketchy

26. Portrait of a Man
(?)lost; clay; 1906

27. Study of a Boy
(?)lost; clay; 1906

21

28. The Redskins
(?)lost; plaster; 1906

28a. The Adolescent
(?)lost; plaster; 1906

29. Repose
(?)lost; plaster; 1906

30. Torment
14¼"; bronze; 1906

piece called, literally, *The Redskins*, is an evidence of sympathy for the plight of the American Indian; it repeats the gesture of *Laokoön Study*, no. 1, and possibly the subject of the dark figure at the back of the studio at 10 Place de la Bourse, which may also be an Indian. More careful in its execution is *The Adolescent* in which a girl, dreaming with her eyes wide open, looks up to heaven. As in *Study of a Boy*, an arm is an important element in the design; the mass below, like portions of the hair in *Pride*, has been touched repeatedly by a sharp tool.

Repose appears to combine elements of *The Redskins* and *The Adolescent*, while abandoning the arm and supporting mass of the latter. But the theme, as we learn from the title and the closed eyes, has become more generalized.

The study of a half-figure of a boy, no. 27, appears in a version in bronze. Brancusi has pushed the head against the right shoulder, dispensed with the left hand, and refined the modeling and the surface. The formerly inexpressive attitude of the head is altered remarkably. We now see a young boy, wincing in pain, who has thrown his head behind his raised shoulder; he is younger and a more appealing type than the boy in the original study. The work is titled *Torment*, and justifiably; a dramatic sense, latent in the title *Pride*, quietly evident in *Bust of a Boy*, no. 22, and clear in *Darascu*, has been given full expression here. But unless Brancusi saw or recalled a child being beaten after he made the first study, the notion of *torment* was created in the studio as he strove to imbue a dull work with some significance.

Torment (in plaster) was exhibited in the spring of 1907 at the Société Nationale. The refinement of the modeling may well reflect an interest in Medardo Rosso. The Italian sculptor had been one of the founders of the Salon d'Automne; in the Salon's second appearance, the exhibition of the fall of 1906 where Brancusi showed three works, Rosso had exhibited a boy's head in wax, the magical *Ecce Puer* (appendix 4).

The theme of *Torment*, or the object itself, seems to engage Brancusi, for he reworks the plaster and casts it in bronze, making this the first of his sculptures which exist in more than one version. The new one is shorter than the first by the height of the left forearm and the inexplicable mass below it. The modeling is the same as that of the previous bronze, but the surface is quite tight, the fresher, more varied surface of the original having been smoothed over. This version concentrates the design.

31. Torment II
11½"; bronze; 1907

In passing from the clay study to the second bronze version, Brancusi has purified the image, changing its specific, personalized interest to one more general and universal. The relation of chunky body, slender neck, and round head is formally dramatic, but it is the poignancy of the attitude that makes this piece memorable. Its intensity is rescued from melodrama and rendered bearable to the viewer by the total absence of contortion in the child's features. The lack of emotion expressed on the face signalizes the distance between this piece and the *Laokoön Study*, and announces a sensibility that, since Manet, we recognize as modern.

A rapidly modeled *Head of a Boy* turned to its left appears to gather a number of Brancusi's characteristics at this juncture: compactness, intensity of expression, immediacy of facture. The tension

32. Head of a Boy
13½"; bronze; 1907

23

in the throat is more successfully realized than in any other head of Brancusi's. The subject here resembles the boy in *Torment*, but with its pertness and nobility, and its questioning glance, it might serve as an imagined portrait of the artist as a boy. Brancusi made three casts of the head, the greatest number so far.

The beginning of 1907 is a critical moment for Brancusi. He is thirty-one years old; he must leave the Ecole des Beaux-Arts because of his age; he is, in any event, dissatisfied with Mercié, his professor of sculpture; he has difficulties in working from the nude model. But he continues to model the head with his usual success.

Portrait of a Young Woman is a careful study of a personage with Oriental features who may have been associated with the Cambodian dancers that Rodin drew. In spite of the realism of the face, the hair is modeled in a tentative fashion, the change of color and texture seeming to raise a problem.

Brancusi carves a head in stone, possibly from the portrait, no. 33. It is worked, not with flat and toothed chisels, which are rather intellectual and tend to dig into the stone, but with a "point" used gently—pecking, in fact, at the material. The method keeps the image unified, preventing sharp definition of forms. The moody head has no neck and rests on its chin, the face emerging impressionistically from the roughly cut mass of hair and covered, like it, with toolmarks.

In a lost portrait of a young unknown woman the sculptor abandons his habitually elaborate treatment of the bosom for a simple, formal design from which the head rises gracefully.

Brancusi assists Rodin, but leaves after a short while. On April 18, he gets a 7,000 franc commis-

33. Portrait of a young Woman (?)lost; plaster; 1907?

34. Head of a Girl (?)lost; stone; 1907

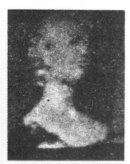

35. Portrait of a Woman (?)lost; plaster; 1907(?)

36. The Prayer
43⅞; bronze; 1907

sion for a monument for the grave of Petre Stanescu in Buzau, Rumania: a portrait and a figure.
With a 500 franc advance he takes a new studio
and sets to work. In April he shows four sculptures
at the salon of the Société Nationale.

Yet, by the end of 1909 he will show only three
more pieces in the salons of Paris. The monument
for Buzau (appendix 4a) occupies him, and having broken with Rodin he is determined to find his
own path. His production is small in the years
1908 and 1909—he is ill much of the time and takes
a trip to Rumania—but each step is important.

At a time when Brancusi is unhappy about his
progress in figure study, he sets out to do a figure
for the Stanescu monument. It is of a nude young
woman kneeling with the left leg somewhat in advance, the body leaning forward, the head inclined
further, the arms over the chest in a gesture of
crossing oneself. The mood of the sculpture is seri-

25

ous and elegiac; here is a femininity from which the erotic is absent. The breasts are not visible, the only sensual note being a fullness in the thighs. The face is impersonal, the fingers of the right hand are not delineated, the left arm is cut off above the elbow. The rough surface and clear shapes avoid imitation of skin and flesh; the surface itself is a marvel of sensitivity and variety, "felt" at every moment (appendix 5).

The sculptor has subtly altered the anatomical truth (if this creature were to stand erect, its proportions would be most unnatural), and while these forms still compose a female figure, they insist on their role in a more purely sculptural conception. They are connected in a serial progression, their axes clearly changing direction at several points. The composition is grasped in a glance. The left arm is cut off in order to eliminate an unwanted axis, the right arm is pressed close to the body, its gesture giving a fuller content to the compact torso while gently breaking its profile and supplanting the breasts. The attitude of the figure is poised between rest and tension. The smooth profile on the back contains, as within a shell, the smaller elements of the front as though to symbolize a relation between public dignity and private emotion. The impersonal, overhanging head, whose gaze is frankly on the ground, is a tactful, poetic innovation on a theme of mortuary sculpture that is usually banal; at the same time that this young female figure shuns the erotic, it is bent in an expression of grief that escapes the morbid. *The Prayer* speaks in a calm quiet language of forms.

Begun in 1907, not yet finished toward the end of 1909, it was exhibited in Paris in March 1910, probably in plaster. It is altogether possible that the

piece changed but little after it was begun; at any rate we may imagine it as the presiding spirit of Brancusi's studio for several years.

The *Portrait of Petre Stanescu* was done mainly from photographs, though the subject's brother posed for Brancusi. It is modeled with a bold touch in large pellets of clay that leave a broken surface (appendix 6). But while the skin of this sculpture is rough and scored, the form is large and firm. Like *The Prayer*, this portrait avoids the rendering of flesh and the naturalistic surface effects of earlier work; it shows Brancusi not so much modeling as shaping and structuring, and benefiting from the classic structure of the lost portrait, no. 35. At the same time that we have here a clear progression of forms, Brancusi escapes the symmetry inherent in the inevitable design by an extraordinary distortion of the chest, especially at the rear, and by the unusual angle at which the neck progresses from it. In spite of being on a very high pedestal, the piece is visible and various from all angles. It is Brancusi's most forceful portrait.

At a crucial point in his career *The Prayer* and the *Stanescu* give Brancusi new confidence in his

37. Portrait of Petre Stanescu
30¼"; bronze; 1907

38. Head of a Girl
(?)lost; stone; 1907

39. The Kiss
11"; stone; 1907

powers. Emboldened by his recent efforts, inspired perhaps by his model, he carves an asymmetrical *Head of a Girl* which he labels, "First direct stone, 190—." It is a nonnaturalistic work whose forms are invented rather than copied. They seem, moreover, to develop from the carving process, from a varied sense of the shaping, cutting and chipping possible in the stony medium. A remarkable liveliness of expression results from its left eye having been incised over a previous carving of the eye; surely this was a head Modigliani saw in 1909, when his friendship with Brancusi began. With its flat nose, "drawn" eyes, stylized hair, and a force of personality emerging from its compact stoniness, it is a work of absolute originality.

The Kiss continues Brancusi's explorations in stone. It marks a great step forward, unpredicated by anything done up to this point except *Head of a Girl,* no. 38, than which it is more daring in conception at the same time that it is more delicately carved. Clearly a modern work, it has that timelessness, simplicity and autonomy which Brancusi and his young contemporaries sought.

Carved in a mass of almost cubical dimensions, two lovers embrace. They are eye to eye, their lips mingle, the breasts of the woman encroach gently on the form of the man. Her hair is wavy and falls down her back, while the man's is short and straight. In this stately, tender image of love, every element is thematic. The unity of the bodies is reinforced by the more distinct modeling of the paired arms. If there is a problem here, it lies in the round, rope-like *separable* character of the arms which violates the continuity of the stony matter. But the musically ordered sizes animate the difficult blockiness of the mass, the composition focusing inevitably on

28

the details of the faces sheltered under the arch of the hair.

In spite of the clear stylization Brancusi has managed to invest the piece with a force of sentiment surprising in so "stony" a work, and his sensitive chisel has created a number of touching details.

One of these is the fact that the man's eyes appear dark because they bulge slightly, while the woman's seem light because they are shallow. We note too that, at the meeting of the brows, the hair of the man and woman does not exactly design an arch. The man's hair falls over his brow, much as Brancusi wore it in 1904 (appendix 7). The line of the hair starts at a higher point on the woman, giving her a somewhat longer face than the man, and making her appear slightly taller (and Brancusi was short). It is reasonable to speculate that this carving, in contrast to the little work standing in front of *Study for Pride*, no. 19, celebrates a consummated kiss. If it does, we must conclude that what seems to be a set of formal variations has a biographical origin.

The head of *Wisdom of the Earth* has an affinity with the portrait, no. 33; but the title, the attitude of the arms under the breasts, the symmetry of the pose, the simplicity of the forms, all strike a chord of the primitive and earthy. Seated on the ground, looking straight ahead, this personage is an image of self-containment. In spite of the virtual intricacy of the forms, the actual stony matter is continuous (as it threatened not to be in *The Kiss*); but the compact organization causes a problem at the places where breast and arm and hand meet: the design is soft and indecisive. The piece has two other questionable features: the shelf of the feet projecting dangerously from the mass behind it, and the re-

40. The Wisdom of the Earth
19⅞"; stone; 1907

29

41. Double Caryatid
29½"; stone; 1908(?)

42. Head of a Girl
(?)lost; stone; 1908

ceptaclelike space captured between the knees and the body, always a troublesome motif in sculpture. Yet in spite of these difficulties and perhaps *because* of the general softness of the forms, this figure gains a force—a force of gentleness.

Double Caryatid is a curious object in the Brancusi œuvre. As against the orderliness and decisiveness of his previous work, this piece looks as though the stone had been attacked without plan, the artist making his way intuitively. It is the nearest thing to that contradiction in terms, action carving; no other work of Brancusi's shows so much "unfinished" stone. Across the rough stone Brancusi has worked the file, creating smooth areas that cause the rough ones to appear "left over." Whereas stone is usually smoothed or polished on the outer or easily accessible surfaces, *Double Caryatid* has smooth surfaces in the areas between the figures, where we find an altogether unexpected, long, narrow opening. The smoothing of outer surfaces simulates natural effects; Brancusi's labor emphasizes human decision and artifice.

Double Caryatid is a work of preciosity and playfulness, mimicking, in its artful gaucherie, some unfinished Gallo-Roman carving. The one ogreish face is not at all frightening; the gesture of the arms is that of the questionable *Ancient Figure* (appendix 8).

Dissatisfied, it seems, with the earlier *Head of a Girl*, no. 34, Brancusi recarves it, smoothing the surface somewhat and dividing the mass clearly into face, hair, ears, and neck. The sharp separation of parts, in the small scope of a head, marks a new departure.

Having exhausted for the time being, apparently, the possibilities of a carving mode, Brancusi makes

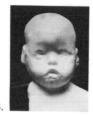

43.   44.

43. Head of a Girl
(?)lost; marble; 1908(?)

44. Child's Head
(?)lost; marble; 1908(?)

a realistic *Head of a Girl* which he designates, "first work in marble." In spite of its realism, the summary cutting of the hair and the disturbing expression of the face relate it to *Double Caryatid*. But while the latter is a work of fantasy, *Head of a Girl* is an exercise in pathology, unique in Brancusi's œuvre. Carved at the same moment is a bust of a full-cheeked baby, a somber representation of infancy. The heads are compact masses, firmly fashioned except for the eyes, which have a broken surface.

An ambitious carving in a porous white stone is a full *Bust of a Child* whose design is much like that of *Bust of a Boy*, no. 23; it has disappeared.

45. Bust of a Child
(?)lost; stone; 1906 (?)

Sleep is a faithful copy of *Repose*, no. 29, and shows differences enforced by the new tools and material. The profile of the total shape is less adventurous than that of *Repose* and is probably intended to emphasize the angle and long axis of the head; but the shelf of stone in front of the face is very deep. Only the left side of the face emerges clearly from the roughly cut surrounding marble. The contrast between smooth and unfinished surfaces and the suggestiveness of the subject mark this work as done under the sign of Rodin. The naturalism of the rendering lacks distinction, but it is rescued by the tasteful overall handling.

46. Sleep
10¼" h.; marble; 1908

Sleeping Child, in bronze, is a wispy effort, as charming as it is fragmentary. It can rest in two positions, flat on its unmodeled right side, or at an angle on the cheek and chin.

A small carving, seemingly copied from no. 47, is also unworked on the right side, though otherwise complete. But the charm of the original is lost

47. Sleeping Child
6¼" l.; bronze; 1908

48. Sleeping Child
6½" l.; marble; 1908(?)

31

49. Child's Head
9⅞" l.; marble; 1908(?)

50. Sleeping Child
6⅞" l.; marble; 1908?

51. Torso
9⅝"; marble; 1909

52. Naiade(?)
11¾"; limestone; 1909?

in the literal translation. A large roundish *Child's Head*, in marble, is an unpromising beginning, and was scored by the sculptor.

Sleeping Child in marble, about the same size as the bronze, no. 47, recovers its charm. It is fully worked on both sides, and symmetrical. This is the head striving to be an independent object: an ambition at odds with its naturalism.

Torso, a carving in a fragment of marble, is a small work extracted, as it were, from the central section of *The Prayer*, no. 36. It shows the left side of the stomach and the left leg and hip, all smoothly carved, fully realized from *one* moment of vision. A change of viewpoint shows that the back of the figure is only sketchily indicated: the flattish surface that joins the back to the stomach is, like the top, of rough stone. This curious effort was probably intended as a fragment more radical than any of Rodin's, lacking, as it does, any reasonable anatomical boundaries or definition of its representation. An object that shifts from utmost clarity to ambiguity, it remains a sensuous invitation to the right hand.

Naiade (a putative title) in marble is more realistic than no. 38 and is probably another portrayal of its model. In spite of the clearly structured nose, the work has a naive inflection. The poet Apollinaire owned the sculpture and it has a simplicity very like that of the portraits of Apollinaire, Picasso, Fernande Olivier, and Marie Laurencin in Laurencin's painting, *Group of Artists*, of 1908; the rimmed eyes, in fact, are similar to those of Picasso in the painting (appendix 9). The sculpture is a fusion of the classical sentiment of the recent works in marble and the "stony" quality of the earlier limestone carvings.

32

53.

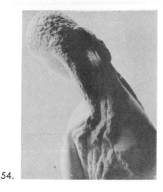

54.

53. Study of Renée
(?)destroyed; clay; 1909?

A study in clay, of a young Frenchwoman whose features beguiled Brancusi for a long time, reveals something of his manner of working. The large planes of the face are struck off firmly and intelligently, a wire cutting tool having gone over some areas modeled by the hand. The eyes are worked in a tentative fashion, the lower lip is in the process of being studied, the shock of hair piled on the head is in a rather amorphous state. Incomplete as it is, this study has a clear structure and a quiet intensity. Like others of the same model, it was destroyed.

Brancusi's most ambitious carving so far is a life-sized marble bust, *Woman Looking into a Mirror*. The head is inclined forward almost as strongly as that of *The Prayer*, but the form and features have a fluid drawing that signalizes a new sophistication. A right arm and hand are pressed against the bosom; there is no left shoulder or arm. While the parts designating skin are smoothly finished, the hair is roughly cut. There is much of it—on the head, knotted at the nape of the neck, and falling in cascades down the back and over the left breast —and the too artful contrast of smooth skin and ubiquitous, textured hair supplies us with a reason for Brancusi's impatience with this piece. For he decides to carve into it.

Baroness R. F. (Renée Frachon) derives from the clay study, no. 53. In the carving the character of the features has been intensified; these are now not only physiognomic indications but motifs as well. The long, firmly modeled nose has become a straight sharp ridge, and the arched eyebrows have

54. Woman Looking into a Mirror
(?)recarved; marble; 1909?

55. Baroness R.F.
(?)size unknown; stone; 1910

33

been daringly accentuated. The projecting lower lip has been suppressed and lies close to the general plane of the face. The mouth and the eyes, the more mobile parts of the face, are carved in a more tentative fashion than the rest; the sharp peak of the left side of the upper lip, a seemingly accidental note in the clay study, has been retained. Indeed Brancusi has found a way of translating into carving some of the extemporaneous results of modeling. Every element here is marked by the same sophistication that appears in *Woman Looking into a Mirror;* but the mass of hair on the brow continues to be troublesome, now a disturbing mop which looks quite detachable. Oddly enough, the design of the mask and coiffure has a remarkable resemblance to a self-portrait of Marie Laurencin (appendix 9).

Sleeping Muse, which had the same model as *Baroness R. F.,* shows some important differences from it. The chignon on the forehead has been moved to the back of the head; at the front, the hair continues the sweep of the brow without a change of plane; the neck is short, ending well above the level of the chin at the nape; the ridge of the nose is the chief motif that counters the general curvature of the head.

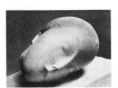

56. Sleeping Muse
11½" l.; marble; 1910

The facial features compose a formal declension as brow converges to nose, which drops to upper lip, itself separated from the slight elevation of the lower lip by a shallow, open groove; between cheek and brow the eyes are a gentle modulation governed by the large tapering ovoid of the head. The skin of form is broken only in the neighborhood of the ear, which rises sharply; in a gentle overlapping of forms, the hair seems to pass over the cheekbone. In short, the content of the human head is developed under a continuous, moving surface—an excellent solution to the problem of registering the blond, transparent beauty of the model.

An organic, vital quality in the stone *Baroness R. F.* has been rendered more absolute in the colder marble; the effect is of a calm, slightly asymmetrical Hellenism. It is possible that Brancusi had been influenced by the sculpture of Elie Nadelman, who held his first exhibition in Paris in April 1909; a bronze head by Nadelman, long considered lost but recently brought to light, shows a treatment of the mass of the head and of its parts (except for the mouth and chin) which appears in the carving (appendix 10). However that may be, *Sleeping Muse* reveals Brancusi in a new mood—sweet, serene, formal, detached, with an echo of Greek perfection.

In closing the eyes, suppressing the personality and concentrating on the ovoid of the head without neck, Brancusi has abstracted his subject and pitched the design exactly to the point where it is an *object* that yet has human resonance. The image is at once close enough to the human and just enough removed, so that *Sleeping Muse* miraculously avoids the appearance of a severed head and gains independent existence. Brancusi made several casts of this piece in bronze, working a great deal on both the metal and the intermediate plaster, and the bronzes display much variety in size and surface treatment.

57. Sleeping Muse
11″ l.; bronze; 1910

He carves a *Narcissus* in alabaster. The work, now lost, shows a round compact head on a strong, arched neck supported below by the dangerously thin shelf of the right shoulder. The attitude of the head, forward-leaning and downward-gazing, is one we have seen many times, but the emphatic,

58. Narcissus
(?)lost; alabaster?; 1910(?)

35

59. The Kiss
35¼"; stone; 1910

bulging eyes introduce a neglected motif, the round eyeball, for which Brancusi has found a dramatic pretext.

At Cimetière Montparnasse in Paris is a tall version of *The Kiss*.* The attitude is the same as in the smaller work, but here the figures are complete; the two bodies touch for their entire length and the legs of the woman embrace those of the man. To arrive at this design Brancusi has added to the early version the motif of the lower part of *Wisdom of the Earth,* doubled in order to accommodate two figures. This *combining* of motifs from distinct works is a new procedure, unlike the *development* of earlier forms which has been Brancusi's usual method. It is a procedure much used by Rodin, resulting in his case in dazzling *tours de force* which defy reason. Brancusi's *Kiss* is a *tour de force* of reasonableness, his own work reflecting upon itself fruitfully and intelligently.

This columnar *Kiss* is more noble, less intimate, than the smaller version. It accomplishes the weaving of forms without destroying the integrity of the stone; indeed the continuity of the stiff stony surface in spite of the multiplicity of forms marks an advance here over the first *Kiss* and *Wisdom of the Earth;* we note that at the bottom of the piece Brancusi has accomplished the progression in depth of thigh, foot, and foot, while avoiding an appearance of layers of stone. The composition is conceptual enough to be transmitted over the telephone; it is rescued from sheer design by charming nuances in drawing, and in the touch of hand and chisel.

* The sculpture, made before the middle of 1910, was later placed on the grave of Tatiana Rachewsky, who died Dec. 5 and was buried Dec. 12, 1910.

Frank, pagan and chaste, this image of two figures locked in an embrace is a permanent expression of the unity of love, which Plato called "the
desire and pursuit of the whole."

Enchanted by a Hungarian artist, Margit Pogany, whom he sees in a *pension* in Paris where he
occasionally takes his meals, Brancusi carves a portrait in marble from memory. The spherical head
is balanced on a short curving neck; there is a snail-
like chignon at the back. The primitivism of *The
Kiss* and *Wisdom of the Earth*, the vitalism of *Head
of a Girl*, no. 38, and the naiveté of the so-called
Naiade, no. 52, are all absent here. This little head
reveals a new, lean geometric quality, an interest in
curved rather than flat construction (as in the
Montparnasse *Kiss*), and a facial detail that stamps
it as a development of *Narcissus*, no. 58. The large,
slightly bulging eyes—Mlle. Pogany saw it as "all
eyes"—are defined by a series of precisely curved
planes and edges; between them rises a fin of a nose.
A venture in absolute design, the piece is saved
from being a mere *exercise de style* by the slit of
mouth, which alone seems to carry the burden of
personality. Brancusi exhibits it as *Danaïde*.
Pasarea Maiastra is a Rumanian title and means
both "master bird" and "magical bird." It refers to
an episode in Rumanian folklore, recounted in the

60. Danaïde
11⅛", reworked; marble;
1910(?)

37

following words by Brancusi: "Prince Charming was in search of Ilena Cosinzene. The master bird is the bird that spoke and showed the way to Prince Charming." The sculpture is a sleek symmetrical stylization of an erect bird in white marble; from the large ovoid of the body rises a long sinuous neck that curves forward to a head whose beak is open; the eyes are hemispherical depressions; the tail is a flattish tapering mass; joined to it and the body is a square column that represents the legs. The dramatic difference in size between the body and the other parts, and the energy of the neck as against the geometry of the rest, save this piece from being an exercise in simplification. Although only twenty-two inches tall, it rises to over seven feet, mounted on a base that includes *Double Caryatid*, no. 41, and two blocks of stone (appendix 12).

Pasarea Maiastra is a design that results from the intersection of two views—a front, and a side which is repeated in reverse—interpreted by flat and curving planes. The back is the formal product of these views; a large curving surface, it tells little of what is happening at the front and nothing of the side. Labor and information are arranged in a strict hierarchy: the greatest amount is concentrated on the front, less on the sides, and the least on the back. This strictness is something like that of *The Kiss*, but with the curving system there is greater variety—achieved by a greater expenditure of effort. The sculpture is a clear sign that Brancusi, while wishing to leave the planar realm of *The Kiss*, seeks another that is equally ordered and principled, and not governed by inspiration or chance.

Another *head as object* occupies Brancusi in 1911, the small marble *Prometheus*, in which the

61. Pasarea Maiastra
22⅛"; marble; 1910

38

rather spherical head falls back and to the right in a
gesture of pain which Brancusi has used before.
Squarish protruding ears break the smooth transition from head to neck, while the features of the
face are revealed by barely perceptible changes on
the surface. In the polished bronze they are more
visible than in the duller marble, but in neither case
does this piece have great expressive force. Formally, the compact head is a reflection of the head
of *Narcissus*, but *Danaïde* laid on its side produces
its composition or attitude.

62. Prometheus
7″ l.; marble; 1911

While *Sleeping Muse* is the head become an
ovoid, *Prometheus* is a precious orb endowed with
a suggestion of humanity and a tenuous poignancy.
Surprisingly, it had a human model, a Rumanian
boy, now a doctor, whom it still resembles.

63. Prometheus
7″ l.; pol. bronze; 1911

In the same year Brancusi carves a portrait of
George Farquhar, the infant son of an American
businessman and his Rumanian wife. It is in marble
and shows a child sleeping with its head on the
right side and its clenched fists against the body.
The boldly carved head is very like no. 47, although
it is larger; and in fact *Portrait of George* looks
like a copy of no. 47 with a chest and arms added.
The naturalism of the head, the hands in a different
style of representation, and the not quite convincing neck suggest that this work is composite. Especially when seen from above, it is a touching
rendition of a sleeping child.

64. Portrait of George
9¼″; marble; 1911

It appears that having made a sharp separation
between the little fists and the arms, Brancusi is
compelled to make other such distinctions for the
sake of unity. As a result this work has the curious
feature of a deep groove all around the face, between the arms and between the left arm and the
chest. The exposed portion of the chest thus ap-

pears designed rather than merely "left over." In using this device Brancusi seizes the familiar image for art as against the claims of nature; and he shows again, as in *Head of a Girl*, no. 42, the need to make sharp distinctions between elements.

A third *Kiss* makes its appearance, its proportions less massive than the first, less columnar than the second. The arms and tapering, petallike hands are in only slight relief, and, in each case, lie on the same plane. The heads are now quite four-square, and the piece is blocklike and tight in its transitions. The eyes have become a raised design of opposed semicircles where they were formerly incised and gently rounded. Altogether *The Kiss III* loses the immediacy of the earlier versions as it moves toward pure design. The only relaxation of the rigorous stylization is in the relatively deep groove at the meeting of the bodies, which at this point are modeled more tenderly and suggestively than before.

It would seem that Brancusi decides to compose by addition, repeating the practice initiated in *Portrait of George*. For the head of *A Muse* is the same as *Sleeping Muse*, upright now and a fraction smaller. The knotted mass of *Portrait of George* is opened up into a relatively frontal organization in which four clear shapes—head, arm, neck, bosom —happily create a human presence. These forms blend the organic and the geometric, and they pre-

sent a small gamut of kinds of joinery, inner modulation, and surface treatment. The bulging neck is
a startling invention, seeming to move across even
as it moves upward and forward; the arm is placed
where it stiffens the design and strengthens the
stony material.

66. A Muse
17½"; marble; 1912

A Muse shows Brancusi at a height of invention
and poetry; it is a work of cool untroubled beauty
that takes full advantage of its precious material to
create a vision of Woman as Inspiration. Though
the head faces forward, the gaze is not outward; we
look at *A Muse*, it does not look at us.

The sculpture is very carefully named, the title
in French—*Une Muse*—implying "one muse." Since
carving *Sleeping Muse* or *The Sleeping Muse*,
Brancusi has been inspired by another muse. She is
the painter, Margit Pogany (1879–1964), who has
been studying in Paris.

In December 1910 and January 1911 Brancusi did
a number of studies in clay directly from Mlle.
Pogany. The marble, completed in 1912, shows the
same accumulation of elements that resulted in *A
Muse*. Brancusi has taken the *Danaïde* and added
arms and a portion of the right shoulder; the short
neck has become long and sinuous, the chignon at
the back more elaborate. The relative frontality of
A Muse is here succeeded by a twisting composition, as the shoulder, head, and curving neck envelop the arms. *Mlle. Pogany* is a constantly
changing image; it takes longer simply to see this
sculpture than any that Brancusi has created so far.

67. Mlle. Pogany
17½"; marble; 1912

The complication of the piece is not without its
troubles. The space at the meeting of head, neck
and hands is dangerously deep, and Brancusi's tendency to design each element distinctly makes their
joinery difficult. Ultimately he manages to keep

69.

the handsomely fashioned, sharply differentiated shapes from flying apart.

Brancusi's treatment of "depth" here differs from his handling of *A Muse*. The head of the latter delivers the sense of inner forces and content by a modulated surface; the head of *Mlle. Pogany* implies an interior by the rimmed, bulging eyes and the deep groove of the mouth.

A brief memoir by Mlle. Pogany gives us an insight into Brancusi's working method, and a photograph and a self-portrait painted in 1913, before she saw Brancusi's sculpture, permit us to see something of the workings of his imagination (appendix 11). He has emphasized her salient features: the fine, slightly curving nose, the round face, the small mouth and large eyes that reportedly lighted up when her interest was aroused, and a characteristic gesture of her arm. Brancusi's portrait was the result of repeated effort, distilled by memory and sustained, it appears, by a personal sentiment.

Of 1912 is a marble *Torso*, similar to no. 51 even to the edges along the top, though the piece is a third again as large. The profile of the leg, complete on both sides in the smaller version, is here broken at the front, making the work even more fragmentary and adding a new ambiguity.

In a second version of the standing bird the neck is much shorter and has only a slight forward

68. Torso II
12¼"; marble; 1912

69. Bird
23¾"; marble; 1912(?)

42

70a. Maiastra
21¾″; bronze; 1912(?)

movement, the tail is thicker and the body relatively smaller. The forms are more closely related; and the meeting of body, tail, and leg, brittle in *Pasarea Maiastra*, is more reasonable in *Maiastra*. The short throat tapering up from the body and the slight cleft of the beak result in a somewhat muted image, lacking the vigor of the arched throat of *Pasarea Maiastra* and its sense of an uttered cry.

71. Maiastra
24″; pol. bronze; 1912

Four versions of *Maiastra* appear in bronze; they show a series of subtle changes worked on the marble. *Maiastra I* is slightly shorter than *Pasarea Maiastra*, though it should be remembered that a bronze cast is always a little smaller than the original since the hot metal shrinks on cooling. Nevertheless the leg is shorter and the body longer by small but noticeable amounts; the piece seems squat. A thin square plate now supports the leg; the head appears to turn slightly to its right because Brancusi has shaved some material from the left side. It was painted blue, it seems, at some time during its first exhibition.

Maiastra II is the same height as the marble; there is no plate under the leg.

Maiastra III and *IV* are progressively taller than

72. Maiastra
24⅛″; pol. bronze; 1912(?)

43

73. Danaïde
10⅝"; bronze; 1913(?)

74. Mlle. Pogany
17¼"; bronze; 1913

75. The First Step
ca. 44", destroyed; wood;
1913

the original, with the leg and tail noticeably longer, and the body both longer and fuller; the sharp outer edges have been rounded somewhat on *III*. The highly stylized design appears to better advantage in the "artificial" metal than in the "natural" stone, and the long neck and slender slab of the tail, both dangerously extended in the original, are strong in the bronze. A precious confection in marble, *Pasarea Maiastra*, like *Mlle. Pogany*, is fully realized in the later polished bronze versions.

Bronze versions of *Danaïde* and *Mlle. Pogany* show that the metal has been much worked. The casts of *Danaïde* are variously gilded and polished; they have a serpentine earring on the left side, and a rotundity in the face has been reduced. The coiffure of *Mlle. Pogany* is not polished as highly as the rest; in two copies it has a blackish patina. A certain fragility in the marble of *Mlle. Pogany* disappears in the bronze as the elements are decisively designed and the surfaces tightened. Casting bestows a unity on the forms that the chisel has a tendency to separate; ultimately *Mlle. Pogany* is more satisfactory in the metal than in the marble.

The First Step is Brancusi's first piece in wood, and was probably worked on for some time; it may have been done from a photograph, now lost, of Brancusi holding the infant George Farquhar upright. It shows a standing child, the left leg bent as if taking a step, the right arm raised to the head, whose mouth is open as though the child were crying; there is no left arm. The sculpture presents a façade rather than the swirl of forms we see in *Mlle. Pogany;* in contrast to the narrow slit in *Double Caryatid*, the openings are large; the body

44

has roughly the same form as that of *Pasarea Maias-tra*. The forms are completely rationalized: there is nothing of the organic and there are no ambiguities at the crucial points of transition between the parts. The system of curving planes and edges first introduced in *Danaïde* is now handled boldly: the nose, cheek, and eye are achieved without being represented as such. Only the mouth is represented, yet in this sculpture Brancusi has moved from stylization as a method of translating form, to what may be called relational imagery, achieved by an imaginative use of a small number of quite formal elements.

76. Head of First Step
10⅛"; wood; 1914

The First Step is thoroughly Brancusian, yet one feels an influence of African carving. It was probably for this reason that Brancusi destroyed it after showing it in New York early in 1914, preserving only the head, which was cast in bronze. The metal versions of the head, designated *The First Cry*, are variously unpolished, half-polished, and fully polished. They are new examples of the *head as object*.

77. The First Cry
9⅞"; pol. bronze; 1914(?)

Sleeping Muse II in alabaster, slightly larger than the first, is even less anatomical. The eyebrows sweep up into the forehead in a daring distortion; the ears, only one of which is seen at a time, are now closer together—a bare two inches apart; and the neck has been reduced to a small projection below the chignon at the rear, hardly disturbing the general ovoid. In its translucent material it is a dreamlike presence, a perfumed suggestion rather than a precise image.

78. Sleeping Muse II
11⅜" l.; alabaster; 1914?

A bronze *Sleeping Muse II* is polished to mirror reflectivity. In this transformation it is a thing of resplendent physical beauty, a sensuous object that constantly eludes definition.

79. Sleeping Muse II
11"; pol. bronze; 1914?

80. Three Penguins
22½"; marble; 1914

81. Two Penguins
21¼"; marble; 1914

Three Penguins and *Two Penguins* are the latest of Brancusi's compact, intricate carvings, compositions which include *The Kiss, Portrait of George,* and *Mlle. Pogany.* The sharp separation between the birds' heads creates a troublesome "leftover" space between the first two birds and again above, where the three heads meet; the latter is not unlike a similar space enclosed by the chin, neck, and arm of *Mlle. Pogany.* With the elimination of one head, these matters are resolved in *Two Penguins,* but with a loss of content. On the left side of *Three Penguins* is an ambiguous enveloping element, one of the few unexplained forms to be found in Brancusi's sculpture. *Three Penguins* has a whimsical humor, attributable largely to the varying axes of head and eye. The piece is held together rather by charm than by formal logic or organic connection.

Working directly in plaster Brancusi designs a fountain intended to honor a Rumanian mathematician, Spiru Haret (d. 1912). Given the girl in *The Prayer* who looks at the ground, and *Woman Looking into a Mirror*, the figure in *Narcissus Fountain* combines both gestures to look down at a sheet of water. The forms are summary and masterfully modeled in large twisting planes that terminate, on one axis, in an ovoidal head. Around the featureless face is incised a scalloped fringe of hair.

In forcing the attitude of the head to the farthest possible point, Brancusi has rendered the sentiment of *The Prayer* theatrical. His most abstract sculpture to date, the work and its reflection would have made a striking image. But the project was rejected, to Brancusi's great disappointment.

Brancusi continues the theme of a standing bird. A *Bird*, in gray marble, is a little taller than the last and more attenuated. Its changes of size are less pronounced than those of *Bird*, no. 69; the resulting compactness, the raised head and the general elongation impart a clear upward movement. As if to give it impetus in its rising, this *Bird* is mounted on an active rhomboidal base, as against the cube and cylinder on which *Pasarea Maiastra* and *Bird*, no. 69, stand.

82. Narcissus Fountain
20½"; plaster cast; 1914(?)

83. Bird
27¾"; gray marble; 1915

84. The Newborn
8⅛" l.; marble; 1915

The theme of a reclining child's head, last seen in the shape of *The First Cry*, reappears in *The Newborn*. The new developments in this small piece are dramatic. Dispensing with the hole of the mouth and the sharp groove along the nose of *The First Cry*, Brancusi has arrived at a compact ovoidal form toward which he seems to have been aiming. In this piece no human feature is represented; the image of a bawling child, its mouth wide open, is achieved by the relation of a very few formal elements. Brancusi has sliced off a section of the ovoid, leaving a small element curving up at the bottom. At the top of this section he has dropped the surface of the ovoid for a certain distance—a delicate task—and removed a small amount of material to create a point (of the nose) that just touches the section. Neither stylized nor simplified, *The Newborn* is the result of a leap of the imagination, of a synthesis of purely formal materials. The work releases a certain humor, and then, by a reversal typical of Brancusi, turns serious as it suggests cell division and the shock of birth.

Two studies in plaster show Brancusi working on curious extensions of familiar themes. He models a columnar figure with a head similar to *The Newborn*, but larger, symmetrical and lacking the chin. A bust, seemingly based on *A Muse*, looks to the right rather than the left; the face is reduced to two planes that meet along a vertical ridge and are marked with curving incisions that serve for hairline, eyebrow, eyelid, and eye. Both works are evidence of a fluid state of thought, modest proposals arising from the recent past.

The Newborn in bronze dispenses with the modulation which earlier produced the point of the nose. The drawing is more exact, and the work as

85. Study for a Figure
60½"; plaster; 1915?

86. Study for a Head
17¼"; plaster; 1915?

48

86.

87. The Newborn
8⅛" l.; pol. bronze; 1915

a whole is more definitive than the marble. Brancusi perfects his motif the second time around.

A unique piece, as thoroughly rationalized as a sculpture could be without being a geometrical shape, is *Timidity*. A design, drawn on the side of a flat piece of stone of a certain thickness, is cut all the way through the stone as though with a band-saw, making the same profile in reverse on the other side of the stone. Whether or not the piece was done this way, it establishes the idea of such a process.

The motif suggests a female figure, and the surprising thickness of the stone—eight and five-eighths inches—gives "body" to a design that could easily have been cut in a much thinner slab—and been a mere pattern.

88. Timidity
14⅜"; stone; 1915

Between 1913 and 1915 Modigliani made a great number of studies on paper for a *Caryatid* in stone, now at the Museum of Modern Art in New York: the profiles of the legs and torsos of the crouched figures very much suggest Brancusi's sculpture. One of Modigliani's studies (appendix 13) has the word "audacity" written across the top in French. Brancusi's *Timidity* may well be a commentary on his friend's drawing; certainly his sculpture seems modest beside the bold *Caryatid* of Modigliani.

But he carves two *Caryatids* of his own in wood that are not crouching like Modigliani's—or Rodin's —*Caryatid*, but upright like the Maidens of the Erechtheion porch. On the taller, we may distinguish a head, neck, body, legs, feet and two flat

89.

90.

shapes that are ambiguously a headdress and arms raised beside the head. The forms are of a geometrical order, though the body is not as decisively designed as the rest. Across the neck is a series of shallow grooves whose section is that of the gouge that cut them out. A curvature at the corners of the head is evident on the outer sides of the feet, and suggests that this piece was carved, not from a square but from a round or roundish beam that probably influenced the shape of the body. The sculpture suffers from a too sharp separation between body and legs, but is at once solid and springy, innocent in its expression, sage in its opposition of curved and flat plane, of blunt shape and fine, bright detail.

In the shorter, more delicate *Caryatid* the long opening between the legs of the larger *Caryatid* is much reduced. The feet are mounted on a carved block, thus simplifying the task of achieving the small opening that penetrates the structure at this point. The figure itself is carved from a square beam and designed frankly on each face (though a feature at the "ankles" allows the front to slide into the sides); the elaborate lower region emphasizes the tension of the long, curved body; and along the back, in relief, is a number of parallel elements connected in an undulating series which suggests wavy hair. The serrations at the side of the head, the undulating series along the back, and the grooves at the neck (of both *Caryatids*) are the first repeated, decorative elements in Brancusi's œuvre.

This *Caryatid* is very *art moderne*, but of a noble order and of the first hour. It contains only a faint memory of the human, just enough to relieve the coldness of its abstraction. The Erechtheion Maid-

89. Caryatid
90⅛"; wood; 1915

90. Caryatid
65⅝"; wood; 1915

51

ens have gone into the service of an elegant, playful functionalism.

A small wood carving, *The Prodigal Son*, is the most intricate of Brancusi's works. The upper mass, a handsome composition of flat and curved planes, is supported on one side by a column of rectangular section, and on the other by an arch that is curved and regular on its inner surface while its outer is faceted and irregular. The upper part demonstrates an ability to organize a complex system which Brancusi has not manifested up to this point. The work is a sparkling counterpoint of bulk and openness, weight and tension, classical order (the column and upper mass) and surprise (the arch). Its open construction and a slight dynamic quality, new to Brancusi, suggest a combined cubist–futurist influence.

91. The Prodigal Son
17½"; oak; 1915

The Prodigal Son is achieved, somewhat like *The Newborn*, not by simply fashioning the mass of material, but by imposing on it a series of cuts which intersect each other. These cuts create planes whose placement is felt as intellectual gesture rather than as the result of labor. The work seems to disclose a process of sculptural thought.

The image of the returning son is not easy to read. It requires a sense of humor to see here a kneeling figure, one hand on the ground, the head thrust forward, a pack on the back. When Alfred Stieglitz exhibited *The First Step*, no. 75, in New York, he called it *The Prodigal Son:* the sculpture disappeared but the title persisted.

Portrait, seen from the rear in the illustration, would not seem out of place in a group of African wood carvings; it illustrates in almost didactic fashion Brancusi's approach at this moment. This *Portrait* bears no human feature, but we are aware of

a head, a comb or knot of hair, and shoulders. Taken separately the parts would not be recognizable for what they are in this relation. The shapes and the process of their making are perfectly rationalized; it would be possible to reproduce this sculpture from verbal directions. The central element, for example, results from taking a portion of a definable ovoid and imposing upon it a flat and a curved plane whose positions may be stated simply and exactly.

Portrait is the first of Brancusi's works to be *constructed;* construction permits him to indulge in surprising relationships and in a playfulness not possible in carving. Only the central feature now exists, and it is possible that the piece came apart. But it is equally possible that he took it apart at a late date—it was shown in 1933—when its synthetic quality had lost its attraction for him.

The curving chignon of *Portrait* turns up again atop an abstract *Portrait of Mme. L. R.* (Léonce Rosenberg?). This piece, like *Portrait*, has an African overtone, is symmetrical and a construction in wood, apparently of six parts. The base (half of a flat ring) and two cylindrical elements look mechanical in their execution. The sectioned cylinders, set on the same axis, seem to penetrate the lower of the two bulky forms and to hold them apart; the implied energy of these forms gives the piece a machinelike quality. *Portrait of Mme. L. R.* is a human machine; it has disappeared.

94. The Kiss
28⅛"; yellow stone; 1915?

95. Study for Column of the Kiss
ca. 57", lost; plaster; 1916

The Kiss in yellow stone accentuates the design which had appeared in *The Kiss*, no. 65, and retains only a minimal humanistic sentiment. The surfaces are without any suggestive curvature; now flat and hard, they are relieved only by a sprinkling of dots left by the bush-hammer. A shallow incision marks the difference between the lovers; the semi-circular eyes have a geometrical exactitude of drawing. The two heads, now larger, seem, at moments, to become one, with one large eye which looks out at the world. The alternation of the sense of two and one gives this version a humorous cast and a cubist flicker. *The Kiss*, like many repeated works, has become increasingly abstract.

Brancusi makes a square column in plaster which is contrived by combining four columnar elements, all alike. Its main feature is a circular motif, divided vertically, which we see to be a version of the eyes of *The Kiss*. This column marks the culmination of Brancusi's interest in the eye as a motif, begun in *The Kiss*, and continued in *Narcissus, Danaïde, Mlle. Pogany* and the *Penguins;* its design demonstrates the extent to which Brancusi read every configuration of his sculpture as motif.

After years of recarving *Woman Looking into a Mirror*, no. 54, Brancusi completes *Princess X* in 1916. Throughout this labor the subject remains unaltered, but the mass of stone undergoes attrition and the conception is transformed: both the gesture of the figure and the stylization of the head are as extreme as in the earlier *Narcissus Fountain*, no. 82. Vanished are the descriptiveness of the original and the "natural," broken surfaces of the hair. The work incorporates developments of the intervening years: all is thoroughly contained under the same tight skin; the elements are few; the piece is much taller than wide; decorative notes are present in the treatment of the hand at the bottom of the piece and in a similar motif on the other side that serves for hair where head and neck meet; the work is taken in at a glance while exhibiting a great variety of aspect.

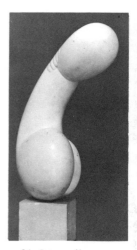

96. Princess X
22"; marble; 1916

But *Princess X* exhibits some new features. The relative tallness of the piece combined with its curving bottom makes this the most precarious looking sculpture Brancusi has yet created. The forms are rationalized into a completely curved system; there are no flat planes. And except in the accents of hand and hair, there are virtually no shadows. *Princess X* seems bathed in light; the polished bronzes —*Prometheus*, *The First Cry*, *The Newborn*—gave the clue to this possibility.

A woman combing her hair has become a very shape of narcissism, curled in on itself. In the marble, *Princess X* is a work of unequaled confectionary luxury, a version of feminine grace whose overarching sweetness is exactly proportionate to its excess of abstraction. The surface is velvety and, at the difficult moments where the crease in the throat meets the great outer curve, exquisitely graduated. Precious, almost perfumed, this *Princess X* seduces. In the bronze, *Princess X* has an elastic quality that seems to be a privileged condi-

55

tion of curving, gleaming metal; at the same time it is Brancusi's closest approach to organic form.

When natural forms are severely rationalized there is no certainty that the new forms will give up the same image as the original ones. A degree of ambiguity is always present, and the special nature of the ambiguity of *Princess X* caused Brancusi some worldly embarrassment: its phallic shape resulted in its being withdrawn from the Salon des Artistes Indépendants of 1920.

The size of a human head, rather like *Sleeping Muse* with its features erased, *Sculpture for the Blind* is the latest of a series of objects that rest in neutral equilibrium. It is neither head nor pebble nor egg, but a man-made construct implying all three, moving from curve to secret plane across a variety of transitional edges. The alternation of hidden structure and luminous mystery keeps the eye attentive: vision is confounded, reverie is alert.

Now in a museum where one may only look at it, *Sculpture for the Blind* was originally intended to be touched. H. P. Roché remembered that it was exhibited at an early date enclosed in a bag that had two sleeves through which the hands could enter. It was a "revelation for the hands" (in Roché's statement the words are between quotation marks and are presumably Brancusi's), but most people thought it a joke. He quotes the sculptor:

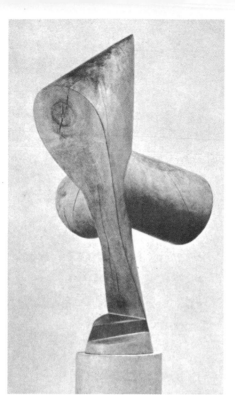

"I put my curiosity of the unknowable into it—an egg where little cubes seethe, a human skull."

The Sorceress is a single piece of wood, and its unusual articulation is due to its having been carved in a portion of a tree trunk from which three branches grew. It could have been carved from a massive block of wood, but at a great cost in labor and material. This wasteful economy would have been visible in the finished work; there would have been no circle of core wood in the middle of the "face," and the angle of the two cylinders would have been illogical with respect to the grain of the wood. The whole piece, indeed, would be illogical if carved from a solid mass, and we may be sure that its design would never have occurred to Brancusi if he had not come upon this particular piece of material.

The placement of the greatest weights in the upper rather than the lower portion of the sculpture is the culmination of an effort to free all-too-mate-

99. The Sorceress
39⅜"; wood; 1916

57

rial sculpture from its usual heavy bottom. Starting with *The Prayer*, this effort had grown progressively bolder in the series: *Maiastra, Bird, The Prodigal Son, Portrait of Mme. L. R.*

Portrait of Mme. L. R., a symmetrical construction, rises lightly and easily on a slender leg which is vertical. In *The Sorceress* the leg is under tension, at an angle that compensates for the asymmetrical distribution of masses. The work is in perfect balance (it can stand without being attached to its base) and is Brancusi's most daring essay in equilibrium to date. With its clearly defined axes and open construction, it is a piece whose composition can be grasped at a glance from any point of view, yet it has great variety of aspect.

Besides being a demonstration of statics and sculptural economy, *The Sorceress* is at once a humorous and haunting conception. The hooded, overhanging head is properly awesome; the two cylinders are sources of secret power, chambers where spells are worked or where charms are kept. Brancusi extracts a poetry from pure form.

100. Torso of a Young Man 19"; maple; 1916(?)

Carved from a fork of a maple tree, *Torso of a Young Man* exhibits the same economy and logic in its use of material that characterize *The Sorceress*; both show two short cylinders in the same relation. The long axis of the body and the shorter ones of the legs follow the real core of the wood; the circular planes of the sections are inscribed by the annual rings. The vertical member does not merely rise from the diagonal ones; it seems to express the release of a pressure they generate. But the piece is not as diagrammatic as it appears to be from the front: buttocks are visible at the back. The meeting of large elements along a sharp edge, such as existed earlier in *Head of a Girl*, no. 42,

58

and *Portrait of George*, is demonstrated here with a new frankness and formality.

Although it represents the central portion of the human body—a version of the torso of the destroyed *First Step*, no. 75—this delicate image of youthful, male vitality arouses no sense of loss, of limbs cut off. It is a self-contained design, the first *torso as object*. We observe, finally, that there are no genitals. *Torso of a Young Man* is itself a phallus, geometrical, rationalized, sublimated.

101. Torso of a Young Man
18⅜"; pol. bronze; 1917

The bronze of *Torso of a Young Man* is about an inch shorter than the wood; material was removed from the top so that the upper plane is markedly less slanted. A high polish and a hard tubular character have replaced the familiar roundness and ingratiating surface of the wood. The polish mitigates even as it emphasizes the geometricality: it aerates the mass, and fills the form with light. A brilliant mechanical image with only a minimal human resonance, it is sustained by the sweetness, simplicity, and logic of its design.

Two casts of *A Muse* in highly polished bronze are taller than the marble, the increase in size occurring in the bosom and arm. The arm has become tubular, the earlier tooled surfaces on the outer side are smooth, and the side of the hand shows a sharp edge where there was a curving one in the original. The upper part of both these versions has been tipped forward so that the head is more salient and the arm vertical. The faint indication of eyes in the marble has disappeared, the gently fashioned meeting of bosom, throat, and arm has been brought forward and thoroughly rationalized, and the surfaces have been tightened generally in the interest of unruffled reflectivity. It is clear that Brancusi has worked a great deal on both the plaster cast

102. A Muse
19¾"; pol. bronze; 1917

59

103.

104.

105.

from the marble and the subsequent bronze. *A Muse* in bronze is dazzlingly "modern," a new kind of hard, shiny beauty, of an order different from that of the marble and related to the bronze *Torso of a Young Man.*

In a third bronze, Brancusi preserves the latest angle of the work but has cut it down to the height of the original marble, leaving, however, a straight edge along the bottom that carries no reminder of the carving. Starting at the shoulder just below the attachment of the throat he has removed a great deal of material from the side of both shoulder and bosom, and has cut off the back along an edge that goes to the base of the arm, leaving visible the hollow interior of the sculpture. This version, then, emphasizes the head, which, with its reduced underpinnings, has a relatively greater forward thrust.

Adam, half sculpture, half base, is a male caryatid crushed beneath its burdens, suffering from compression. It is symmetrical and designed from each face. The recession from the large frontal plane to the neck, and the even deeper recession to the headdress, explore the depth of the block, while the sharp corrugations animate the profile; when the work·is viewed from the side, the rear profile exhibits an elaboration of design and a roundness of form unsuspected from the front. The grooving at the neck has completely lost its decorative character; it seems to be a way of achieving a curved plane. As never before, we feel the touch of the chisel. But *Adam* is unfulfilled.

Chimera is a work whose every aspect is ambiguous: the total configuration is columnar, but composed of three separate sections; it is not clear whether the formal middle section belongs with the base below or the figure above. The upper and

103. A Muse
19½"; pol. bronze; 1917(?)

104. A Muse
17⅜"; pol. bronze; 1917?

105. Adam
34⅞"; wood; 1917

61

106.

107.

middle section both have holes which, however, function differently: graphically in one case, formally in the other. The upper section, like the duck-rabbit illusion, alternates between a birdlike image and that of a girl with a braid. Altogether it deserves its title: *Chimera* is the most unsettling image in the Brancusi œuvre.

Formally it completes a series of essays in statics. After *Portrait of Mme. L. R.*—symmetrically disposed on a vertical leg—and *The Sorceress*—asymmetrically balanced on a slanting leg—*Chimera* shows an unequal distribution of weight over a vertical leg. The piece cannot fall over since the upper mass is hardly larger than the footing. But the unevenly distributed load above is held in place because the material of the leg is strong enough to keep it there, in defiance of the normal sense of balance.

Putting wooden forms one on top of the other, as in *Chimera*, but neutralizing the expressive force of the uppermost element, Brancusi makes a decorative *Architectural Project* which has figural overtones. The progress upward from hollow mass to short block, thick smooth disk and tooled gourdlike shape is slow and serious. In spite of its evident bulk and firm seat on the ground, it is rendered weightless by its open organization and the purity of its conception. The design is symmetrical about a central axis. Thus the work has every characteristic of a column except emphatic verticality. Relatively short, various and widespreading, it is a curious extension of the idea of the column. *Architectural Project* exists only in a photograph; the three parts were dispersed by the sculptor and have recently (1968) been re-assembled in the Brancusi Studio at the Musée d'Art Moderne in Paris.

108. Endless Column
80"; oak; 1918

109.

Using an ax with the same easy touch he favors lately, Brancusi carves *Endless Column*. The motif is present on porch posts and in the woven work of his native region of Oltenia (appendix 14); it appears in his pedestals as abstract support and is repeated here till it achieves independent identity. The planes have a slight fullness, the lively surface relieving their geometry. The totally abstract image is ambiguous and fruitfully so, the elements organizing themselves as a succession of paired truncated pyramids now apex to apex, now base to base, with a constant flicker and sense of movement.

The rhomboidal module is a little less than five inches across its narrow width, ten inches at its wide dimension and twenty inches high. These measurements approach a ratio of 1: 2: 4, but Brancusi has not insisted on it: the *Column*, when seen from the side, measures nine and five-eighths inches, resulting in a module of ratio 1— : 2— : 4. Moreover, when the *Column* is viewed from a corner instead of a face, the width increases and we have a ratio of 1+ : 2+ : 4. If Brancusi had wished to make a column the proportions of whose module remain constant from any point of view he would have made a column of circular section. Such a design would have entailed an increase in labor and a reduction in content—a faulty economy.

Vertical, repetitive, rationalized, *Endless Column* has the artistic distance, objectivity, and impersonality that are the common denominators of Brancusi's œuvre. Distinct from his sculptures of subjects in nature, it is a work of high decoration in which one yet feels the shaping hand and mind.

110.

111.

112.

An unusual subject for Brancusi is a *Cup,* a solid hemispherical mass, with a thick disk for an ear. It exists in four versions whose measurements are worth observing. Their heights are 6 1/4″, 7 1/2″, 9″ and 10 1/4″; their diameters are, respectively, 8 7/8″, 11 5/8″, 17 3/8″ and 16 1/2″. Only in the third is the height close to the radius; in the others the height increases by about a quarter of the radius. Their ears are close to a fifth of the diameter of the bowl, except the second which is somewhat larger; the third is square, perhaps not completed. Thus the first and fourth, although varying greatly in size, are similar; relative to the others, the third is low, the second has a large ear. If we consider the smallest one to be either the first or the norm of the series, the others embody all the worthwhile variations: the second, a change in relation between the two masses; the third, a change in relation between the height and the width; the fourth, a change in absolute size.

Cup is a modest creation modeled upon a commonplace artifact; by the simplest of means it releases a poetry of the object. After the *head as object,* and the *torso as object, Cup* is the *object as object;* the gambit is quintessentially Brancusian. Beside *Development of a Bottle in Space,* 1912, of

109. Cup
10⅞″ w.; wood; 1918?

110. Cup II
14⅜″ w.; wood; 1918?

111. Cup III
20⅞″ w.; wood; 1918–20?

112. Cup IV
19¾″ w.; wood; before 1925

113. Little French Girl
49"; oak; 1918?

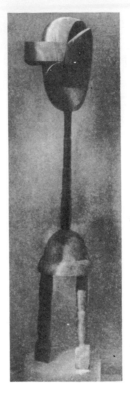

114.

Boccioni and *Absinthe Glass*, 1914, of Picasso, *Cup* has a monumental innocence.

Cup, sometimes called "Cup of Socrates," was intended to be displayed, not on a pedestal, but casually, in a dining room, possibly on a pillow, sitting flat or at a tilt. At the very time that it was made, Erik Satie, the composer and a close friend of Brancusi, was occupied with "furniture music," music intended to serve as a background for conversation.

Little French Girl, once labeled *Mlle. Brancusi*, is a construction that utilizes legs of sectioned cylinders like that of *Portrait of Mme. L. R.* Although it is much fuller in its representation than the related *Study for a Figure*, no. 85, we note—late—that there are no arms. The head is asymmetrical; it combines features of *The Newborn* and *Caryatid*, no. 90. The large head and short legs give the work a look of precarious, childish equilibrium; the varieties of size, shape, and surface contribute to its

66

wit. *Little French Girl*, with its bleak expression and clumsy stance, its delicacy and transparency, is the most affecting of Brancusi's human images.

Another version of *Little French Girl* shows legs which have two, instead of three, sections; a simpler skirt which does not resemble a turtle shell, as the other did; a central column that is without grooving; and a head designed of fewer and larger elements. The work was destroyed by the sculptor.

Torso of a Young Woman, in onyx, takes up the theme of the *Torsos* of 1908 and 1912, nos. 51 and 68, converting the romantic fragment into an essential, self-sufficient fragment; all surfaces are now clear and intact. The front tips forward, the top plane slants downward from front to back, and the back is composed of two planes that meet at the high rounded bulge of the buttocks; the thighs are shallow, giving a small footing to the piece and contributing to its quality of precariousness and lightness. The anatomical distinctions emerge as the result of the faintest incursions on the compact mass. The pubic region, scanted in *The Prayer*, absent in the fragmentary *Torsos*, is here a delicate modulation of the translucent surface. The object creates a reverential ambience.

Not apparent in a photograph (and even Brancusi had difficulty in making one) is the fact that the basic symmetry of the carving is disturbed by a shift of the general plane at the rear somewhat to the right, producing a section that is roughly a parallelogram and causing the piece to appear wide when seen from the right and tall when seen from the left (or, as here, from the right rear). The illusion of a change of proportions as the point of view changes is related to a similar effect in *Endless Column*. Inevitable in the latter, it is consciously

114. Little French Girl II
ca. 43", destroyed; wood;
1918?

115. Torso of a Young
Woman
12⅞"; onyx; 1918

contrived in the *Torso of a Young Woman.*

The treatment of the thighs is then of special interest. Having established on the front the width of two thighs, Brancusi makes their depth one-half of this amount. This strict relation is in the interest of creating an object that is rational, intelligible from any point of view, and as free as possible from natural—here anatomical—contingency. Thus Brancusi offers formal clarity and formal illusion in a conjunction at once witty and wrenching.

The theme of the erect bird is resumed. Like the gray *Bird*, no. 83, *Yellow Bird* does not simply stand—it stretches upward, its parted beak seeming to utter a call to the heavens.

The gradual filling in of the spaces below the breast has culminated in a continuous surface; as if in compensation, there is a greater difference in size between neck and breast, and the neck is squarish in section while the rest is circular. The compression of forms is extreme; the unity which results is altogether new. *Yellow Bird* cannot be considered a simplification of the form of a bird, nor as a normal development of a designing process; we must suppose here a leap of the invention beyond the available materials. *Yellow Bird* absorbs a number of previous developments—tight form, imagery from rationalized shapes, emphatic verticality—and contributes a reductiveness so drastic as to be dangerous. The danger is double: to the subject—a bird —and to the object—the sculpture. The success of this venture will depend henceforth on a poetry of form, on the creation of significant images. As descriptiveness decreases, it will depend too, it appears, on an increase in absolute size: *Yellow Bird* is almost exactly one and a third times as tall as *Bird*, no. 83.

116. Yellow Bird
36⅜"; yellow marble; 1918

68

Two bronzes, designated *Golden Bird*, are a quarter inch and an inch and a half taller than the marble. But the taller of these is somewhat smaller in girth, and so is relatively much more slender. The bronzes appear lighter and swifter than the marble and, while lacking its impressive massivity, seem less precariously balanced on their bases. In the bronze, Brancusi draws the surfaces more precisely.

A second version of *Mlle. Pogany* in a richly veined marble reflects Brancusi's new interests. With the elimination of the shoulder, the work tends toward the columnar. The two arms have merged into a single large form; the lower eyelid has disappeared as one plane now describes eye and cheek; the ear remains, a motif in relief joined to an arching upper eyelid; the slit of the mouth is gone; and instead of a chignon at the back of the

117. Golden Bird
38″; pol. bronze; 1919

118. Golden Bird
37¾″; pol. bronze; 1919

119. Mlle. Pogany II
17⅜″; veined marble; 1919

69

119.

120. Mlle. Pogany II
17"; pol. bronze; 1920

121. The Newborn II
10¼" l.; marble; 1920(?)

head, a decorative cascade of arches falls along the neck, ending in a whorl a short distance above the base. At the bottom of the neck are two small passages of rough stone, and the top of the head has a pebbled texture; otherwise the piece is smoothly finished. These changes make for a more unified image, but the meeting of the three main forms at the crease of the throat continues to be a problem.

The joining of arms and throat at the base is a work of wizardry. The area is actually small while seeming ample; this effect is accomplished by a sage overlapping of forms. Whereas most stone sculpture has its heavy base disguised by a multiplicity of forms, the multiplicity of forms here disguises a small base.

The first *Mlle. Pogany* still had the quality of a fragment; *Mlle. Pogany II* has become an independent object. At a cost: the personality in the original has diminished considerably. But the attention lingers over the sumptuous material, the carver's craft, the noble drawing. The experience of the bronze, more abstract, unvaried, is swift; the head rises like a flower over the supporting members.

A larger version in marble of *The Newborn* is less tentative than the first; as in the small bronzes, only one side of the nose has been designated. The work is composed, then, of a large curved surface, the crescent-shaped plane at the nose, the round plane of the mouth, and, joining these surfaces, three edges all equally clear except for a variation

122. The Newborn II
9¾" l.; stainless steel;
1920(?)

where the great outer curve forms the bottom of the mouth, the only melting transition on the piece. This ambiguity is perfectly placed—at quivering chin—and perfectly relieves the precision of the rest. Once again within the confines of a small object and its limited elements, Brancusi has carried an earlier design to a stage of grandeur and plenitude.

Two slightly smaller versions in bronze and chrome steel complete Brancusi's study of the head as object in an essential form.

Brancusi carves an *Endless Column* (1920, preserved in its entirety only in a photograph) for the garden of Edward Steichen in Voulangis, on the outskirts of Paris. Composed of nine rhomboids, with a half-rhomboid at the top and a half-rhomboid and short riser on the bottom, it seems capable of infinite extension. The planes are not flat but swell slightly as if from an inner pressure. The carving process has been rationalized: a photograph shows Brancusi using a saw to cut through a beam to the inner edges of the rhomboids; it was then an easy matter, because of the grain of the wood, to carve the planes connecting the outer edges of the rhomboids, marked off around the beam, with the saw cuts. The twenty-three-foot column rises without effort and unobtrusively against the surrounding foliage. It appears as a repetition without monotony, diminishing perspectively, but ever present in the mind. Stiff where all is swaying, regular where all is varied, it is the shape of intelligence amid floral exuberance, a human gesture in a natural world.

Brancusi cut the column down when Steichen left Paris. Two sections of it remain, along with two other columns in wood: one is ten feet tall; a more slender version rises thirteen and a half feet.

126. Endless Column IV
(—)ca. 285"; wood; 1920

71

126.   123.   125.

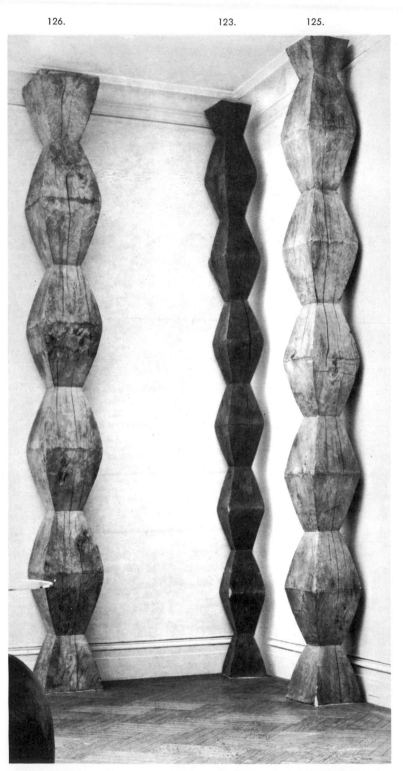

Brummer Gallery, New York, November 1933

Another slender column, no. 124, preserved in a photograph, has disappeared.

The many versions Brancusi carved of *Endless Column* make it clear that the motif had a special place in his affections. From the carver's standpoint it is a delicious one. Once the proportions are established it is only necessary to lay them out on the beam of wood and procede almost automatically; the work goes on like a litany, with no need for invention. Every new *Column* seems to develop its own individuality. From a relatively small effort there is here a great poetic yield. In this sense the *Cup* is the mate and complement of the *Column*, though the economy of its production is not equally advantageous. Here, too, by a simple process and with a form dear to him, Brancusi can produce an evocative image.

King of Kings is Brancusi's largest independent carving. Starting at the bottom, we see the pierced cube of *Chimera;* a helical shape, new to Brancusi's sculpture, but present in his studio in the form of a long wooden screw from a winepress; a cubical mass showing, on three faces, horizontal and vertical corrugations while the fourth shows the surface of the beam; a short, round, tapering throat covered with a grooving Brancusi has used several times before in designating this region; a large ovoid, pierced by two spaces at a right angle to each other, and topped by a narrow band and a large, circular, flamelike shape. Absent from this anthology is the repeated element of *Endless Column*, a motif reserved for that column and for pedestals. The strict formality of the parts here is softened by the gentle surface; the columnar quality is mitigated by the alternating large and small masses. With typical economy Brancusi has facili-

123. Endless Column I
(—)161½"; wood; 1920?

124. Endless Column II
disappeared; wood; 1920?

125. Endless Column III
(—)118"; wood; 1920?

127. King of Kings
(—)118⅛"; oak; 1920(?)

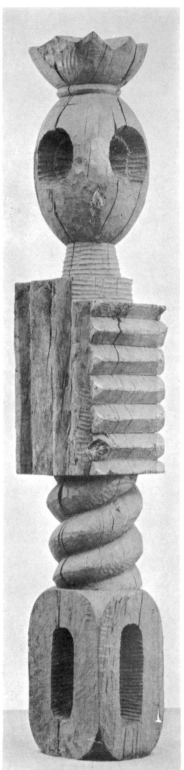

127.

128.

tated the carving of the horizontal corrugations by making preliminary sawcuts across the grain of the wood, just as he did on *Endless Column.*

The changes in size, the implied torsion at the bottom, the flicker of the central mass, and the flamelike crown aim to animate this large work. The similar bulk of the three large masses keeps the sculpture constantly present: it does not taper or move off into space; what was an achievement in the case of *Endless Column* is doubtfully so here. The combination of the figural and the decorative suggests a large chessman.

Brancusi was not satisfied with the work. After referring to it for a time as *The Spirit of Buddha*, he renamed it *King of Kings.* A certain stolidness in the stance and the forbidding quality of the head recommend the allusion to Genghis Khan.

Exotic Plant, similar to the topmost element of *Architectural Project,* no. 107, is a curious sculpture whose middle section is marked by a mysterious horizontal groove. To its muted expressiveness are opposed the deep serrations of the base, which forms a spiky guard around the work. It is a man-made cactus.

128. Exotic Plant
17¾"; wood; 1920

Short, and composed of three globular masses of subtly different girth, it is the most recent essay in a series of columnar possibilities. If *Endless Column* is a study in repetition and *King of Kings* a study in variety, *Exotic Plant* is a study in close values.

Vase is a tapering cylinder with a flat scalloped decoration projecting from opposite sides; again, a formal conception has been humanized by the

129. Vase
11⅞"; wood; 1920?

75

gentleness of touch. Like *Cup*, its interior has not been hollowed out. It can hold nothing, but invokes those flowers which Brancusi loved and which he never made his subjects.

A Hand is a reminiscence of *A Muse* or *Mlle. Pogany*. Carved in a sliver of marble, a variation at the wrist inflects its long taper. It is the hand become object. It seems to embody not so much the anatomical member as the sense of a caress. Inevitably it opposes itself to the individualized, gesticulating *Hands* of Rodin.

130. A Hand
(+)12" l.; marble; 1920

Rejecting the myth of Jupiter turning into the curvaceous swan, Brancusi invents a fable of his own: Leda becomes the swan. And that is how he described his *Leda:* the kneeling girl leans back and as she does so the line of her breasts and head becomes that of the head of the amorous bird.

131. Leda
21" h.; marble; 1920

Ambiguity pervades every aspect of this clear design: it is present in the metamorphic image and idea, in the doubtful equilibrium, in the conjunction of two quite different forms, in the double reading of the upper form as plunging into and growing out of the lower mass. The small joint between the two elements strains the physical properties of stone (and the object has been broken at this point) but nowhere is the Brancusian logic more apparent than in the working out of this joint. The edge created here is not a blending or sliding

of one form into the other; it is sharp, and demonstrates perfectly the meeting of a three-sided column and a complex curve. The seeming inevitability of this edge releases a moral tone; it tells us not only that Brancusi proceeds logically, but also that he faces the consequences of the forms and the vision he projects.

The upper, active element of *Leda* is clearly structured; though round and full in its mode, it is stiff, it tapers downward, it has a triangular top plane and a triangular section. The passive ovoid is organic, subtle, and difficult to grasp.

Ultimately *Leda* composes an image fundamental both to the Greek myth and to Brancusi's own fancy: an image of fertilization. A reproduction of the piece in a Bucharest journal of 1924 is, indeed, labeled "Fecundity."

Of *Beginning of the World*, H. P. Roché said that Brancusi "preferred it placed on a pillow or a sofa—and, especially, placed on his knees, *touched by his hands*, his eyes closed."

More regular than *Sculpture for the Blind*, less organic than the body of *Leda*, *Beginning of the World* is a structured ovoid. Beneath its apparent roundness lies a series of planes, fewer than in *Sculpture for the Blind*, their transitions more subtly contrived. Mere roundness would be slack; it is an underlying planar organization that keeps this sculpture taut, vital, and light-catching.

But *Beginning of the World* does not merely demonstrate a perfect control of minimal sculp-

132. Beginning of the
World
12" l.; marble; 1920(?)

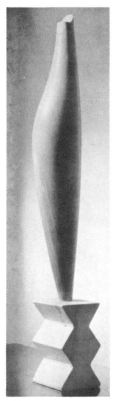

133.

134.

tural materials. While *Sculpture for the Blind* "seethes" at its bulging middle, *Beginning of the World* is stretched tight at this point. The change from its fine to its full end implies a movement, a drama as quiet as the turning of a head. *Beginning of the World* is a mass in the act of extending itself, of acquiring a new dimension. Ezra Pound saw it as about to levitate. At any rate, it is a shape with a future, perhaps, even, the shape *of* the future, its plenitude pregnant with possibility.

A *Gray Bird*, slightly shorter than *Yellow Bird*, is emphatically smaller at the breast; consequently the passage from throat to foot is more direct and swift. The section of the body is no longer circular, but rather ovoidal as a ridge appears along the spine. As against the fullness and relative variety of *Yellow Bird*, *Gray Bird* is slender and unitary. It achieves elevation with ease and speed.

133. Bird
35½"; gray marble; 1921(?)

Adam, 1917, achieves fulfillment in the composite *Adam and Eve*, 1921. The work continues the vertical, serial, symmetrical mode so much favored by Brancusi.

134. Adam and Eve
(—)94¼"; wood, stone; 1921

Figuratively and literally the base of this sculpture, *Adam* has the angularity of form and the directness of facture characteristic of many of Brancusi's bases. *Eve*, on the other hand, is all curves, carefully elaborated, with a general structure reminiscent of *Portrait of Mme. L. R.*, and specific forms like those in *Portrait*, no. 92, and *Cup*. The interplay of curved planes in the upper part of *Eve* is the result of the crossing of two designs, one imposed from the front, the other from the side. The fine edge that develops near the back of *Eve* defines the boundary between the simple curves at the side and the complex curves at the back, and gives *Eve* a delicacy lacking in *Adam*. *Eve* is an image of eroticism and germination, organic, mobile, almost audible.

Adam and Eve shows responsible Man supporting playful Woman, the flower of human existence. Both creatures face the world: theirs is a wedding of opposites effected by their creator's taste and decision. We are at some distance from the essential unity of *The Kiss*, its lovers lost to the world in each other.

A version of *The Kiss* in brown stone is Brancusi's gentlest carving of the theme so far. His chisel, file, and bush-hammer seem to play on the surface, hardly accenting the mass. The outer edges of the heads are gently rounded; the divisions between the bodies and between the arms, and the transition from the arms to the bodies, formerly so clearly rendered, are here indicated with no insistence at all. The rough surface of the hair is divided into strands by a delicate serpentine drawing; the eyes are incised, with no suggestion of volume—on one side of the work; on the other, the eyes and lids are in relief. The surface is variously tight and broken, and again has that dotting that was a feature of *The Kiss*, no. 94, this time not confined to the heads alone, but on the shoulders, between the arms, and on the body. Its effect is quietly glamorous, as of sequins or stars. Late in his life Brancusi mounted the work on a turntable.*

A Kiss, in a slab of stone found with two rings attached, shows Brancusi making his own folk art. His chisel wanders over the stone, alternating its effect with that of the bush-hammer, eliciting the design without seeming to disturb the surface. A pensive, smiling *Kiss* that echoes Donne: "Differ-

135. The Kiss
14⅛"; brown stone; 1921?

136. The Kiss
23¼"; gray stone; 1921?

* In 1933 this *Kiss* was shown without a turntable; see illus. no. 184.

136.

ence of sex no more we knew than our guardian angels do."

Brancusi again essays the child's head as an object. He fashions two longish ball-like shapes which show a slight indentation at the eyes and a slight elevation at the nose. In the white stone head, which, like *The Kiss*, nos. 135 and 136, bears Brancusi's toolmarks, a small round plane below the nose has been reserved for the mouth; in the black stone, which is smoothly finished, no sign of a mouth is evident as a large plane drops from the point of the nose. The latter is a variation of *The Newborn*.

Here is Brancusi attempting to avoid both the naturalism (no. 47) and the inventiveness (no. 84) of his earlier children's heads. He seems now to wish to render only the infant's first full sleepy roundness. The result is touching and tender, if of limited interest. It is difficult to focus on so minimal a representation.

Torso of a Girl is, like *Torso of a Young Woman*, no. 115, a study of the female pelvic region, but it appears to take as its point of departure the earlier work rather than a human model. It wipes out that torso's anatomical indications, keeps its forward tilt and bulge at the rear, and emphasizes its precariousness to the point of real instability. Brancusi's ovoid of origin, *Beginning of the*

137. Sleeping Child
7½" l.; white stone; 1921?

138. Sleeping Child
7⅞" l.; black stone; 1921?

139. Torso of a Girl
12⅞"; onyx; 1922

81

140. Torso of a Girl II
13"; onyx; 1922

141. Fish
16⅞" l.; veined marble; 1922

World, is here upright in a section that implies a container of other beginnings. With its one flat plane, its single edge and large curving surface, it is one of Brancusi's most reduced images.

A second *Torso of a Girl* is approximately the same height and width as the first. But the upper plane is smaller and the depth has increased significantly.

Even more minimal is *Fish*, a sheet of marble cut to a long ellipse that is pointed at one end. From the bulge that runs along the axis, the form tapers to the surrounding edges at constantly varying speeds: swiftly to the head, less so to the tail, slowly to the ventral and dorsal ridges. A flawless drawing of the surface makes possible this image of resistanceless matter.

Brancusi has had to go low on the zoological order to find a subject on which to exercise his concern for unity, close relations, and graphic limitation. But *Fish*, while a poetic version of the natural forms, is essentially an image of fluidity, of floating, of passage without friction.

Fish is hardly a sculpture in the sense in which Brancusi has up to now conceived it, that is, as having gravity and mass, as mounting upward from its base. Moving across rather than up, it presents a mode new to Brancusi, one less proud, less anthropocentric. Unstable, lacking gravity, it is of all Brancusi's works the most dependent for its existence (or stance) on a base. At the same time, that base is a circular mirror, so that *Fish* is reflected and seems to float. The whole creates an image, indeed a universe, whose limits are not confined by a skin of form.

Brancusi now places a plaster version of *Yellow Bird*, no. 116, on a marble footing, as he explores a new image of the bird, one that absorbs the sense of movement previously found in the bases.

Completed in 1923, though probably begun several years earlier, *Socrates* is a unique work at the same time that it displays a number of familiar features. It has the cylindrical sectional leg of *Portrait of Mme. L. R.* and *Little French Girl*, but this leg supports a very large mass. The mass itself is pierced, like *Chimera* and *King of Kings*, but at two levels. The voids themselves are complex, the result of the intersection of different hollowing processes. A plane has been dropped around both edges of the larger cavity, and at both sides of this cavity, and on the front of the lower, large notches have been cut; one senses the step-by-step process. The large overhanging mass and the openings combine to produce a sense of lightness, as of a balloon on a string, rather than of a great weight dangerously held aloft.

Like all the works that engage the issue of equilibrium, *Socrates* has a special feature in the footing. The footing of *Portrait of Mme. L. R.*, no. 93, is frankly adventitious; that of *The Sorceress*, no. 99, modulates through several transitional planes to become the upright member; in *Chimera*, no. 106, and *Socrates* (which must have been begun soon after) it is again a distinct feature while being formally

142. Study for Bird in Space 44¼"; plaster, marble; 1922(?)

143. Socrates 51¼"; wood; 1923

83

143.

144. Torso of a Young Man
16⅞"; wood; 1923

related to the rest; and in *Eve*, no. 134, it is similar to that of the *Mme. L. R.*, its forced transition to the vertical member being justified thematically rather than formally.

The footing is actually the crux of the top-heavy sculpture. To secure such a sculpture at any angle whatever to a base is too easy and a shirking of the problem. So that Brancusi's option for a footing that is part of the total conception is moral rather than practical. It puts a strain on invention: for to elaborate a footing is to obscure its function and its low position in the hierarchy of values in a work; to reduce it to a merely functional mass is to separate it from the rest. Self-contained equilibrium, unity of conception, subordination of the footing, and variety of design present the difficult course.

Erik Satie wrote his opera *Socrate* in 1918 at a time when he was friendly with Brancusi, who was then reading Plato. Satie, a wit and a conversationalist, called Brancusi, ten years his junior, "the little brother of Socrates." Is *Socrates* a portrait of Satie or Socrates? It appears to be a head in the act of talking or singing.

Actually, *King of Kings* is Brancusi's last venture in the "void." After that point real openings hold no interest for him; his sculpture will be "transparent" while monolithic and unpierced.

A new version in wood of *Torso of a Young Man* shows no open space between the sculpture and the base. The uppermost plane is more nearly parallel to the base than in the first version, but it

145. Head
12"; wood; 1923

slants now to its own right. As a result of the slightest changes in drawing from the original, and of
a reduction in size, *Torso of a Young Man II* becomes the more delicate, less declarative version.

Probably in 1923 Brancusi separates the head
from *Little French Girl*, no. 114; it is henceforth
an independent object, a construction of interlock-
ing masses.

The *Bird in Space* which develops from no. 142
is new in both form and significance. No longer
standing or stretching, it seems to propel itself upward. The open beak is replaced by a single small
plane; the tiered footing has been rationalized as a
smooth conic shape. *Bird in Space* is over forty
percent taller than *Bird*, no. 133; its body alone is
almost nine inches longer than *Bird* and has exactly
the girth of *Bird*, which it may be considered to
contain, extend and refine.

The footing is not integral with the body, but a
separate piece of marble joined to it by an internal
rod. Only the strongest conviction about his design could have moved Brancusi to the extraordinary expedient of joining two pieces of stone.

Instead of the head : body division of the previous *Bird* and the head : body : foot division of the
transitional study, *Bird in Space* shows a body :
foot division. The body, which earlier took rise
with some difficulty, relying on assistance from the
active zigzag of the base, is now sped by the double
movement of arching breast and straight spinal
ridge, and given elevation and release by its own
tapering footing. The base is a quiet cylinder.

146. Bird in Space
50⅝"; marble; 1923

Speaking of some changes he had made since the first bird, Brancusi said, "I wanted to show the *Maiastra* as raising its head, but without putting any implication of pride, haughtiness or defiance into this gesture. That was the difficult problem and it was only after much hard work that I managed to incorporate this gesture into the motion of flight."

No longer descriptive, *Bird in Space* achieves significance by the relation of pure forms. It is, indeed, very little like a bird (which rarely moves in vertical flight) and several years later a version was in fact deemed not to represent a bird by a sector of American opinion.

The reductiveness of the body of *Bird in Space* is like that of the recent *Fish*, both in degree of abstraction and in absolute design; they are long and have only slightly inflected contours. We may conceive the former as produced by stretching *Golden Bird;* the latter may be seen as resulting from a stretching and flattening of *Beginning of the World*.

147. Fish
16⅝" l.; pol. bronze; 1924

A polished bronze *Fish*, a quarter inch shorter than the marble, no. 141, is a shiny, decorative object. Lacking the sense of facture of the marble, it is perfectly impersonal, a flash of light. Brancusi said he did not wish to render a fish, but "the flash of its spirit."

48. Beginning of the World
1¼" l.; pol. bronze; 1924?

Unlike the marble, the bronze of *Beginning of the World* is highly polished. Its tight reflective skin cannot retain the subtle variation of the marble, in which the gradual changes of light are carried along by the crystalline structure. The bronze is handsome, disembodied; eventually it is shown on a polished disk, attached to its mirror image.

The long effort to find essential form has led to

monoforms. Brancusi now turns about and confronts the problem of a variety more challenging than that sustained by the simple columnar mode of *King of Kings*—the problem of formal disparity.

Having added an element to the ovoidal *Sculpture for the Blind* in order to arrive at the *Leda*, having removed a portion of that ovoid to create *Torso of a Girl*, Brancusi now converts the ovoid into an ellipsoid, stands it on end and adds three small, quite different elements to it. The oval of the lips, the disk of the chignon, and the pointed ornament at the rear (which resembles the flamelike crown of *Kings of Kings*) are attached to the central mass in frank fashion and all lie on the edge of the plane of bilateral symmetry.

149. White Negress
15"; veined marble; 1924

The joinery is as varied as the forms: the ornament lies along the plane, the lips lie across the plane, and the chignon is askew of the plane. The chignon is thus the only deviation from symmetry, having, besides, a curving development on its right side.

White Negress rests on its chin, set forward of the center of a cylindrical base that does service for a throat. Unlike *Mlle. Pogany*, where the eyes and the slit of the mouth give the sense of an inner content, *White Negress* offers no illusion. Brancusi attempts to achieve both unity and depth by a sheer constellation of elements. The lack of organic relation and interiority causes perception to shuttle between an image of a head and a set of shapes.

New and difficult as this venture is, Brancusi forces the issue by employing a white marble. The piece was inspired by a young African woman who had been pointed out to Brancusi at a reception by a girl called Eileen. He had earlier done a portrait of Eileen (1922–23?, lost), and they laughed over

87

150. Bird in Space
50"; pol. bronze; 1924

the fact that it was in black onyx while the new work was white.

The energetic body and strong footing of *Bird in Space*, no. 146, are considerably reduced in girth as Brancusi designs a more slender version in metal. In the process the relation of complexity and simplicity in the body and footing of the marble is reversed. As the footing becomes more energetic the body is rendered swift and unitary, by both the reduction of its median bulge and the flattening of the oblique angle formed by bevel and frontal curve.

If the curving surfaces of *Bird in Space* are projected upward, a pointed form is produced; we may consider the bevel as cut across this complete —too complete—form, creating the present image. The bevel thus introduces a situation more complex than that of the representational open beak of the previous *Birds*. It creates a slightly truncated image which the mind completes by an act of imagination that moves along the same path as that of the sweep of the *Bird*. *Bird in Space* fulfills itself in moving upward.

The Cock continues the relative complication of *White Negress*, as though Brancusi would counter his tendency to an extreme reductiveness. If *The Cock* is more successful it is partly because the forms of the lower orders are more amenable to rationalization than complicated human form. Besides, Brancusi is less precious with wood than with stone; wood has length, an orientation in which he is always comfortable.

The Cock is composed of two lengths, two axes; its structure takes advantage of a portion of a trunk of a tree and a branch. With the grain of the wood running along each element, the strength of the slender leg quite naturally supports the large body, which in its turn easily accepts the form into which it is fashioned. As in the case of *The Sorceress*, this sculpture would be difficult if not impossible to render in an ordinary block of wood.

This work reminds us that points are rare and blunted in Brancusi's sculpture, and never aggressive. We note that the back of *The Cock* curves down from a central ridge and that the planes of the repeated teeth are on the underside, protected, as it were, like the intimate features of *The Prayer*, by the sheltering back.

The rear edges of the serration lie approximately on the same plane as the upper triangle; the front edges lie on another plane which, as in *Bird in Space*, meets the projection of the back at a point outside and above the sculpture.

The long pointed head, the heavy balancing tail, the repeated frontal motif, make an image of a cock crowing that is one of the magical creations in Brancusi's œuvre. Magical, surely, because there is no beak, no comb, no feathers; instead, a series of features which have no counterpart on the animal, but which suggest its stretching, its crowing, its nervous energy. Tense, alert, surprising, intelligent, the very shape of thought, *The Cock* is an expression of Brancusi's highest art and craft, made accessible in its most public form.

Brancusi embarks on a large-scale version of *The Cock*, apparently starting the first study in clay and later working on the cast directly in plaster. *The Cock II*, about eleven feet tall, is almost one and a third times as tall as *The Cock I*. Aside from size, the most notable variation from the wooden original is the much greater verticality of the plasters: whereas the back of the wood makes an angle of

151. The Cock
36⅛"; walnut; 1924

89

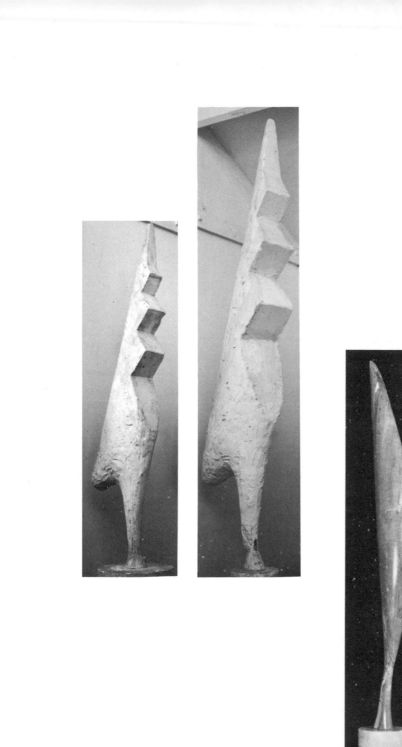

154.

about 55° to the horizontal, the backs of the plaster *Cocks I* and *II* make angles of 77° and 72°, respectively. The triangular plane at the top of the plaster is much smaller, proportionately, than in the wood, as are the legs. The half-ellipse on the front of the plasters is considerably longer than in the wood; the dentation is deeper. Altogether, the plasters achieve a rather forced élan while appearing angular and brittle, their solidity threatened.

In the summer of 1924 Brancusi creates a "Temple of the Crocodile" on the beach at St. Raphael. It is a playful production, abandoned to the elements after having been photographed by the sculptor (appendix 15). Its title, if not its form, reveals an ambition that looks beyond the making of isolated sculptures.

For *Bird in Space* in yellow marble Brancusi designs a footing of undulant form, his best solution to date of this feature, and related in its slenderness to the leg of *The Cock*. This may be a bird that Brancusi tried to make in one piece and that broke. The delicate meeting of the upper and lower elements has been repaired; these probably did not meet in the abrupt fashion of *Bird in Space*, no. 150, but in a continuous curve. The latest *Bird* is shorter than the last two, its footing is longer, and its girth markedly reduced; also, the angle formed by the bevel and the frontal curve is much flatter. These changes make for a generally slender *Bird* of great elegance.

Torso of a Girl III, in marble, is one-fifth shorter than the version in onyx, no. 140, but only one-tenth less wide and one-eighth less deep. It is thus the smallest and the squattest of the three versions of this motif, which progress from relative flatness to relative roundness.

152. The Cock I
(—)100¾"; plaster; 1924

153. The Cock II
(—)131⅞; plaster; 1924–33

154. Bird in Space
45¾"; yellow marble; 1925

155. Torso of a Girl III
10⅜"; marble; 1925

91

Torso of a Girl III is an ideal pear, sliced across the top. Like the last versions of *The Kiss*, nos. 135 and 136, and the second versions of *Sculpture for the Blind* and *Torso of a Young Man*, it is a gentler, less incisive image than the earlier ones.

All features are missing from *Head of a Woman*, marble, except a small whorl of a chignon at the back. The skull is a smooth globe undifferentiated but for a slight flatness at the face. Its perfect formal autonomy is that of a diagram, rejecting anatomy, resemblance and psychology. It seems certain that *Head of a Woman* is *Danaïde*, no. 60, reworked years later. Mlle. Pogany visited Brancusi in 1925, and it is likely that the alteration of the work had a more than merely formal significance for the sculptor.

156. Head of a Woman
11⅛"; marble; 1925

Once again, Brancusi stands his ovoid on its smaller end, and causes a knoblike form to develop from the top. The representation is even more neutral than that of *Head of a Woman*.

Eileen, in stone, is a portrait of a young woman who wore her hair pulled back and gathered in a small bun. With all human features erased it requires an effort to be read as a head, but we observe the fullness of the frontal profile and the flatness of the rear, where the back of the neck rises to meet the bun. Yet it remains an ambiguous image, avoiding the biomorphic by its perfect symmetry and the precision of its drawing, and by the fact that the curving forms are regulated by the clear vertical and horizontal axes within.

157. Eileen
11¼"; white stone; 1925?

In the bronze of *Leda* the ovoid is tautly drawn so that the light may flow smoothly on the polished metal; the shape is more tense than in the marble, yet it retains an elastic quality by contrast to the stiffness of the upper form. The smallness of

158. Leda
21" h.; pol. bronze; 1925

the joint of the forms is more reasonable than in the original, while the perfection of drawing and the high reflectivity make this a dazzling object in every respect. A golden mass penetrated by light, it joins craftsmanship to poetry in a work of wonder. Some time after it was completed it was mounted, like *Fish*, on a polished metal disk arranged to revolve slowly.

In *The Chief*, a thick neck and a small cranium reverse the usual relations of Brancusi's heads, and create a stolid mass of inelegant profile. Brancusi removes a slice from the melon of a head, adds a piece of rusty iron, and achieves a monumental expression of vulgar authority. The means are few and large; one feels their order and their effect: the column indented to form the head and neck, then deeply cut to create the mouth, the whole then passing under the metal. The sculptor's sense of humor, delicate in *White Negress* and *The Cock*, is broad and malicious in *The Chief*. Brancusi apparently intended to satirize the Pope rather than a military or political leader.

159. The Chief
20"; wood, iron; 1925

*Portrait of Nancy Cunard** is topped by a wonderfully fashioned, systematically twisted chignon that is attached to, not integral with, the strictly symmetrical head and neck. On a generally precious design it is a striking "note," parallel to a style of modern elegance, precarious and con-

---

* Miss Cunard, poet and patron of poets, was a gay and intelligent adornment of the artistic life of the twenties.

93

160. Portrait of Nancy
Cunard
20⅜"; wood; 1925

161. Little Bird
16½"; colored marble; 1925

trived; the work has the alternate title of *Sophisticated Young Lady*.

In *The Chief*, the large central form of the head has undergone the subtraction of the gaping mouth; in *Portrait of Nancy Cunard* it bears the addition of the extravagant chignon. The two works are commentaries upon excess; but *Portrait of Nancy Cunard* has no sharp edges.

The relation of chignon to head may have been suggested by the "Temple of the Crocodile." Brancusi thought enough of this construction to send four snapshots of it to his friend Roché, and to mention it to the editors of *The Little Review*.

If the *Nancy Cunard* is turned on its head with the chignon removed, and a bevel is cut at a point below the joining of the neck, *Little Bird* is produced.

Little Bird is the nest-bound fledgling, all stomach and open beak. The work has the same straight back, tipped forward, as *The Chief* and *The Cock*; the straight rear profile, though tipped to the rear, appears on the body of the first marble *Bird in Space*, no. 146. The last work to have an elaborate back was *Adam and Eve*, 1921; since then Brancusi's means are more economical. The total image is apprehended more quickly.

Little Bird is situated morphologically between *Torso of a Girl* and *Bird in Space*; it has the beak and bodily form of the latter, in the state of youthful, undifferentiated, unstable plumpness of the former. At first glance a merely handsome shape of limited expressiveness, it is also a demonstration of Brancusi's interdependent language of form. Made after *Torso of a Girl* and *Bird in Space*, it "fills in" the series while seeming to evolve from the later *Nancy Cunard*.

94

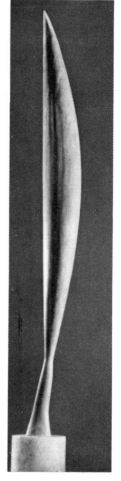

162. Bird in Space
52¾"; gray marble; 1925

A *Bird in Space* in gray marble is, like the white marble *Bird,* no. 146, not of continuous material but of two joined parts. It is the tallest bird Brancusi has made, with a relatively slight increase in fullness over no. 154, and a spine that is almost vertical; the oblique angle at the meeting of bevel and frontal curve is more oblique than in previous versions; the footing, 16.4 percent of the total height, is quietly flamboyant. These changes make it much the slenderest of all the *Birds,* with an elegance and sense of elevation greater than those of the *Bird* in yellow marble, no. 154, and altogether different from the bulging, energetic *Bird* in white marble.

In a dramatic and exhilarating change, *Bird in Space* in white marble rises to a height of seventy-two inches, or more than a third taller than the *Bird* in gray marble. The girth increases proportionately, but the footing increases so little that it is only 13.98 percent of the full height and thus is relatively shorter than in the two previous marble *Birds;* with respect to the recent *Bird* in gray marble, the body has been lengthened by about seventeen inches, the footing by an inch and a quarter.

Surprisingly, the tallest *Bird* Brancusi has carved so far is a continuous length of marble, while the meeting of body and footing is relatively fine. The design at this point is not the gentle transition from one form to another, as in the last few *Birds;* instead, the bottom of the body slightly overhangs the top of the footing.

Brancusi has at last found the technical means of carving this long form without causing it to break or to be breakable at its fine section. It was probably a technical consideration that led to the rather short footing; the relatively large and heavy body

163. Bird in Space

164. Sculpture for the Blind
12¾" l.; onyx; 1925

would seem to have suggested the slight bulge at the joint.

A second version of *Sculpture for the Blind* alters the proportions of the first in a striking manner. Elliptical in section, rather than round like the early example, the object is relatively flat and rests on its base in a relaxed fashion instead of seeming to rise from it. Its dimensions indicate a systematic deviation from the original, whose width and thickness are equal; in flattening the work Brancusi has retained this thickness and chosen a width approximately midway between length and thickness.

In its later stages *Sculpture for the Blind* was fashioned with a bushhammer, not with a chisel, and it is likely that the two earlier variants of this shape were worked in the same way.

A second *Bird in Space* carved in a single shaft of marble goes to a height of 74 3/8 inches. The footing is relatively the longest so far, or 16.5 percent of the total height. As compared with the last *Bird*, the body has increased 1 1/2 inches in length, the footing 2 3/8 inches.

A recent (1966) repair of the sculpture has revealed its inner structure:

Inside the *Bird* was a round brass rod five-eighths of an inch in diameter, held in place by a thin layer of cement. The rod was 55 1/2 inches long, of which 43 1/4 inches were in the *Bird*, progressing upward to the middle of the body, the remaining

163. Bird in Space
71"; marble; 1925

96

12 1/4 inches penetrating the cylindrical base (6 3/4 inches) and descending into the pedestal. The rod is perpendicular to the base and passes close to the front of the footing and the rear of the body. Only the strict verticality of the rod would prevent the stone from breaking by its own weight or because of a shock. (The sculpture was broken by a violent shock—a fall.) The body slants back at only a slight angle from the vertical, and a vertical rod entering it would be, for a long distance, close to the skin of the stone; it was therefore necessary to penetrate the body to a great distance in order to set the end of the rod in an area where there was enough stone surrounding it to provide strength.

At the elliptical section of the joint there is just over a quarter inch of stone before and behind the rod, and just under a quarter inch on either side. Almost exactly a third of the section is metal and cement, and two-thirds marble. The section has an area of one square inch and supports a mass over sixty-two inches long.

There is no doubt that, in carving this and similar *Birds*, Brancusi first drilled a long hole in a column of stone, then set the supporting rod, then shaped the column, adjusting his design to the lay of the rod. Much of the carving, especially toward the end of the work, was done with a pneumatic chisel, which has a short, light drive and therefore shocks the stone much less than a hammer-driven chisel, removing small amounts of material with great speed; the final form and surface were achieved by filing and abrasion.

The tall monolithic *Birds in Space* are not only marvels of art and dazzling examples of craftsmanship, they are engineering feats whose tolerances are as small as those of the design.

165. Bird in Space
74⅜"; marble; 1926(?)

97

167. Blond Negress
15⅛"; pol. bronze; 1926

166. Bird in Space
53¼"; pol. bronze; 1926

A bronze *Bird in Space* is based on the gray marble *Bird*, no. 162; footing and girth increase, while the length of the body decreases, over the earlier version by small amounts. The footing is about 18 percent of the total height, relatively the longest of all of the *Birds*. The rather full body and long slender footing are in sharper contrast than before —a contrast accentuated by the gleaming metal— and produce an image of elevation that is *emotional* rather than energetic like no. 146, or elegant like no. 162.

Blond Negress is the bronze of the marble *White Negress*, no. 149, and would seem to be an advance upon it. The attachment of the chignon to the head no longer appears fragile in the metal; the lips and the ornament at the rear appear more integral with the mass of the head. The ornament has undergone a change in design, not the first time such a change occurs in the bronze: whereas in the marble its central peak rests on a flat plane, here the plane is broken inwards, making the upper and lower wedge shapes longer and thinner, and the whole element more delicate and brilliant.

Four bronze *Fish* vary slightly but systematically the proportions of the original marble, no. 141. One *Fish*, no. 168a, increases in height by a half inch; another, no. 168b, decreases in length by seven-eighths of an inch; another decreases in length by three-eighths of an inch; and the fourth decreases in height by a half inch and in length by three-eighths of an inch. The height : length ratio here varies from 1 : 3 to 1 : 3.67, making the first relatively

168a. Fish
16⅝" l.; pol. bronze; 1926

168b. Fish
16" l.; pol. bronze; 1926?

168a.

168b.

the shortest of all Brancusi's *Fish*, and the last the longest. All are mounted on shiny metal disks, and the first two were provided with elaborate pedestals by the sculptor.

A tall bronze *Bird in Space*, developed from the marble no. 163, is taller than the original, the additional height and more having gone into the footing. This *Bird* is a breathtaking object, with a powerful upward surge that irresistibly moves the spirit.

Two bronze versions of *Bird in Space* seem to be derived either from the bronze no. 166 or the marble no. 162. The versions in bronze were made by taking a plaster cast of a previous *Bird;* dimensions

169. Bird in Space
72½"; pol. bronze; 1927

99

169.   170.   171.

were altered by manipulating both the mold and the cast. When a radically new image occurred to Brancusi, he carved it in stone. But, as we have seen, the footing of no. 150 appears only in that bronze; it was designed in the plaster.

The *Birds in Space*, nos. 170 and 171, are progressively taller than no. 166, by small amounts. The former is fuller of body; the latter is more slender, more vertical, and has a shorter, thicker footing, resulting in a reserved stately expression. No. 170 is situated, morphologically, between nos. 166 and 171: it has the great sense of elevation of the former, and partakes of the greater solidity and unity of the latter.

170. Bird in Space
53¾"; pol. bronze; 1927(?)

171. Bird in Space
54"; pol. bronze; 1928(?)

A version in bronze of *Little Bird*, no. 161, reduces the dimensions slightly. Not of the brood of the marble, its speed and lightness relate it to the creatures of Brancusi's other, shiny universe. The polished metal has effects which are absent in the stone: the flat plane, catching reflections differently from the curving surface, at moments gives the illusion of an opening to the interior, then reverts to its hard actuality. This alternation between illusion and reality creates a sensation that is cubist.

172. Little Bird
15⅝"; pol. bronze; 1928

173. White Negress II
15⅞"; marble; 1928

A second version in marble of *White Negress,* no. 149, shows Brancusi making a multitude of fine changes and adjustments in an object of small size.

White Negress II is taller than *White Negress* by a small percentage; its base has increased by the same percentage. The chignon has gained in height relatively more than the head; it incorporates other changes: it is smooth on both sides, its vertical plane is closer to the plane of symmetry of the head, its vertical axis continues that of the head (that is, it does not appear to tip forward) and emphasizes the slight rearward slant of the head, and its bottom is rounder (that is, does not deform its curvature to meet the top of the head as in *White Negress*) and seems almost to be floating. The tangential meeting of two curving surfaces results from the fact that this chignon is *attached* to the head, strength being provided by an internal rod. The ornament at the back of the impressive ellipsoid maintains the design of *Blond Negress,* no. 167, but is more fragile; the upper and lower wedges, probably carved with a pneumatic chisel, are even longer and thinner. The whole work is placed further forward on the base where it is more precarious and distinct.

Each element in this sculpture is fashioned with a masterly decisiveness and exactitude learned, it would seem, from the version in bronze. The white marble, like the polished metal, has a clarity and abstraction which are absent from the somewhat vegetable, veined marble of the original.

The slight increase in size, the counterpoint of sharply differentiated elements, the clarity of form and color—all combine to give *White Negress II* a quiet nobility and a champagne wit.

Large Little Bird, in marble, is taller and wider

102

by a half than *Little Bird*, no. 161, while its depth increases by only a quarter. The spinal ridge is closer to the vertical, and the piece is more elongated than *Little Bird*. Taller both relatively and absolutely, *Large Little Bird* has outgrown the fledgling state and assumes serious proportions. Monumental in stature, simple in design, it transcends its imagery to attain a realm of pure form.

Between the bevel and the great curving surface lies a narrow plane intended to take the edge off the meeting of the large surfaces, an edge that at the top of the sculpture is potentially dangerous both to the sculpture and the viewer. Thus there is no transitional plane at the bottom of the bevel, where the surfaces meet at a wide angle and the material is strong. It starts at the sides of the bevel, where the large surfaces meet at almost right angles, and from these fine ends goes to its greatest width at the top, where the form is sharpest and weakest. This plane must make its own design while mediating between the drawing of the other two. It is a work of tact and sculptural science, the final refinement on an already rarefied object. It appears on all the *Birds* that present the bevel.

Portrait of Mrs. Eugene Meyer, Jr. presents three clear sections: the head which takes up slightly more than half the height, the long throat, and the bosom which serves for a footing; the head itself has a delicate inner division. The head and throat meet at a clear acute angle and the throat and bosom at a clear obtuse angle, while within the head there is a melting transition in the obtuse angle between the upswept coiffure and the brow. These angles help to compose a movement not unlike that in *Bird in Space* and *Portrait of Nancy Cunard*: a movement from below, upward and into the

174. Large Little Bird
25¼"; colored marble; 1929

175. Portrait of Mrs. Eugene Meyer, Jr.

103

175. Portrait of Mrs. Eugene Meyer, Jr.
52⅝"; black marble; 1930

work, then a release outward and upward along the main mass. Swift and sweeping in *Bird in Space*, erratic and fanciful in the *Nancy Cunard*, this movement is controlled and majestic in the *Mrs. Eugene Meyer, Jr.*

Like everything since *Prodigal Son*, 1915, except new versions of *Mlle. Pogany* and *The Newborn*, and works of slightly disturbed symmetry, *Portrait of Mrs. Eugene Meyer, Jr.* is symmetrical; from the dynamism implicit in asymmetry, Brancusi has moved to the calm and orderly statement of balance.

Unusual is the contrast between the front and rear profiles, animated in the one case and straight in the other. We are at the culmination of a series of works in which Brancusi carries to a new point his thoughts on the *axis* and the relative *elaboration of the back* of the sculpture.

As against the large number of works—the columnar sculptures, *Leda, White Negress, Torso of a Young Man*, etc.—with a centrally situated axis, whether straight, bent or bifurcated, Brancusi has recently made a series of objects in which the axis has moved, as it were, to the surface and to the rear. This spine is to be seen on the body of *Bird in Space* and *The Cock*, on *The Chief, Little Bird* and the head and neck of the *Nancy Cunard*—works of the period 1923–25—and it finds its clearest form in the *Mrs. Eugene Meyer, Jr.*, where it runs along the whole work and is perfectly vertical. Although completed in 1930, the *Mrs. Eugene Meyer, Jr.* was conceived five or six years earlier.

In moving the axis to the rear, Brancusi has subtlized the serial organization of earlier work—*Endless Column, King of Kings, Exotic Plant*—and eliminated the elaborate development of the back of the sculpture such as we see in *Caryatid*, no. 90, and for the last time in *Adam and Eve*. The rear profile is rendered simple and regulatory, all forms being projected forward from it. The sculpture achieves greater unity and greater speed of apprehension.

In the *Mrs. Eugene Meyer, Jr.*, the large, overhanging mass of the head is not made lighter by piercing, as in *Socrates*, nor is it balanced by another form, as in the *Nancy Cunard;* it is held in space by the verticality of the face, parallel to the spine. The calm face and springy throat are familiar treatments, and once again the color of the material apparently provides the sculptor with a stimulating contradiction (the model was a full, fair beauty).* With the large cube and cylinder, also of black marble, which constitute its base, the *Mrs. Eugene Meyer, Jr.* rises to over ninety inches. The great size, the high style, the easy unity of sculpture and mechanically made base, create an image of suave, distant, sumptuous elegance unique in Brancusi's œuvre.

The wooden version of *Portrait of Mrs. Eugene Meyer, Jr.*, probably begun in 1924 and completed after the marble, lacks its tall proportions. The bottommost form, reduced in size, no longer suggests the bosom; the piece resolves itself into an image of head and throat, with the head daringly projected.

We may suppose that the projection of the head and the smallness of the foot are at the limit permitted by the stability of this object. If the same design were to be made in a taller version, the pro-

176. Study for Portrait of Mrs. Meyer
32⅞"; wood; 1924–30(?)

---

* Mrs. Eugene Meyer, Jr., of the *Washington Post* family, is a collector of Chinese art and has owned five Brancusis.

105

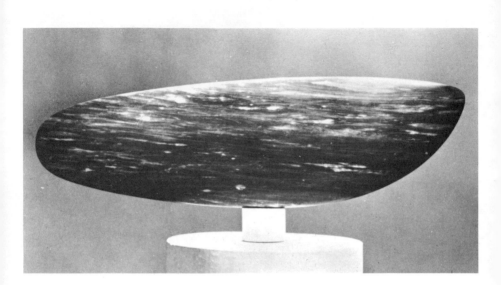

177. Fish
(—) 71¼" l. blue marble 1930

jection of the head would have to decrease, or that of the foot increase. In fact Brancusi chose to incorporate both these changes in the later version in marble. This aspect of the work relates it to others that explore equilibrium—*Portrait of Mme. L. R.*, *The Sorceress*, *Chimera*, *Socrates*, *The Cock*.

The almost six-foot-long *Fish* in blue marble is flatter across the top than the early small versions, it has lost its pointed nose, and it tapers back from the full "head" rather than from the middle to each end as the small versions do; like them, it is balanced on a point slightly forward of its middle. In spite of the passage of time since the first marble version, no. 141, in spite of the changes of proportion in the intervening bronze *Fish* and the great increase in absolute size, the blue marble *Fish* recovers the proportions of the first version.

The sculpture is symmetrical on the vertical plane running through its long axis, or when viewed from any edge. But if Brancusi's handling of form in many works obscures the fact of their symmetry, with *Fish* he has, for all purposes, eliminated the fact by the brevity of the moment of symmetry. The unusual width of the curved surfaces of *Timidity*, no. 88, (a symmetrical work!) is reduced in

Fish to an edge, mass being achieved by a bulge on the lateral faces.

Fish of 1930 is an image of a large, blunted submarine creature which seems to hover on its small mounting. The polished and veined surface carries an illusion of passage through water. Its size and seriousness declare it a public work rather than one meant for private delectation; it brings to the public genre an uncommon reserve.

Considered as mere shape it has a constantly engaging subtlety that belies its initial simplicity. One follows the taut upper edge forward to the turn of the nose; the leading edge is less tightly drawn but is thin and sharp; with a certain ambiguity it turns into the soft bottom edge which returns to the upper edge by a large, slow curve. The sections are no less varied, if more difficult to follow; this much-reduced form demands a keen attention. It can be read as an object (an immense *coup de poing?*) as well as representation with more success than is often the case in Brancusi. It is the form of the idea of Fish.

The axis of *Nocturnal Animal*, as in *Portrait of Mrs. Eugene Meyer, Jr.*, lies on its surface; here, running the length of the bottom. Like the *Fish* in its horizontality, unlike the *Fish* in its deep section, it is a typically ambiguous variation of a clearer, earlier image. Its form is roughly produced if we imagine *Fish* turned over, shortened, cut open along its bottom edge and then spread outward. The changes of contour and section are of the order of *Fish*, but the suggestiveness and minimal elaboration of this wooden form make it one of the

178. Nocturnal Animal
27¼" l.; wood; 1930?

quietest and most disquieting of Brancusi's creations. In a Brancusian contradiction it is mounted on a turntable.

A sculpture in plaster, no. 179, shows a full round form which is achieved by modeling or addition, and several angular forms which result from elimination, from the intersection of a number of sawcuts in a mass of material—an excellent example of Brancusian economy.

Plaster Form seems at first to be an austere study of opposed angular and curving elements, of full contact and tangential meeting with the base. It is undoubtedly an extreme stylization of *Narcissus Fountain*, no. 82, and an instructive example of Brancusian transformation: the chief features of the early work have been submitted to the scope of *Nocturnal Animal*. Whereas we may imagine the latter produced by a series of external operations on *Fish*, *Plaster Form* may be conceived as resulting from an intimate redesigning of *Nocturnal Animal*. The two works have surprising metrical relations: the plaster is about the same length, roughly one and a half times as high and twice as deep as the wood, "roughly" signifying here "with an increment of a centimeter in each case."

Plaster Form was probably intended for a "Tem-

180. Mlle. Pogany III
17¾"; marble; 1931

ple of Love" that Brancusi had projected some time since.*

Twelve years after *Mlle. Pogany II,* a third version appears which goes further along the path taken by its predecessor. The height remains the same—there would be no point in changing it—but every element in the design is carried to its ultimate point. The stepped arcs of the hair, now close to the neck, descend to the bottom of the work, ending in a circular motif. The two arms have clearly become one, the section across the bottom of the arm lying on the same plane as the contiguous throat; the upper surface of the arm is not broken at the wrist. The eyelids are more pronounced, descending to the bottom of the nose; the hand is shorter, stopping at the sweep of the eyebrow. Importantly, there is no area of rough stone, all elements being contained by a tightly drawn surface. *Mlle. Pogany III* is a sinuous, self-contained universe of infinitely varying aspect.

Brancusi said of it, "Perhaps I may think of a still

* Ezra Pound to William Bird, in a letter of Nov. 11, 1926: "However, you can let your fancy play as to the course of modern art if I had had an income, esp. during the 1912–14 period, Epstein, Gaudier, Lewis. . . . And, later, Brancusi's temple etc."

109

181.

182.

183.

better interpretation some day. Who can ever say that a work of art is finished." But he never thought of a better or other interpretation. On the threshold of pure design, the piece has only a distant human reverberation; to have progressed to an even more formal mode would have meant going out of sight of the original inspiration. What had started as a portrait would have become an unspecific, generalized abstraction, an end already achieved in *Head of a Woman*, no. 157.

In the translation to bronze, *Portrait of Nancy Cunard* submits to a number of formal changes. An inch and three-eighths taller than the wood, no. 160, the difference in height is accounted for by the more vertical angle of the chignon and by a lengthening of the neck. The mass of the head remains the same, except that the joint with the neck is smaller. The neck itself, unlike the rather cylindrical wooden neck, comes forward to a sharp edge at the front, a feature more feasible in metal than in wood. The rather conic neck and the verticality of the chignon create a more stable sense of balance than exists in the slightly forward-falling version in wood. The wooden chignon, imposed on the head, meets it sharply; in the metal, with its actual continuity of material, Brancusi allows a gliding transition between the elements.

Blond Negress II and *Mlle. Pogany III* undergo no unexpected transformation in the bronze casts, the *Mlle. Pogany III* achieving, possibly increased clarity in translation from the dun-colored stone. A hardness of design and a diminished sense of facture, which usually appear in the bronze, were already evident in the marble originals. And they had been influenced by previous bronzes.

A notation beside the entry for *Column of the*

181. Portrait of Nancy Cunard
21¾"; pol. bronze; 1932

182. Blond Negress II
15⅞"; pol. bronze; 1933

183. Mlle. Pogany III
17½"; pol. bronze; 1933

111

Kiss in the Brummer catalogue of 1933 reads, "Part of project for the Temple of Love."

From the small early version, no. 95, the column has grown to commanding size and has acquired a wide-spreading capital. The areas adjacent to the circular motif have been somewhat altered, most notably by a deep crescent-shaped groove cut above and below it; the central, divided element projects slightly beyond the plane of the column to suggest a contained ball. Like the early version, the column is assembled from four equal parts.

The width of the capital is twice that of its height, which is the same as the width of the column. But the simplicity of these relations is not apparent because of the stepped character of the capital, the perspective distortion of the sizes, and the projecting circular motif. The capital itself is a masterful decoration, exhibiting the animated geometry that Brancusi reserves for his pedestals and his public designs. (Several years later he would make another cast of it and place it upside down on the first to create a model of the interior space of a "Temple for Meditation" projected for the Maharajah of Indore; appendix 16.)

Brancusi carves two *Birds in Space* in white and in black marble which are his final explorations of the theme in this material. The white *Bird* is two inches shorter than the last marble, no. 165, and relatively larger in girth and longer in footing. *Bird in Space* in black marble is two inches taller than no. 165, and thus the tallest of the *Birds;* it is relatively fuller of body and shorter of footing, by small amounts, than no. 185. Both are constructed of two pieces of marble.

In a statement made to H. P. Roché in the spring of 1936 and probably intended to be sent to the

184. Column of the Kiss
(—)118"; plaster; before
1933

185. Bird in Space
72½"; marble; 1933

186. Bird in Space
76½"; black marble; 1933

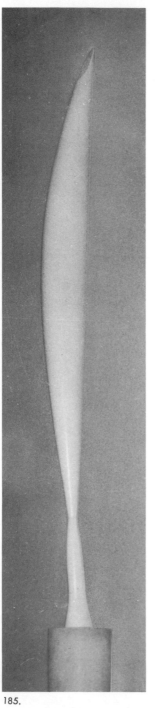

185.

186.

Maharajah of Indore, Brancusi said:

"The height of the *Bird* tells nothing in itself. It is the inner proportions of the object which do everything.

"In the last *Birds*, the differences between them hardly appear in photographs. Each, however, is a new inspiration, independent of the preceding one. I could show your friend their subtle differences on some plaster casts.

"My birds are a series of different objects in a central research which remains the same.

"The ideal of the realization of this object would be an enlargement to fill the vault of the sky.

"My last *Birds* in black and white are the ones where I most approached the right measure—and I approached this measure to the degree that I was able to rid myself of myself."

The Cock in bronze is only four inches taller than the wooden version of 1924, no. 151, but seems much more so because the leg is disproportionately longer, the angle of the back is almost ten degrees nearer the vertical, and the tail projects less strongly to the rear. The change may be stated another way: the profile of the wooden *Cock* may be inscribed in a rectangle almost exactly twice as high as it is wide, that of the bronze in a rectangle more than three and a half times as high as wide. The four projecting edges on the front lie neatly on a plane, as do the four inner edges, a relation only approximated in the wood. This precision, the reduction of the mass of the tail, the greater elevation, and the polished metal itself combine to dematerialize this *Cock* with respect to the wooden version.

A new creature in the Brancusi canon, *The Seal*, appears in 1936. As with several other works, a

187. The Cock
40⅝"; pol. bronze; 1935

small body of mythology accompanies this sculpture; nevertheless Brancusi studied the animal, as a number of excellent photographs found in his studio attest.

Almost as minimal in its elements as the *Fish*, *The Seal* like the *Fish* imposes itself by its size. Nor is it an altogether new image: the disposition of its volumes is similar to that of *Leda*. But instead of a joining of two forms as in the earlier work, we have here a single continuous form whose effective feature is its bent axis. The work is symmetrical and its section is generally round except where the lower part of the body dips to produce a mass of flatter section—the tail—and at the head, where the curving form is intersected by a flat plane whose graphic function is much like that of the bevel on *Bird in Space*. Sitting on its curving bottom, leaning far forward, this precarious shape needs the assistance of a wedge at its underside to maintain balance. But the fluid image is held in space, as it were, by two vertical planes: the invisible plane of symmetry on which its axis lies, and the visible plane of the head, at a right angle to it.

Although the facial plane is similar to the bevel on *Bird in Space*, it is just different enough to raise the question: What has been cut off? In the case of *Bird in Space*, as we saw, the bevel may be conceived as cut across the slightly longer form produced when the surface of the *Bird* is projected upward. Our first impulse is to project *The Seal* forward from its "face"; but no such projection could produce a Brancusian form which we can imagine being sliced off. However, if the neck of *The Seal* is projected beyond the head, the facial plane bears the same relation to the tapering mass thus produced as the bevel to the *Bird*. (The last

116

Birds and *The Seal* taper at the same speed.) The curving top of *The Seal* is then seen to begin (or end) at this plane. Indeed, the head of *The Seal* is a motif created by *cutting across* the earlier motif. It recapitulates the upward and forward movement implicit in the diagonal neck (appendix 17).

Unitary, unaccented on its great surfaces, *The Seal* is situated formally between *Leda* and *Bird in Space*, the bent axis of one lying under the continuous skin of the other. Complex in its curvature, its equilibrium and its spatial orientation, this elusive form approximates the fluid muscularity of its subject.

In preparation for a monumental *Endless Column* at Tirgu Jiu, Brancusi makes a study in plaster which is almost ten feet high. Its modular rhomboid measures approximately 30 centimeters across the top and bottom, 60 centimeters at its wide

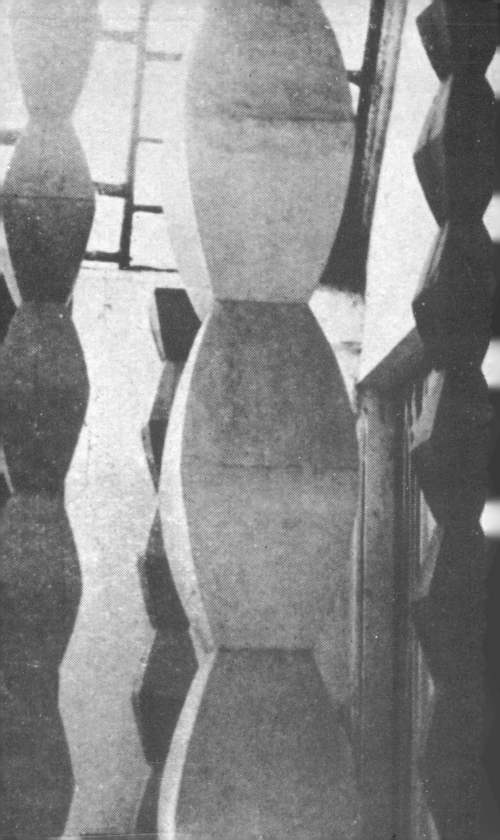

point, and 120 centimeters in height, thus preserving the 1 : 2 : 4 relations of the earlier wooden *Columns*. But a slight (accidental?) increase in the horizontal dimensions and a marked curvature of the lateral planes cause this study to appear airless and earthbound by comparison with the wooden *Columns*.

A detailed and carefully executed plaster model for the *Gate of the Kiss* is made with Brancusi's characteristic economy: both columns are cast from the same model, carved in stone; the lintel, likewise, is assembled of two equal parts.

Early in June 1937, Brancusi goes to Tirgu Jiu to work on the war memorial. The "Temple of Love" is an abandoned dream, the "Temple of Meditation" is a project for the near future. In the park of Tirgu Jiu he will realize for the first time a large public conception.

Gate of the Kiss was scaled up from Brancusi's precise model, while the *Table of Silence* and its stools were cut according to his dimensions in 1938. Both are in a travertinelike stone called *bampotoc*. The carving on the *Gate* was done in 1938 by an assistant from Brancusi's full-size drawings.

189. Study for Endless Column **detail**
237½"; plaster; 1936(?)

190. Model for Column of Gate
13¼"; stone; 1937(?)

191. Model for Gate of the Kiss
20⅞" h.; plaster; 1937(?)

The *Table of Silence* has a rough surface, caught more firmly at the edges. It is 31 1/2 inches high and just over 7 feet in diameter. It is composed of two cylinders of about equal height, the lower recessed 3 inches. It is encircled, at a distance of some three and a half feet, by twelve round stone stools, equidistant from one another. These monolithic stools are 17 3/4 inches in diameter and 21 5/8 inches high. In an early stage of the installation Brancusi had set them in pairs at a practical distance from the *Table;* later, it seems, they were moved away from the *Table*, still in pairs. It is not clear when or by whom they were placed in their present position.

The *Table* resembles the plaster dining table and work space of his own studio, and the base for a number of the large sculptures. Brancusi said that he got the idea for the stools when he placed two halves of an orange, one above the other, with their curved surfaces touching. The stools, while appearing to be made of the reassembled halves of a sphere, are almost four inches taller than the sphere of their diameter.

The *Gate* has a tooled surface, broken by the pores of the material; while appearing to be made of two columns and a massive lintel, it is actually constructed of a number of blocks and slabs of stone. It is approximately 17 and a quarter feet high

and 21 and a half feet wide. The columns are 5 1/2 feet square; the opening is 10 feet wide and just under 11 feet high. In contrast to these large dimensions, the coping plate overhangs the lintel, and the lintel the columns, by 4 centimeters, or about an inch and a half. The lintel is incised with a schematic rendition of *The Kiss* repeated sixteen times on each wide face, and four times on each narrow face. Both columns are deeply carved on their four sides with a motif very like that of the opposed eyes of *The Kiss*. At the sides of the *Gate* and a few yards from it are two low stone benches designed by the sculptor.

The columns of the *Gate* are, of course, developed from the *Column of the Kiss*, no. 184. In the columns on the *Gate*, the space above the circular motif has all but vanished, the crescent-shaped groove appears only below the circular rim, and the inner circle does not project beyond the plane of the column; the column is much shorter proportionately than its first version, no. 95. When the *Gate* is seen from a distance, only the motifs on the columns are visible on the massive forms; at a closer approach the incised *Kiss* motif becomes

194. Gate of the Kiss
(—)17' 3½" h.; stone; 1938

distinguishable. The incised lines that designate the hair, the eyes, and the broken vertical line where the lovers face each other are carved less deeply than all other lines, establishing thereby a subtle hierarchy of form projection and separation. There are some slight changes from the model: in the lintel, the vertical line that separates the thigh from the lower leg is omitted; the narrow vertical plane at the corners of the column does not continue up beyond the circle but goes around it.

The division of space on the lintel and indeed over the whole *Gate* has a surprising variety. Except for the motifs which the sculptor repeats, no dimensions on the *Gate* repeat each other. Thus, the legs are longer than the heads, which are longer than the arms. Of the long forms we note a number of widths from the narrowest, the border below the lovers, to the circular rim, the arms, the bodies, the vertical corners of the columns, and the coping plate. There is one correspondence: the height of the lintel is the same as the width of the columns; the sense of weakness or thinness that would result from its greater length than the columns is compensated by the addition of the coping plate. Altogether there is here a nicety of calculation which not only permits the space to accommodate the design, but which varies all the elements while keeping them closely related. The most poignant effect of Brancusi's calculation is the fact that in this *Gate* which is wider than it is tall the opening is slightly taller than wide.

At the end of July 1937 Brancusi goes to Petrosani to design the *Endless Column*.

195. Endless Column
(—)96' 2⅞"; cast iron; 1937

Working with a Rumanian engineer, Stefan Georgescu-Gorjan, who is to be in charge of all technical and structural matters, Brancusi arrives at a size for the *Column* that is fitting for the site, and carves a wooden module of the repeated elements. These will be cast in iron and threaded, like beads, over a square internal steel column. The whole will be composed of fifteen full elements, topped by a half element and based on another half element continuous with a short square columnar element below, around which lies a low molding. The column will have a flaring steel footing, set in concrete sunk in the ground.

The module, square in section, the lateral faces being slightly bulging planes, is 180 centimeters high, 90 centimeters at its wide central point, and 45 centimeters across its top and bottom. Thus, with the short columnar element of 45 centimeters at the base and the molding, the *Endless Column* is 29.33 meters tall, or three inches more than 96 feet.

Having completed the module Brancusi goes to Paris and returns two months later in time to see the first cast elements threaded down over the bottommost third of the internal column (appendix 18); he leaves for India as work continues. The column is fully assembled by the middle of November, and in 1938 is covered with a coat of golden-yellow brass, the molten metal having been shot out of a special "gun" in the form of a spray. Originally, then, the *Column* was a bright metallic yellow that gleamed in the sun. After having lost this surface for many years, during which it had a dark appearance spotted with large areas covered with rust, it was given a coat of bronze paint in the spring of 1966. The *Column* now stands a few degrees off the vertical, in spite of being anchored in a five meter cube of concrete.

The *Table* and the *Gate* are in the public park at

Tirgu Jiu, connected by a walk bordered by square stone seats made from Brancusi's design. Behind and below the *Table* runs the river Jiu; a few feet from the *Gate* and outside the park is the street. A little over a mile east of the *Gate*, and in line with it and the *Table*, is the *Column*, not visible from the *Gate* because the Church of the Holy Apostles lies in the same line. Beyond the *Column* is another table of stone, smaller in diameter than the *Table* but of the same height; it has no stools and is probably an earlier, rejected version.

The proportions of the module of the *Column*, I : 2 : 4, would lead one to suspect that Brancusi worked according to mathematical formulae or had a belief in the mystical properties of number or proportion, but there is nothing in his life or work to support this suspicion. Brancusi did seek the absolute proportions of any form he was developing, and it seems that the proportions of the repeated elements of the *Endless Column* are absolute and at the same time able to be expressed in very concise terms. Increase the first term, and the *Column* gets dense, stuffy; increase the second term, it loses its nobility; increase the last term and it becomes thin, etc.

Marvelous is the fact that the elements of the *Column* do not diminish in size as they mount. The persistence of size and of shape, the constancy of the repetition, causes the *Column* to remain near to the mind as it moves off from the eye. We have

here a poetry of the actual, without illusion or compensation, without tapering or entasis. The tension between the sameness of what is *known* and the perspectival variety of what is *seen* is unique in art. When seen from nearby the apparent changes in the drawing, resulting from the different angles of vision at which the different elements are seen, are remarkable. And these, of course, change again according to the distance of the viewer from the *Column*. Unlike Brancusi's intimate works, the *Column* while apprehended immediately, offers a surprising variety of aspect; its great size is not easily enveloped by the mind, and powerful optical and psychological phenomena come into play.

Taken singly or together, the three parts of the ensemble in Tirgu Jiu arouse almost endless reverie and interpretation. Rumanians see millstones in the two slabs of the *Table*, situated close to the Jiu. The *Table* is possibly intended as a monumental version of a little, low, round wooden table, with three or four legs—the *masa joasa*—found in some Rumanian peasant cottages, although the stone stools have no counterpart there. The decorated lintel of the *Gate* is reminiscent of the dowry chest —the *lada de zestre*—a standard article of furniture in the countryside. But these chests almost never have figurative decorations, being incised with geometrical designs; a motif (occasionally encountered) of large half-circles on opposite sides of vertical lines bears a formal resemblance to the opposed eyes of the incised *Kiss*. Most Rumanian peasant work in wood is richly decorated, but *Gate of the Kiss* is the only work of Brancusi's at this point to have any decoration. The motif of *Endless Column* bears a resemblance to the capitals of the posts on the porch of a little wooden church in his native village, and to other such posts elsewhere in Oltenia; linked diamond shapes are to be found in the borders of peasant rugs in Rumania, but they occur in the textiles of many other cultures too. In the end, it is appropriate that the only work of Brancusi's that echoes Rumanian formal and stylistic modes, abstracted, ennobled, and mythified, should be the ensemble at Tirgu Jiu. In adjusting his personal vision to the demands of a local situation, Brancusi created one of the few public styles that have proved viable in our time.

At the same time that it calls up a set of correspondences with the artifacts and native lore of Rumania, the ensemble synthesizes many aspects of a universal symbolism. The table with its twelve stools may be read as a cosmic center surrounded by its satellites, as the sun and the twelve months or signs of the zodiac, as a stone clock, as Christ and the Apostles, as the symbol of familial or group relations, as mother and children.

The *Gate* appears to focus on love and generation, humanity seen two by two, upheld by sexual energy. The motif on the columns can be read as the combined male and female genital organs.*

The *Column*, its repeated elements towering to the sky, creates a sensation of pulsation, regular breathing, upward flight, infinite ascension. An image of mounting prayer and aspiration, it alternatively suggests a connection between the upper regions and the earth in a downward movement.

* Brancusi showed Malvina Hoffman, the American sculptor (1885–1966), a photograph of the model of the *Gate* in the fall of 1938 and asked her what she saw. "I see the forms of two cells that meet and create life," she said. "The beginning of life . . . through love. Am I right?" "Yes, you are," Brancusi replied.

Brancusi told a friend that to understand it he should lay his hand on it.

The table and stools are round and have a vegetable closeness to the earth. The *Gate*, standing on two legs and with its contained imagery, adumbrates the animal world. The *Column*, like a thought that proliferates in one direction, is pure crystalline structure.

Solid form may be considered to have three fundamental modalities—the mass or bulk, the sheet or wall, and the rod or column—and the *Table*, the *Gate*, and the *Column* are versions of them.

Taken as a whole, the ensemble is a symbol of human existence: the beginning of life, earthly matters, the round of days; passage to adulthood, social responsibility; ultimate transcendence and sublimation. Endlessly suggestive, widely inclusive, it lingers in the mind long after having been seen. Neither sculpture nor architecture, it is an idea of the world made visible in metal and stone and space.

Tirgu Jiu is the climax of Brancusi's career, and he felt it to be so. Writing about the project early in 1935 to Militza Patrascu, a sculptor and former student of his, he said, "Now all the things begun so long ago approach completion, and I am like a workman's apprentice on the eve of getting his papers. So the proposal could not fall at a better time."

A *Bird in Space,* probably cast in bronze years before it was finished, depends, like nos. 166, 170 and 171, from the gray marble *Bird,* no. 162. It is slightly taller than the marble and appreciably smaller at its greatest circumference, making it clearly the slenderest of the four bronzes which derive from the marble and, in general, closer to it

196. Bird in Space
53⅜"; pol. bronze; 1940

127

197. Bird in Space
ca. 72"; pol. bronze; 1941(?)

formally than the other three bronzes.

Two versions in bronze of *Bird in Space* are casts of the white and black marble *Birds* of Indore. Little has been done to vary them from the originals beyond a reduction of the elliptical meeting of the body and footing.

The more slender *Bird*, whose spine was at first almost vertical (as in the illustration), now leans back as if rising up and to the rear; it was bent far back in an accident and was later straightened somewhat to its present surprising angle.

Bird in Space, no. 198, its fuller body rising in a gush from the exquisitely modeled footing, is the perfect finale of a research that spanned three decades.

Starting with *Pasarea Maiastra*, a bird that stands and speaks, Brancusi makes a sequence of *Birds* that are ever taller and more slender in proportions; as a result of these changes the *Bird* stretches upward and its open beak now calls to the heavens. The addition of a footing gives new life to the sequence, the *Birds* now becoming taller and more slender. A measure of the progress of this elongation in seventeen successive *Birds* is the fact that the last unfooted *Bird*, no. 133, has a circumference and length of roughly 19 and 36 inches while the corresponding measurements of the last *Bird* are roughly 18 and 75 inches (appendix 23).

If the increase in slenderness proceeds at an orderly pace, another relation, that of footing to total height, fluctuates. In general the principal means by which Brancusi varies the expression or character of *Bird in Space* is the body : footing relation. The bodies have differing height : girth ratios, the footings change crucially in relative length, and these two factors are combined variously.

The footing undergoes two distinct changes in the existing *Birds*, with variety of curvature in the final design. And the stance varies from the strong slant of the white marble, no. 146, to the verticality of the gray, no. 162, to the slight slant of the later *Birds*.

The bevel itself changes from the wide, short design of the white marble, no. 146, to the long narrow ellipse of the final *Birds*. In fact, the apparent desire of the sculptor to keep this reflective plane magically close to the arc of the frontal curve was instrumental in elongating the *Bird*. Theoretically, a short *Bird* might be designed with the same arc of great radius as the last marble *Birds*, but it would be so thin as to make impossible the setting of an internal rod. As Brancusi implied, the elongation of *Bird in Space* was no mere enlargement, but the result of pursuing the logic of an idea to its ultimate point. At this point the structural necessities, "the right measure" and Brancusi's fantasy coincide.

These measurements, relations, and changes in design, their variety and combination, and the number itself of the works chart an intensity of research unparalleled in Brancusi's long effort. In *Bird in Space* idea and image are one, not for the first time in his œuvre, but never after so long a study or to such luminous purpose. As he said, each version has its own inspiration. And each creates its own kinaesthesia. *Bird in Space*, in its later examples, releases a euphoria of elevation. Its shaping ultimately answers the needs not of a poetry of the avian, but of an imagination of flight—flight as ascent, as effortless rising, as freedom from gravity, as transcendance of the earthly human.

Bird in Space is unique among Brancusi's creations in the manner in which it departs from its

198. Bird in Space
74¾"; pol. bonze; 1941

129

natural model. It leaves observable nature behind at the moment it comes into existence—when the elongated *Bird* acquires a footing and becomes the first *Bird in Space*. This vertical image, as I have observed, resembles neither flying bird nor bird flight. The special nature of its fantasy—and of that which sustained the earlier series of *Birds*—is finally clarified in the version, no. 154, which has an undulating footing. *Bird in Space* is the shape of dream flight, in which no effort seems necessary but the slight propulsion afforded by the feet on leaving the earth. The classical counterpart of this image is Mercury, the nightly messenger, who has tiny wings attached to his heels, and who moves through space—rather vertically, too—by means of a power surely not supplied by them. The power is that of man's aspirational, ascensional nature which achieves imaginative and nocturnal fulfillment, at once voluptuous and beneficent, in the widely known dream of flight.

The Seal II, sometimes called *The Miracle*, is a
fraction higher and longer, and somewhat greater of section in the lower part, than *The Seal* of 1936, no. 188. Instead of the previous subtle change of taper, there is a marked drop from its new fullness as it narrows to the tail. The increased fullness in the area of the bent axis has the effect of making the change of axis ambiguous where it was clear in the white marble, and the greater bulk of the lower region seems to stabilize the sculpture and remove the need for the earlier, improvisatory wedge. The frontal curve has developed a slight concavity below the facial plane, suggesting a forward development of the head which was not the case in the first version.

Altogether Brancusi here expended a great labor

130

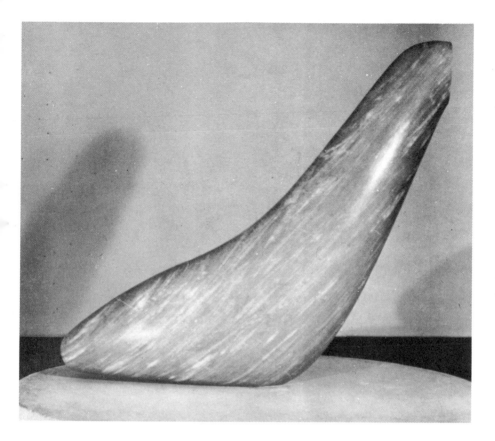

in order to achieve a set of small variations whose cumulative effect is a more compact, less incisive image that yet suggests a greater internal energy. A close-valued image like this was also the result of reworkings of *The Kiss, Torso of a Young Man, Torso of a Girl*, and *Narcissus Fountain*.

The Turtle exists in complete form only in a plaster cast, the original in wood having been destroyed since Brancusi's death. It is formally one of the most venturesome of Brancusi's later works, at the same time that it maintains their symmetry. The legs and head radiating from the body create an image more lively than any since *The Cock* of 1924; the parts are assembled in a manner that recalls *Torso of a Young Man*, no. 100, since *The Turtle*, like it, was carved from a part of a tree where two branches left the trunk. In this new

image no element is quite new, all being variations of motifs used earlier.

But more novel than its absolute design is its spatial orientation. Low, spread out, meant to be seen from above, *The Turtle* enters a dimension untried by Brancusi up to this point, though approached in *Nocturnal Animal* and *Plaster Form*, nos. 178 and 179. In the series *Bird in Space, Fish, The Turtle*, the first is perpendicular to the horizon, the second parallel to the horizon, and the third parallel to the earth; these are all the extensions that define a three-dimensional world.

The Turtle has a grim humor that comes from below. It echoes the last-ditch tenacity that sustained Brancusi during the war years; it rested on the ground in his studio.

In *Flying Turtle* (appendix 19) Brancusi drives the image to a point just this side of geometry and total abstraction, rationalizing not so much the shape of the animal as his own sculpture of it in wood. Instead of being composed of a mass and three outward-radiating axes, *Flying Turtle* gives the impression of the powerful union of two shapes, a square shaft and a section of an ovoid with a large wedge removed. The extensions from the mass of the body submit to the structural demands of stone: the long head is necessarily strong, squarish in sec-

201. Flying Turtle
36⅜" l.; marble; 1940–45(?)

tion, tapering as it progresses outward, and blunt at its end; the "feet" are short and of such section as to be pointed and yet not structurally weak. The head is a rare instance in Brancusi's œuvre of a form making its way between two others. *Flying Turtle* composes an image more dogged, more earthbound than the wood. Like *Bird in Space* and *Fish*, it is a creature that moves in a fluid medium, satisfied to plane determinedly in low flight, a foot above the ground.

Long after he carves it, Brancusi decides to turn the sculpture on its curved back where it rests unsteadily at an angle to the earth. Never, it seems, had he so toyed with a conception. He had probably become disenchanted with the original earth-hugging image. At a moment it had truly reflected his thought and the state of his spirit, but eventually it did not express his unquenchable urge to elevation. *Flying Turtle* flies, but in doing so becomes an elegant "modern" object.

Disturbed by the loss of Rumanian territory during the war, Brancusi carves *Boundary Marker*, calling into service again *The Kiss* of the Cimetière Montparnasse, no. 59, and even maintaining its

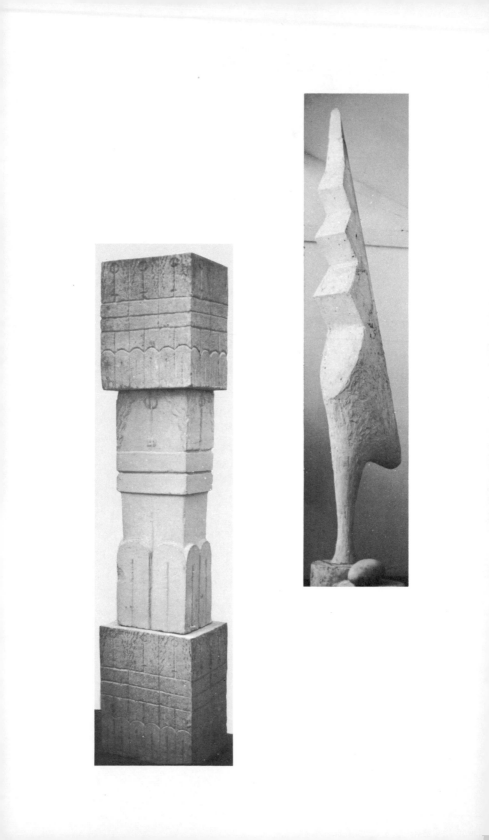

overall dimensions. But he hardens its elements in the almost geometrical manner of *Gate of the Kiss,* and adds a capital and base incised with the same motif. A column now, slightly wider than deep, *Boundary Marker* faces the four cardinal points of the compass.

In the large central figures the demands of representation on four sides have forced some changes in the design; Brancusi absorbs them without resistance. Like the *Gate,* this conception is stable, architectural, and decorative; lacking nuance, unmarked by personality, it is suitable for repetition by other hands.

But whereas the *Gate* reveals its final message—in the incised figures of the lintel—only at a close approach, *Boundary Marker,* whether distant or near, delivers always the same message: love—at the center, above and below, and on all sides.

In the Brummer exhibition of 1933 Brancusi showed a plaster *Cock* that had a stubby and graceless leg, obviously cut down to accommodate the work by a scant inch to the height of the gallery ceiling; later he lengthened it by about a foot. *The Cock III* is approximately the same height as *II;* its back makes an angle of approximately 74°, that is, halfway between those of *I* and *II.* The half-ellipse was lengthened after the Brummer exhibition, but even so it is shorter and of more open curvature than in *II;* the dentation is less deep. These two features mark a return to the relations that pertain in the wood and bronze.

What was surely the definitive version, both by the authority of its form and proportions, and the clarity of its drawing and surface, is *The Cock IV,* just under sixteen feet tall. It is four feet taller than *III,* or more than one and a third times as tall. After

202. Boundary Marker
62¾"; stone; 1945

203. The Cock III
(—)133⅛"; plaster; after 1933

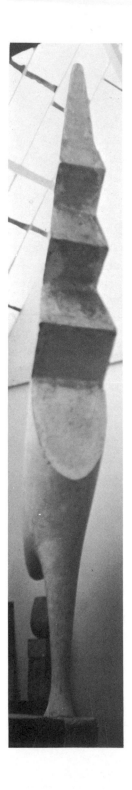

noting the depth : height ratio of the wood and the bronze *Cocks* as 1:2 and 1:3.6 respectively, we note that in *IV* it is 1:4.85.

The final plaster keeps the same angle at the back as that of *III*, but its leg is relatively longer than that of *III* and of the other plasters; the triangular plane is relatively the shortest of all the plasters. Thus there has been a gradual rising of the toothed elements and the plane below them. The dentation has the relative depth of *III;* this fact and a slight increase in width give *The Cock IV* an amplitude that was lacking in the three previous versions.

In a long and painstaking research that involved not only great variation in absolute size, but minute adjustment of pitch and internal relations and angles, Brancusi made a series of six *Cocks* culminating in a monumental version. In retrospect the wood and bronze versions were unsuited for enlargement because of their relative horizontality and high perch on the leg. The monumental form of the conception was achieved mainly by a great increase in verticality over the original and by a reduction of the outward thrust of the tail. Brancusi compressed the elements to almost columnar scope, or, in other terms, transformed the two axes of the wooden *Cock* into the virtual single axis of the plaster *IV*.

It makes its way upward by the double movement of the swift back and the energetic, stepped front, aimed at a point high above itself. "I am *The Cock!*" Brancusi had said.

204. The Cock IV
(—)191"; plaster; 1949

137

Reflections

The history of modern art presents the rare spectacle of two œuvres, parallel to each other in time, whose evolution is marked by an exemplary continuity and reasonableness—those of Brancusi and Mondrian. But while Brancusi's work after 1907 is sharply different from his production of the previous few years, Mondrian's development shows no break or leap of style; long in extent, fine in grain, it is the model of the idea of artistic evolution.

The biographies of these artists, as distinct from their abilities, shed some light on their difference in this respect. Mondrian was born into an artistic milieu, whereas the young Brancusi had to find one. The move to Paris was easy for the Hollander; for the Rumanian it was an uprooting—which he sought.

Brancusi makes himself over in 1907 by an act of the same will, intelligence, and ambition that made him leave his country four years before. Never again did his skill in faithful portraiture manifest itself, though the human head was long to remain an important motif for him. A mimetic talent that he had exercised on the skin of things would henceforth be applied to their spirit.

But his tact survives his change of mind and focus. It had been evident before 1907 in his relation to his models, his task, and the style under whose influence he worked; it, rather than talent, rescues his portraits from the mass of histrionic Rodinesque portraiture of the early years of the century, and it serves to contain the emotionalism of his own *Nicolae Darascu* and *Torment*.

After the studious beginnings, one feels in the *Petre Sta-*

nescu and *The Prayer*, for the first time, *l'air de Paris*. From now on Brancusi proceeds with tact *and* audacity, and his audacities will be the most gracefully, the least sensationally, offered in modern sculpture. Indeed, the tension between the boldness of his thought and the gentle fashion in which it is presented gives the work of Brancusi its particular *frisson*.

Brancusi never spoke of tact, but in later years he often used the word *"mesure." Mesure* is tact shifted from the moral plane to the visual; it is the tact of dimension.

In 1907, with *The Prayer*, Brancusi attempted to go beyond the influence of Rodin. His gesture, though similar to that of a whole generation of sculptors, was complicated by an involvement with the Master unmatched by most of his contemporaries.

In the effort to move along a road that seemed blocked by Rodin, only the Frenchmen Duchamp-Villon (who was Brancusi's age), Despiau (who was two years older), and Matisse (who was seven years older) went through him. The foreigners in Paris all resorted to the more radical solution of taking another path; of them, Brancusi alone submitted to Rodin and then changed course, forever carrying with him the effects of his passage. In his revolt against Rodin, only Picasso, Nadelman (who had settled in Paris in 1903), and Derain, in a few pieces, preceded him. The rest of an amazing constellation of sculptors—Laurens, González, Modigliani, Lipchitz, Csaky, Orloff, Archipenko, Lehmbruck, Zadkine, Freundlich, Gargallo—either began their "new" work or arrived in Paris between 1908 and 1910.

Whether primitivistic, cubist, or "hellenistic" in character, the new sculpture proclaimed its freedom from Rodin by the abandonment of theatricality and an accumulated sculptural rhetoric of touch and gesture, and the adoption of formal hardness and clarity. Much of it still displayed a Rodinian complication of theme or construction, and in this respect

Brancusi made a cleaner break from Rodin than his contemporaries did. Yet his own efforts toward simplicity and reductiveness were made possible by the daring truncation of the human form that Rodin had initiated. He was probably referring to the partial figures of Rodin when he said, in 1928, "Without the discoveries of Rodin, my work would have been impossible."

In pre-World War I modernism, the reaction against Rodin was one aspect of the general search for vital sources in the primitive, ancient, and folk arts. In Brancusi this turning to the past took the character of a return to beginnings, of a dream of beginning that linked primal innocence with sculptural simplicity. The stylistic archaism and the direct carving (as against "pointing") of the works of 1907 and 1908 announce the mood; it is continued in the many early sculptures of children and infants, and later in *Beginning of the World*; and it finds explicit statement in one of Brancusi's aphorisms: "When we are no longer like children, we are already dead." His sketch, *The Redskins*, indicates a moral attachment to the primitive, and in his brief relations with the Abbaye de Créteil in 1907 we may read a return to beginnings on the social plane.

A similar effort in the opening years of the century marks the work and thought of Gertrude Stein and Erik Satie, who rebel against the examples of Flaubert and Wagner. Miss Stein spoke of beginning, of "beginning again and again." She achieved a fresh, childlike tone in her writing by using the present tense. By this device she produced, not a separation of the chronological present from the past and the future, but an artistic *now* without temporal resonance, a continuous present that corresponds to the actuality, the nonillusionism of Brancusi's surfaces. The concern over beginnings led Gertrude Stein to an examination of words, verbal relations, and the very parts of speech; it led Brancusi to find a clear and limited sculptural syntax.

Satie, for his part, eschewed sonorities, made each note audible, looked back to Greek and medieval modes of composition. His work is brief and witty, and in this too both Stein and Brancusi resemble him. He and the sculptor were to be joined, after the First World War, in a friendship based on perfect sympathy for each other's art; he was also a friend of Miss Stein, who wrote a "portrait" of him.

Satie, Stein, and Brancusi were the strict and elegant extremists of the new spirit. Going beyond primitivism, they sought an art that was fresh, clean and unencumbered. In the realm of painting their closest counterparts were the Fauves; their precursor was Gauguin; their innocent exemplar, le Douanier Rousseau.

Brancusi's work in the years immediately after *The Prayer* may be regarded, not merely as un-Rodinian, but as anti-Rodinian. With *The Kiss* of 1907, on every score the antithesis of *The Kiss* of Rodin, he turns against the master of Meudon. His squat block of ordinary limestone accuses Rodin's tall gleaming marble. It is cut directly, by the sculptor, into a composition that is clear and periodic. The Rodin is cut and enlarged by technicians employing a "pointing" device; its composition is intricate and elusive. Rodin's protagonists are a man and woman, frankly energetic and erotic; they imply a past and a future. The gender of Brancusi's personages is indicated by gentle variations in design; his *Kiss* in enacted in an eternal present, without memory or anticipation. Rodin's marble lovers are continuous with the marble "ground" they rest on, fictions in a fictional space; Brancusi's terminate at their own extremities, stone designs set in real space.

In the following eight years Brancusi was to create works entitled *A Muse, Danaide, The Prodigal Son*, and *Caryatid*, and, a few years later, *Hand* and *Adam and Eve*. These are also the titles of works by Rodin (though it is Brancusi's *Sleep* and *Sleeping Muse* which resemble Rodin's *Muse*, and though Rodin made *Adam* and *Eve*); and while they are not uncommon in the catalogues of the period, the coincidence of seven titles in the work of the two men is surely not accidental. Rather, it appears programmatic on the part of the younger sculptor. We note Brancusi's *Gate of the Kiss* as against Rodin's *Gates of Hell*. Eventually Brancusi's anti-Rodinism went beyond matters of form and spirit: he opposed Rodin's faithfulness to nature ("art is not copying nature") and famous trust in *work* ("Work is a Biblical curse").

Brancusi's early vision is of a universe seen with childlike innocence and rendered with archaic simplicity. Intuition rather than intellect guides his hand. This impulse turns classical (and is signalized by the change from limestone to marble) and then absorbs the formal component of archaism, first glimpsed perhaps in *The Kiss* of Cimetière Montparnasse. Brancusi reforms his initial attitudes in response, it seems, to the needs of his intellect and sense of humor. In the following years he makes a number of quite round sculptures in marble and bronze, then a number of long sculptures in wood which establish the large elements that he will vary and combine during the rest of his artistic life. The quasi-geometrical replaces the "sensitive," intuitive motifs of his first stone carvings; he now has a lean lexicon of forms that will engage some fundamental matters within a slowly developing syntax.

In shedding his early archaism, he preserves his innocence of vision, but his means are no longer innocent. Intelligence, rationality, and precision are his new tools; the effort to create through them a joyful view of the world is the chief feature of Brancusi's modernity. His formalism is not a dogma but a means. Rationality is to be in the service of intuition, aesthetic delight and reverie; it is intended to cut through the dross and habitual excess of things in order to arrive at the essential. Brancusi seeks *essences* which by their clarity, unity, and immediacy will be apprehended in joy. "I give you pure joy."

In assimilating the shapes of the natural world to the uses of art, the twentieth century has seen much of a kind of stylization that is simplification; it consists in the reduction of the number of forms in the subject, and in the suppression of detail. In some instances, forms are joined under a continuous skin, as though by the abrasion of projections and the filling in of crevices, and this has been possible whether curved or flat surfaces are employed. Most of these modes of simplification are mannerist. Brancusi proceeds by other means: he redesigns the shapes of the visible world and presents them in a *rationalized* form.

Rationalization is reduction to quasi-geometrical form, to surfaces and edges that may be plotted, that meet and progress unambiguously, moving along their paths in logical fashion. It brooks no mysteries of articulation, whether of surface or axis (as in Arp or Moore), and its gentle or sliding transitions are as strict in design as the abrupt changes.

Rationalization is the method of the scientist who reduces the chaos of facts to intelligible form; it is the method of the craftsman who "sizes up" a job so that he can work without wasted effort. And it is the method of much primitive sculpture and of many sculptors contemporary with and after Brancusi. But in no body of sculpture is it employed as rigorously and exclusively as in his. We observe in Brancusi the almost complete absence of decoration such as exists in primitive sculpture. Absent, too, is intricacy of articulation, the very number of the elements being contained by a rationalization of the total shape. Rationalization is not only evident in the formed object, it makes itself felt as an act of mind and as a movement of the shaping hand; Brancusi's mental chisel, its effort must satisfy the demands of poetry on the one hand, and of a strict economy on the other.

Brancusi criticized an ever-growing simplicity in sculpture, which he called *"pompier,"* and declared: "Simplicity is not an end in art, but we arrive at simplicity in spite of ourselves as we approach the real sense of things."

Brancusi's syntheses did not lead him to a simplistic system of forms. There is no sphere, no cube, no easy oval, in all of Brancusi's sculpture, geometry being reserved for the ensemble at Tirgu Jiu, for *Architectural Project,* and for his bases and pedestals. Only in the vertical column of *Torso of a Young Man* do we find a cylinder, and here the slanting plane at the top has the effect of distorting it.

Thus, while the mind swiftly acquires an impression of a particular sculpture by Brancusi, it is not lulled by the automatically accepted forms of Euclidean geometry; it is held, in fact, by the deviations from them.

Likewise, there is no system in Brancusi for translating natural forms into sculpture. In the long series of portraits— *Sleeping Muse, Mlle. Pogany, Eileen, White Negress, Nancy Cunard, Mrs. Eugene Meyer, Jr.*—no one work supposes any of the others. All, while clearly from the same hand, have unique structural bases.

Brancusi was not occupied with fashioning either handsome shapes or stylish versions of the natural world. His artistic seriousness lies in his demand that a sculpture carry meaning in its shape—that it be the shape of meaning. In spite of the near geometry of his forms, there is no Brancusian method; there is only Brancusian thought or intelligence, and a Brancusian absoluteness where idea and effort, design and process, are one.

Rationalization produces an object, an essence, and an effect. Its immediate result is thingification (a formula, a sentence, a shape), and Brancusi had no hesitation in referring to his sculptures as "objects." His reliance on the object is a reliance on the goods of the earth, on the glory of what is given. The object is magical for Brancusi; it contains meaning, it concentrates energy, it is a locus of power and poetry, it speaks. And it speaks of something beyond itself. As Brancusi's friend and fellow-countryman Benjamin Fondane said, ". . . the object is not real, but *a good conductor* of the real."

Rational form is essential form, and this was the aim of Brancusi's imagery after, say, *Torso of a Young Man.* "I seek the essence of flight," said Brancusi of *Bird in Space;* henceforth from the multiplicity of the data of nature he means to extract pure distillates. Time suggests refinements in the process, whence the repetitions, the series in Brancusi's œuvre, as he seeks to distill further, to achieve a realm of purest essence. His trials are supported by one certainty: he must avoid resemblance. Reality could not possibly reside in the appearance of things; it can only lie in those few large eternal forms from which all the visible and transitory variations depend. "They are fools," he said, "who call my work abstract. What they think to be abstract is the most realistic, because what is real is not the outer form, but the idea, the essence of things." Mondrian, being of the same mind, would say, "Brancusi, that great realist!"

By the clear conjunction of object and essence, avoiding resemblance which is their mutual debasement, Brancusi's later sculpture induces an effect like a flicker of the mind. Matter is spiritualized—before your eyes, as it were. The movement between that which is seen and that which is understood is like an effect of cubism. Between the data of the world and an intuition of their significance, the sculpture mediates as a sign pointing both ways. The concision of the sculpture gives rise to a euphoria of intuition.

The primary experience on seeing a sculpture by Brancusi is that of knowing it at once. Prolonged attention or the accumulation of a series of views from a series of angles of vision adds nothing or little to the initial knowledge. Time only confirms what the first instant revealed; time continues to reproduce the first sensation. Many works of sculpture

146

induce immediacy and totality of impression, but Brancusi's œuvre after 1907, almost in its entirety, enforces them to an absolute degree.

The intuition of instantaneous knowledge, of complete and sudden cognition, is, in short, *revelation*, and this would seem to be the mode in which Brancusi saw the world when he saw it significantly, and in which he wanted his work to be seen.

The enormous influence exercised by Henri Bergson (1859–1941) in the opening years of the century cannot have failed to touch Brancusi. *Introduction to Metaphysics*, published by the "artist's philosopher" in 1903, was translated into a half-dozen languages in the space of a few years, and there is every likelihood that Brancusi, who we know read Bergson, was acquainted with it. At any rate, the opening paragraph of the *Introduction* sounds like a brief for Brancusi: ". . . philosophers . . . agree in distinguishing two profoundly different ways of knowing a thing. The first implies that we move around the object; the second, that we enter into it. The first depends on the point of view at which we are placed and on the symbols by which we express ourselves. The second neither depends on a point of view nor relies on any symbol. The first kind of knowledge may be said to stop at the *relative;* the second, in those cases where it is possible, to attain the *absolute*." A few paragraphs later, we read: ". . . an absolute could only be given in an *intuition*, whilst everything else falls within the province of *analysis*."

This language and the whole essay so exactly define the Brancusian area of expression that we are tempted to think that the sculptor found in them not only an inspiration but a kind of program.

Besides Plato, he read other Greek classics; his library included Rabelais, Renan, Panaït Istrati, and a number of Rumanian works. An old photograph of his studio shows a small table on which lie volumes by Homer, Bergson, Gide, and Henri Poincaré. Brancusi read the mystical early nine-teenth-century philologist Fabre d'Olivet. He was fond of Rumanian folk tales, and liked to quote the Chinese sages. He fell under the sway of Milarepa, the Tibetan saint, a transla-tion of whose biography was published by Jacques Bacot in 1925; we may suppose he read Bacot's excellent introduction. At Brancusi's death, dictionaries of many languages were found among his books. By his bed hung a globe of the world.

Given Brancusi's intensity of purpose and the amazing connectedness of his œuvre, it is difficult to assess the effect upon him of the work of his contemporaries; his sculpture often has the appearance of generating itself. It is certain that, after an academic training based on the antique and a tradition of faithfulness to nature, he went to Paris to im-prove himself and to enlarge his vision. He expected, one may imagine, to see and learn from the sculpture of Rodin. He did not, one may also imagine, anticipate the develop-ment in himself of revolutionary tendencies. Nor could he have expected to see the sculpture of Gauguin at the Salon d'Automne of 1906 where he himself exhibited, or the few daring stone carvings of Derain, shown at a moment that preceded or coincided with his own original ventures in this medium. It seems likely that as early as 1906 he was much affected by Rosso, and he once asked Jacques Lipchitz (who arrived in Paris in 1909) to go with him to the Luxembourg Museum to look at the Rossos there. His admiration of the Egyptian works at the Louvre may be reflected in *Wisdom of the Earth;* at the Musée Guimet he falls under the spell of Asian sculpture, whose influence may be discernible in the head of *Mlle. Pogany*.

While he clearly was an influence on the sculpture of Modigliani, we may see in the stiffness of *The Kiss* of Cime-tière Montparnasse the sign of an influence going the other way. An exhibition of Nadelman seems to have the effect of classicizing, at a moment, Brancusi's tendency to gracile design. Since he was a friend of Léger, Braque, Apollinaire, and Picasso during the first days of cubism, it is no surprise to discover it, in however transmuted a presence, in his sculpture after 1912. Indeed, a cubist device of his own, the groove along the eye and nose of *The First Cry*, appears in the same place on the head of the boy in Matisse's *Piano Lesson* a few years later; yet this motif appears with a certain suddenness in *The First Cry*, and we may wonder if Brancusi was not stimulated by the example of Matisse's *Jeannette IV* and *V*, 1910–11.

Like many of his friends he was struck by the power of African sculpture, declaring later that only the Africans and Rumanians knew how to carve wood. But he declaimed against its influence and told Epstein that he had destroyed work where it had appeared. Immediately, African sculpture had the effect of intensifying the rationalization of his forms, and ultimately of reminding him of the carving of his native Oltenia.

There are curious correspondencies between the early sculpture of Epstein and Brancusi. In 1904, while studying at Beaux-Arts (which Brancusi attended the following year), Epstein made several children's heads, one of which a later head of Brancusi's resembles remarkably. Epstein's *The Sunflower*, 1910, and the insistent motif of braided hair at the back of *Maternity*, 1911, seem echoed in Brancusi's *Adam*, 1917, no. 134, and the back of *Caryatid*, 1915 (appendix 20); Epstein met Brancusi toward the end of 1912 and may have shown him photographs of his work. The similarities do not end here: in the same year, 1914, Epstein carved several pairs of *Doves* and Brancusi two *Penguins*, all in marble and themes never again broached by either artist. And both sculptors projected a "Temple of Love," Epstein in 1904.

The openness of *The Prodigal Son*, 1915, is clearly cubist. At the same time a subtle dynamic quality in the work may be traceable to a futurist influence and Boccioni's exhibition of sculpture in Paris in 1913—which may be said also of *The Boxers*, 1913, by Archipenko and *The Horse*, 1914, by Duchamp-Villon, however much the work of these three men may have affected Boccioni in the first place.* It is surprising to learn (from a letter of Brancusi's at the end of 1920) that he knew very little of the work of Duchamp-Villon, especially since the latter was a constant exhibitor at the Salon d'Automne from 1904 onward and was given a memorial exhibition there in 1919. The work of these sculptors shows several unexpected resemblances, of which the most perplexing is that between the male figure of Duchamp-Villon's *The Lovers* (appendix 21), shown at the Salon d'Automne of 1913, and Brancusi's *Narcissus Fountain*, no. 82, probably not made before 1914.

The spirit of Dada, mediated for Brancusi by the character of Satie, is evident in *Cup* and *Socrates;* the latter may be a commentary on a humorous self-portrait by Satie (appendix 22). But the friendship between the composer and the sculptor had for both men an artistic importance that cannot be overestimated. Recalling the insistently repetitive mode of *Endless Column*, 1918, we read Roger Shattuck's description of Satie's *Socrate*, 1917–19: "*Socrate* . . . goes along by an absolute refusal of development . . . in figures that are endlessly repeated and scarcely varied at all. Yet the music never stands still . . . a new balance between monotony and variety."

Finally, it is interesting to speculate on the relation between surrealism and *Bird in Space*. I have described the latter as a dream image, and we note that its first version, no. 146, was completed in 1923, several years after *Yellow Bird*,

---

* Gino Severini: "Before returning to Milan, after his trips to Berlin and Brussels [June 1912] for our exhibitions, Boccioni spent a few days in Paris, showing at this moment a very great interest in sculpture. . . . I took him to visit Archipenko, Agero, Brancusi, and even Duchamp-Villon, who were the most audacious sculptors of the avant-garde at that time."

a stylized standing bird. In between, and certainly prior to the creation of *Bird in Space*, Brancusi was very much aware of the early manifestations of surrealism (page 4) and he may even have had more intimate connections with the movement.* Brancusi's capacity to dream needed no stimulation from the Surrealists, still the surrealist preoccupation with "psychic automatism," the subconscious, and the dream world may have provided Brancusi with exactly the suggestion he needed to turn the standing bird into an image of flight which is dream-flight. Otherwise, *Bird in Space* is an example of *zeitgeistlich* coincidence.

If any or many of the possible influences to which I have pointed did affect Brancusi, it is clear that they were assimilated by a mentality that transformed them boldly and radically and always to its own purposes.

Rarefied as the atmosphere of Brancusi's art may appear, it is a realm of certainty that offers real rewards. It is intended to give pleasure and create joy, rather than raise intellectual problems or existential doubts. "Don't look for obscure formulas or for mystery," said the sculptor.

Joy has thematic limitations: pleasant or pretty subjects, the elimination of conflict, the banishment of trouble of any kind. Brancusi's first subjects are children, beautiful young women, and parts of young bodies; a *Vieille Heaulmière* by Brancusi is inconceivable. As time goes on the animal kingdom increasingly supplies him with motifs, and these belong to the lower orders. Man and the quadrupeds are neither shadowless nor bright, and are carriers of conflict and trouble in direct proportion to their physical complexity.

The pursuit of joy in art imposes problems on the artist: he must be in the proper mood. We may take as perfectly autobiographical Brancusi's statement that, "Things are not

* André Breton in a letter, probably of 1923, to Francis Picabia: "Clearly, I cannot face going to Brancusi's studio with you."

difficult to make; what is difficult is to put oneself in a state to make them." He did not work nearly as constantly as is generally assumed, and needed strong reasons to set him in motion. When the mood is upon him he is irrepressible. Describing a chance meeting with him in Apollinaire's apartment, Chirico writes, with a certain asperity, "Brancusi . . . said, to anyone who cared to listen, that he felt a great inner joy." His favorite model claims that she "never saw him with his face contracted or looking tired; he worked in a state of joy." Belief in joy as the end of art leads him to reject, after undergoing it, the influence of African sculpture, which he felt to be demonic; it causes him to say, outrageously, "Who could imagine having a Michelangelo in his bedroom, having to get undressed in front of it?"

In the Brancusian vision the need to project joy has formal consequences. It avoids situations involving complicated joinery or the meeting of several forms, always the sign in sculpture of opposition or conflict. It shuns an intricate play of edges and planes, and the multiplication of axes.

The pursuit of essence, for its part, keeps the sculpture in a crisis of unity which provides the main drama of Brancusi's formal effort. Having achieved the modulated ovoid of *Sleeping Muse*, Brancusi embarks on a series of more complicated massive works—*Portrait of George, A Muse, Mlle. Pogany*, the *Penguins*—while still pursuing the unitary shape in works like *Prometheus, The First Cry*, and *The Newborn*. After the open, axial, and relatively disorderly organization of *The Prodigal Son* and *The Sorceress*, Brancusi will never again undertake a massive composition of any inner complexity or a complex distribution of axes. Unity will be achieved by the concentration of mass in a single form—a monoform—or by the long axis which will join such forms serially. A late solution will be the radial grouping of forms with respect to a central feature.

The question of unity has an extreme form: Since a work

of sculpture is one thing, how many parts may it have? A clear tendency in Brancusi's formal strategy leads us to think his answer would have been, unqualifiedly: one. The later works are a noble and touching record of his attempts to achieve oneness.

Unity is troubled by the very nature of solid form, which is multiple in having a top, a bottom, sides, and edges, and which contains shadow and presents variety of aspect. A sphere, from this viewpoint, may be considered as the ideal shape of unity: one surface, one center, one image regardless of the angle from which it is viewed. Brancusi's œuvre does not include a sphere, but he is never far from its influence, while refusing its geometry. The works of cubical or faceted mass are few, whereas many of the sculptures in stone (and, consequently, in bronze) and parts of some works in wood, may be understood as variations or distortions of the sphere, or as incursions upon it. The unity of spherical and ovoidal masses reinforces the sensuous attraction that curved surfaces undoubtedly held for Brancusi. Of his *Leda* he said, "It is Leda, not Jupiter, changing into a swan. A man is as ugly as a frog; a swan has exquisite curves like those of a woman's body."

The blocklike sculptures of Brancusi are created early and remain few in number; they are succeeded by the more numerous ovoidal forms. The direction of this progression would seem to be the normal one for the process of abstraction, a process which moves toward ever-greater simplification; we note that, superficially, a cube has six sides, eight corners, and twelve edges, while an ovoid has a single complex curving surface.

Abstraction results from continuous meditation on form, and, in Brancusi's case, from the pressure of thought upon form. This action appears to be closely related to the physical process in which a cube is reduced to a sphere by tumbling or by abrasion of its saliences.

The preponderance of ovoidal shapes and their derivations

over blocklike shapes in Brancusi's sculpture is thus not simply a function of his taste for the curvaceous. Essentially it is the result of the frictional quality of his imagination. His preferred form may be described as rubbed, curved, unified.

Artistic economy is a special case of that constant search for simple means which is a practical necessity for the sculptor as he attempts to wrest an image from recalcitrant material. Artistic economy is, like any other, the relation of means and ends, of input and output. In Brancusi's case one has the sense of a perfectly balanced economy, of a result exactly commensurate with the effort that went into it. Precisely what has been put in the work has come out; there is no sense of lost, unnecessary, invisible, or even magical labor. However much we study a sculpture by Rodin, there is no possibility of reconstructing the steps by which it was made; the miracle of expression outshines the miracle of modeling, and both are beyond comprehension. But in a sculpture by Brancusi one sees the form and at the same time has the intuition of the thoughts and acts that went into its making; often, indeed, their very order. The sculptor, it seems, has made only such form as carries thought, and has had only such thoughts as he could form; there is nothing else, no embellishment, no unexplained, gratuitous, or neutral areas.

It was to economy among other things that Brancusi was referring when he said, "High polish is a necessity which relatively absolute forms demand of certain materials. It is not compulsory; indeed it is very harmful to those who do *bifteck* sculpture." Harmful, because in this case it tends to confuse rather than clarify forms, and because the labor of polishing such a sculpture is enormous and creates an imbalance in its economy. In his own sculpture the surfaces are amenable to the polish, accessible to the polishing hand, and, indeed, easy to polish.

The decision to make a polished bronze is not haphazard. Only four out of some two dozen designs in wood achieve the state of shiny metal. Most of the works in wood, like the early stone heads, *Wisdom of the Earth* and all versions of *The Kiss*, would be unintelligible in metal. Of twelve marble *Birds*, four have no polished metal versions and these four may be considered transitional versions. The remaining eight marble *Birds* lead to fourteen metal versions, and eleven other motifs in marble produce some thirty-five polished bronzes. The versions of *Child's Head* would be unreadable in shiny metal; the large *Fish*, *Seal*, and *Turtle* might have proved to be distorting mirrors. *Mrs. Eugene Meyer, Jr.* in shiny bronze would have necessitated casting the large geo-metrical base, which would have looked like metal stock. Finally, Brancusi cast none of his six carvings of the female torso in metal; three of these are in translucent onyx, and it is possible that Brancusi thought the metal too hard and cold for these images.

Brancusi's gleaming surface is his ultimate invention. While having the traditional quality of splendor both in craft and material, on his highly rationalized sculpture it takes on a radically modern appearance, and becomes the absolute state of absolute form. The form of every marble, except perhaps *A Muse*, is perfected in the succeeding bronze; and later marble versions—of *Bird in Space, Mlle. Pogany, The Newborn*, and *White Negress*—learn from the intermediate bronzes. At the same time, the dense material is rendered transparent by reflectivity, and Brancusi's realm of certainty is invaded by a glamorous element of chance.

In polished bronze no fault of touch, no deviation from exactitude of drawing, is possible. The merciless exposure to light demands of form nothing less than perfection.

The absolute is subject to a law of inner necessity: It can-not be other than what it is, a change in a part changing the whole. Perfection is its natural condition, and Brancusi de-cried comparisons of his sculpture with that of primitive and prehistoric artists who did not know "how to work with such a precision up to the end as I do now." His perfect drawing and perfect surfaces are never the result of mere polishing, but constitute a fine and final carving which envelops the form in an unflinching exactitude. Perfection is commonly the pride of craftsmanship. Brancusi's perfection is the pride of the absolute. "My motto has been: all or nothing."

A remarkable text informs us that in a conversation with Alfred Stieglitz on March 4, 1926, "Brancusi said that when he worked it was as if an Absolute expressed itself through him, that he as a person did not count, that the individual did not matter, and this was the relation of the artist with the world."

A dozen years later he would complain that "aesthetes have an aversion to biography."

Surely this concern with the biographical, the particular, is at odds with an urge to the absolute, the timeless, and the ahistorical. Yet it is one of the surprises of the case of Brancusi that his life and work—like the sculpture's curving surface and orthogonal orientation—are perfectly joined. Valéry, who was embarrassed by his "life," was struck by a statement of Wagner's: "I composed *Tristan* in the grip of a great passion, and after several months of theoretical meditation." Valéry continues: "What is rarer, I thought, and more enviable than this singular coordination of two modes of vital activity, commonly considered as independent and even incompatible." For Brancusi the flow of outward event seems always to be assimilated to his changing artistic preoccupations. The sculpture feeds on itself and on his life too, and this life, so devoted to sculpture, is in turn formed by it. Who shall say that Brancusi, or any artist, in exchanging the attractions of one inspiration for those of another is moved more by the ordinary affections than by the revelation of new and untried formal properties?

But in spite of his criticism of "aesthetes," Brancusi often eludes the biographer, and, it seems, by design. The game was difficult in view of his care in dating and recording his work, especially during the early years.

Absolute form is independent of contingency, and Brancusi attempts to free his sculpture from the prime natural contingency, light. He aims at an art that is shadowless, and achieves it in the polished bronzes, where the material carries the light equally to all parts. Seen in the light, his sculpture gives back all of light. "I have eliminated holes," he said, "which cause shadows." But his forms are such as could be known by the touch, with the eyes shut, or in the dark. It is worth noting that Brancusi made no low reliefs, that type of sculpture that disappears when the lights go out.

In this respect it is interesting to consider the lintel of the *Gate of the Kiss*, where the incised motif of the paired lovers is repeated forty times, without interval. The design, once recognized, is not read—it is known, even where it is not seen. Thus the lintel decoration, shallow as it is, is not a low relief (a continuous surface modeled by light), because it is both unvarying and incised. The columns of the *Gate* are decorated with the same motif on all sides, and they too avoid the sense of planar relief by the depth of the cutting and the strong implication of contained forms.

Brancusian form is freed from reliance on nature with its painting of light and dark. It is form seen by the light of human intelligence.

But it is wise for sculpture in general to avoid the most ordinary onslaughts of the contingent, and Brancusi's sculpture is a model of this principle. It should, for example, declare its difference from other objects, and offset the possibility of mistake as to its identity. It should repel the possibility of being used in some fashion or of being grasped like an object of use. It should demand and deserve special attention. And it should be so made as to maintain itself in the world in its pristine state. In respect to this last condition it is helpful for sculpture not to have large horizontal surfaces

157

or such concavities as will invite or accept other objects or hold snow, rain, or dust. To the extent that sculpture is deformed or invaded by nature, it belongs to nature.

The Kiss presents a relatively large, relatively horizontal surface at the top, but this situation is not repeated in any other subject, that surface itself is irregular, and a late version of the subject shows a rounded top. After *Wisdom of the Earth*, which, uniquely, has a receptaclelike space between the chest and legs, Brancusi made only one sculpture with a pronounced horizontal plane—*Architectural Project*, no. 107; the work was disassembled by the sculptor, very possibly because it had too often been mistaken for a table. *Adam*, with its flat top, was clearly unsatisfactory; *Eve* is not flat at the top. The *Table of Silence* and its twelve stools are most susceptible to fate in the form of snow, objects, and men; these works are themselves close to the earth and at the "natural" end of the ensemble of Tirgu Jiu.

Apart from these few works, the tops of Brancusi's sculpture present points, edges, and curving surfaces intended to shed all manner of deposit, especially dust. This sculpture means to defy change or alteration of its original condition and remain always what it was at the first. In escaping the contingencies of nature it separates itself from nature and seeks to insure its own preservation.

Materials have sensuous qualities and structural properties, but no intrinsic artistic content, and a mystique of materials is limiting, delusive, and finally a concern of craftsmen. "Love of material" is a psychological, not a sculptural, affair; "truth to material" is a truth which changes from style to style and sculptor to sculptor.

There is often thought to be an original rectangular block of stone which the sculptor emphasizes or expresses. Do the several versions of *The Kiss* "express" the rectangular block? We do not know. Does *Beginning of the World* "express" an original large pebble of marble? Again, we do not know.

What is likely is that Brancusi, in these cases, wanted a blocklike and an ovoid sculpture, and would have carved them out of any piece of stone of sufficient volume. We do know that the *Endless Column* in Edward Steichen's garden was a tree—therefore round—that was trimmed to an almost square beam before Brancusi carved it. There is no reason to think that Brancusi was involved in Michelangelo's moral problem of thinking his way into a given piece of stone; or that, with the possible exception of *Torso*, no. 51, he exploited accidental or unusual shapes of stone; or that he "found" an image in the stone. In *The Sorceress, Torso of a Young Man, The Cock,* and *The Turtle,* construction is dependent on a special condition of the material. But it seems that Brancusi either arrived at a more or less preconceived image by a series of cuts, or went to a preconceived image directly, which is not to say unfeelingly.

Materials are only more or less useful, more or less adaptable to certain ends. Beyond that, a simple negative principle comes into play: it is unwise to violate the structural properties of a material if the sculpture is to exist at all.

There is no doubt that after the initial period of the "stony" work in limestone, Brancusi carved marble, with few exceptions, to emphasize its sensuous character, disregarding its structural properties. The finlike noses break, edges chip, unstable masses slip from their mountings, smooth and heavy shapes are almost impossible to grasp. It is not that Brancusi is simply unwise—he wishes to go beyond the material. In fact, he dissolves it: the attenuation of *Bird in Space* provides a thrill of the dangerous, the impossible. Ultimately the aestheticism and structural difficulties of the marbles are redeemed by the versions in bronze.

The sculpture in wood, unforced and "natural," is one of the classic handlings of the material. Born in a region with an ancient heritage of woodworking, a whittler since childhood, trained in carpentry, Brancusi was completely at home in this medium, and it responded easily to his thoughts.

Wood is the medium of his deepest nature; it is the material of *Endless Column,* his most "Rumanian" work, and it occasions his only artistic sentimentality—he cannot resist old oak beams. (This partiality has since raised problems in conservation.) Brancusi loved their aged ruggedness, and, of course, they responded beautifully to the chisel. Marble was to remain for him the material of artistic aspiration, of "fine" art; polished metal is the emblem of his modernity.

If, in certain wooden works, form is dependent on material, there is no play of grain or blandishment of patina. If the bronzes and marbles dazzle, there is no mystique of materials here. Brancusi's description of high polish as "a necessity which relatively absolute forms demand of certain materials" establishes form as the first cause. The *Mrs. Eugene Meyer, Jr.,* in stone and wood, has no emphatic stoniness and woodenness. In the many sculptures of birds, from *Pasarea Maiastra* to *Bird in Space,* the changes in form and size from the marble to the bronze are never dictated by considerations of material except that the meeting of body and footing in the bronzes is usually finer than in the corresponding marbles. In the wooden *Cups,* material is suppressed as Brancusi explores a language of form. And so forms are translated from wood to wood, marble to marble, bronze to bronze, marble and wood to bronze and steel, and from white marble to black. Brancusi insisted that once a form was achieved, it could be repeated, without change of proportion, in any size (but *The Cock?*), and it is clear from his œuvre that he thought it could be repeated in any material, within the structural possibilities, of course.

Brancusi is, to be sure, susceptible to the beauty of materials, and his tendency is to make them appear precious; but the form is already so. "Sensuous beauty," said Santayana, "is not the greatest or most important element of effect, but it is the most primitive and fundamental, and the most universal. There is no effect of form which an effect of material could not enhance. . . . Nothing is ravishing that is not beautiful pervasively." And Brancusi would be ravishing. But in his sculpture the gratification of the senses, like the flash of revelation, is not an end in itself: it serves to "fix" the image in the memory. "The beauty of materials," he insisted, "is my last concern."

What is significant in Brancusi's attitude toward materials is that after 1907 he made only a limited number of works in clay and plaster, and used these media mainly to study his subject before carving, as an oil painter might make sketches in watercolor. He used them, however, to the end of his career, always keeping his clay workable, and dispensing it to other sculptors. The monumental *Cock* of 1949 was modeled in clay, as was a portrait of a child in the early 1930's; both were cast in plaster.

Clay and plaster are amorphous in their original states; they are essentially painterly mediums, best suited to temperamental natures. At a given moment Brancusi feels the need to develop his thoughts within the confines, both physical and psychological, of a hard and resistant material. In stone and wood he can achieve the tight surfaces and sharp edges he seeks more easily than in clay, since hard materials are susceptible to minute correction and refinement in a way that clay is not. His mind is orderly and calculating, and the rigor of the carving process echoes the strict formal and artistic limitations he sets himself. Besides, a work in clay is chancy, it might have happened, while a carving is clearly *made*. "Direct carving," he says, "is the true path to sculpture." It is a process that is irreversible, pointed toward an end. Carving has a destiny, modeling has only a history.

The pleasure, if it is one, derived from touching a sculpture is very much like the pleasure of touching other things; that is, it is not a specifically sculptural pleasure. This kind of touching has a certain validity when it serves to dispel the strangeness of the sculpture and reduce the distance between it and the observer; but in most cases the palping of sculpture is only a voyeurism of the hands. It makes more sense, as far as learning anything is concerned, to touch a painting.

Brancusi's sculpture is pleasing enough to the touch. Yet it is certain that he did not intend the sizable number of works in polished bronze to be touched; the sensitive metal tarnishes at the contact of the hand. *The Prayer* does not invite the touch, nor does *King of Kings*. *Pasarea Maiastra* is mounted too high to be reached, as are the six-foot marble *Birds in Space*. Brancusi made two pieces that were meant to be handled, *Sculpture for the Blind* and *Beginning of the World*, in their marble versions. It is possible that the small heads in stone, nos. 137 and 138, the versions of *Sleeping Muse* not in polished bronze, and the *Cup* were also meant to be handled; all are intimate objects which often rested on cushions. In general, however, the tactile impulse is satisfied by vision; the forms, touched so carefully and intelligently by their maker, communicate their sensuousness without the need for physical contact.

But the tactile quality is powerful in Brancusi. If "form is congealed movement" (Reich), Brancusian form recapitulates a movement of the mind while the polish recalls the movement of the hand. A gamut of tactility is suggested by the later works—touching, caressing, rubbing; and a psychology of Brancusi would have to take into account the hours and days of his life spent in rubbing and polishing his sculpture.

The Kiss and *The Wisdom of the Earth* have the stability of permanence. A series of feminine images—*Mlle. Pogany, Eileen, White Negress, Torso of a Girl*—is unstable, and we may suppose that this fact had a significance for Brancusi. But if equilibrium is an index of meaning, it is also one of the chief determinants of the formal changes in the œuvre.

The statics of *The Kiss* leaves little room for exploration— Brancusi may vary the external features of the design, or stretch the mass upward as in *Endless Column* and other works—and after 1915 brings forth no new design. The stable horizontal mass appears only twice, in *Nocturnal Animal* and *Plaster Form.*

With the abandonment of the flat heavy bottom Brancusi has the various alternatives of the curved, the edged, and the pointed bottom, the top-heavy form, and the precariously tall form. The first of these may be in neutral equilibrium, or changeable and stabilizable, or essentially unstable but stabilized by the shearing of a plane on the underside (*The Seal, Leda*). Sculpture resting on a point occurs in one motif, the *Birds*, and that resting on an edge finds one motif in seven versions. The top-heavy form achieves stability by means of its footing, and the tall form, *Bird in Space*, requires a base for security's sake.

In all these cases form and stability *act upon each other,* and this is not so in the case of *The Kiss.* We have noted that questions of stability account for the differences between the large and the small *Mrs. Eugene Meyer, Jr.*, and between the first and second *Seal. Fish* rests on its center of gravity—it will turn at a touch. In short, changing statical conditions give Brancusi new and real forces with which to contend. As gesture, in the early work, reveals human psychology, in the later works the condition of equilibrium reveals the secret life, the psychology, of mass. Equilibrium is the law of nature to which the sculpture constantly submits; the sculptor himself is governed by demands of a moral order.

There is a clear pattern in the occurrence of types of equilibrium employed by Brancusi. From 1907 to 1918 the number of original works that stand firmly without support is twice that of all other original works. A similar reading from the end of 1918 to 1949 shows the number of stable sculptures to be half that of all other objects.

Along with Brancusi's increasing interest in instability, we see polish destroying density, reflective bases attacking gravity, and movement, real and illusory, questioning fixity. In

the ever-encroaching disequilibrium, mobility, dazzle of surface, and suggestion of suspension—and the final gesture of
turning the marble *Turtle* upside down—we see Brancusi approach dematerialization and dissolution of form in aerial
and luminous effects. To a group of amazed listeners in his
studio in 1948, he said, *"Mais la sculpture, c'est de l'eau, de
l'eau!"*

Brancusi for many years made a hobby of photography,
taking excellent photographs of his sculpture which for a
long time were the only ones published. The snapshot
("l'instantané"!— revelation in a box) held a fascination for
him and his relations to photography took some interesting
forms.

He did portraits from photographs, and began to record
his sculpture regularly by photography as early as 1905. He
had his own darkroom, which Man Ray helped him build
around 1921. Militza Patrascu reports that it was impossible
to use his bathtub because prints were always washing in it;
she was once given a camera by Brancusi, but he took it back
because she did not know how to use it. He was very demanding of a photographer who took pictures of his work
at an exhibition in New York. He took a close-up photograph of himself, and occasionally used a bulb and a very
long hose, as when he took a shot of himself with Mary
Reynolds and Marcel Duchamp relaxing at Villefranche in
1929. There is only one published photograph of him wear-
ing eyeglasses, taken from the rear. He made a trick print,
a double exposure of *Architectural Project*, and he had an
album of photographs that included good pictures of seals.
He made a large print (or had it made) that shows *The Kiss*,
no. 135, almost at full size. When Victor Brauner was introduced to Brancusi on arriving in Paris in 1932, Brancusi put
a camera in his hands and told him to take some pictures: he
wanted to know what Brauner "saw." And when he was in
Tirgu Jiu in 1937 to work on the *Endless Column*, he

sketched a column in ink on a photograph of the field in which it was going to stand (appendix 24).

This last evidence makes it seem possible that, in the absence of clearly distinguishable working drawings, Brancusi used photographs in developing some of the variants of his sculptures. In the case of the blue marble *Fish*, which maintains the proportions of the small early one in white marble while changing radically in size, it is tempting to suppose that Brancusi drew over a photograph of the first *Fish* to design the later version.

Of the drawings of sculpture which exist, it is not clear whether they were made before or after the sculpture was created. Most like working drawings are three studies of *The First Step*, one of which shows the image at about thirty-two inches, or about six inches shorter than the (destroyed) work which it resembles; the other two are somewhat shorter, and one of these has both arms over the head, unlike the sculpture and suggesting priority for the drawing. A number of works were certainly designed on the original block of material. Brancusi did make full-size drawings on paper for the motifs on *Gate of the Kiss*.

It is worth noting what is *not* revealed among the many photographs of Brancusi's studio and sculpture, and the several taken of him "at work." The only motif which appears under his hands in photographs is that of the *Endless Column*. *The Sorceress* and *The Chief* are to be seen with their surfaces unfinished, but otherwise fully designed. *Study for the Portrait of Mrs. Meyer* and *Flying Turtle* are visible in a "roughed-out" state, and a photograph shows *Caryatid*, no. 90, not quite completed and marked in chalk by the sculptor. From 1924 onward, the large *Cock* in several sizes and states of completion was photographed in the studio. There can be no doubt that this paucity of photographs of unfinished or roughed-out objects was intentional and, like so much else in his life, controlled by Brancusi. And among the many objects left in Brancusi's studio at his death there appears to be only one which is unfinished—a shaft of marble on which a profile of *Bird in Space* has been roughly cut.

In short, Brancusi would hide the labor and the steps and stages on the way to full realization, for the pleasure he wishes to produce is not to be qualified by a knowledge of attendant problems. No *gradus ad Parnassum* here; only the revealed object. The new work makes its appearance in the world with the same surprise and suddenness as on those later occasions, often repeated, when Brancusi would whip away a white sheet to reveal it to an astonished guest. The trials and hesitations of his art were his secret alone. "A work of art should be like a well-planned crime," was the way he put it.

Like a well-planned crime his work was usually done swiftly. At the Ecole des Beaux-Arts he did a figure a day, and he could make a portrait in a single sitting. He claimed to have modeled three pieces in an afternoon. In 1920 he said of some recent carvings that the work on them had seemed "endless," but a friend who knew him for long after this period reported, "He worked very quickly, but thought out his compositions thoroughly and then executed them straight off." Given his great technical skill, his disdain of labor, his relatively small production, and his love of travel and companionship, the picture emerges of an artist who dreamed and planned his work a long time, who often executed it in a concentrated rush of labor, and who then appeared in public, calm and smiling as always, outwardly sociable, inwardly occupied with his next or continuing projects.

According to a growing legend, Brancusi was always alone, working, in his studio. He contributed to the legend by saying, "A sculptor's toil is slow and solitary." But we may now assemble a long list of students and assistants (appendix 25), one of whom stated that "he loved working with other people." We can only conclude that he felt himself to be solitary, like many another artist.

As for the constancy of his labors, we have his statement concerning the difficulty of being in the mood to work, and it seems there were years when he was seldom in that mood. He suffered frequent periods of illness when he was unable to work, and in the last eight years of his life produced nothing new. Between 1909 and 1939 at least fourteen trips abroad (appendix 26) and many visits to the coast and to friends in the country caused him to be away from his studio, though sometimes for the sake of his work.

The Impasse Ronsin was a friendly, peopled place, and if Brancusi lived alone, his studio, even apart from assistants, was no hermit's retreat; in the 1920's it became one of the attractions of the Parisian art world. Brancusi must have been visited by perhaps thousands of people, countless numbers of whom have described the occasion.

Brancusi's studio was intended to be visited. A sculptor's studio is, in any event, more dramatic than a painter's; it is, indeed, a *place* in a sense in which a painter's studio is not. Sculpture cannot be stacked away neatly like paintings; it takes up space and, standing about as it does, it creates an ambience. Brancusi made the most of this fact, and was constantly rearranging both sculpture and blocks of material with a view to their effect and to the impression on a spectator. It should be remembered, too, that Brancusi had no dealer in Paris and that prospective buyers had to seek him out in his studio.

It may be said that in paying as much attention as he did to the appearance of his studio, Brancusi created the idea of the artist's studio in our time. No studio has been more famous than his and, since it has been installed in a neat version at the Musée d'Art Moderne in Paris, none will be more visited. The original made an impression which, as many writers have attested, was overwhelming, with its white walls and the light falling on precious objects gleaming among rough blocks of wood and stone. It seemed at once a temple and laboratory of art, the site of a confrontation of man-made order and natural chaos.

The need to envelop his sculpture in a total atmosphere was expressed by Brancusi in 1925 when he was reported as saying that for his exhibition in New York the following year he hoped to "build or rebuild a room in which his work may be properly seen." Seen singly, most of Brancusi's sculptures are gentle, quiet, and undeclamatory; they need one another, and numbers enhance their effectiveness. The concern for the relation between his pieces is mirrored by his concern for the relation between any single piece and the world: in this relation the pedestal is the mediating factor.

Brancusi brought all the resources of his talent for decoration to the teasing problem of the pedestal. In its simplest terms the problem is: how to get from the sculpture down to the ground. If the sculpture is tall, there is no problem since it stands on or near the ground. But when it is a question of a small piece, or a large piece not intended to stand on the ground, how is the transition to be made? The pedestals available to the modern sculptor are banal, a makeshift; they leave the sculpture suspended and isolated. On the other hand, a pedestal in close relation to the sculpture may fog or overwhelm the sculptural statement. We lack a period style that can embrace both.

Brancusi made all kinds of pedestals, simple and elaborate, solid and pierced, smooth and surfaced, in flat and curving planes, in wood, stone, and plaster, and in combinations of these. Most have a vertical axis, some are in the form of brackets. The pedestal of *Pasarea Maiastra* includes a pair of figures; for an early carving and a bronze *Maiastra*, stone capitals serve as bases. Because most of the sculptures are small, many of the pedestals are more voluminous than the objects resting on them; several are far more complicated, finally, than the sculptures they support.

But regardless of their degree of elaboration, of their

beauty and aptness, they are not, as many claim, works of art but decorative objects of the same kind as picture frames. The sculpture can exist without them; the reverse is not true. They are adjustments to the primary fact of the work of art and bespeak an area of choice or option precisely that of all designers and decorators. Made after the sculpture, they are rarely specific to it, different works having the same supports and similar works having different bases and pedestals. In no sense are they governed by *necessity*, as the sculpture is. Those critics of Brancusi who consider his sculpture to be an exercise in decoration* have only to compare it with the pedestals—true decorations—to be aware of its expressive character.

None of Brancusi's five works at the Armory Show, 1913, had pedestals, and the same is true a year later of at least five works in his exhibition at the Gallery of the Photo-Secession. Brancusi specified to John Quinn that *The Kiss*, no. 65, was not to have a designed setting or base. *Pasarea Maiastra* acquired its elaborate pedestal soon after its creation; the bird itself is on a plain block. The bronzes from it are on more elaborate bases, as is *Bird* of 1915, no. 83, but none of these have pedestals. In 1914 Brancusi introduced some variations at the back of the tall column on which the *Stanescu* rests, but the companion piece, *The Prayer*, was set on an unrelieved block.† *The Sorceress*, 1916, acquired its pedestal (not the present one) long after its date of creation; *Torso of a Young Woman*, 1918, is on a simple block of stone without pedestal.

Indeed, not till 1918, when Brancusi carved the first *Endless Column*, his only decorative work, did he achieve a motif which served excellently for a pedestal, and which led to the

* For example, Douglas Cooper: "the hollow decorative artifacts of Brancusi."

† The base of *The Prodigal Son* appears in a much larger version as the shell of the new Whitney Museum of American Art, New York; Marcel Breuer, architect.

designing of other pedestals and eventually to other modes of presentation than the conventional base. The designed pedestal makes its appearance, then, after *Endless Column,* which it often resembles. It appears, besides, at a moment when the sculpture becomes thoroughly rationalized and begins to lose its iconographic force: it is most elaborate where the sculpture is most simplified—*Fish, Beginning of the World.* The pedestals usually function as counterpoint to the sculpture, their size, vigor, and lack of nuance providing Brancusi with a respite from the subtleties of sculpture. *Double Caryatid* serves the same formal function with respect to *Pasarea Maiastra:* in a customary joining of contrasts Brancusi places one of his most rigorous designs over his most undesigned work.

"Art" and "life" remain somewhat discontinuous, and the real ambition of those who fear isolation by the pedestal is to design or redesign the whole world, since anxiety does not stop at the foot of even the best pedestal. Total control being impossible, a reasonable solution is to create a limited world, which the studio was, or to occupy a piece of the world, and this Brancusi accomplished in Tirgu Jiu. Later he addressed himself to other public projects none of which came to fruition.

Brancusi's concern over the manner in which his work came into contact with the rest of the world is like that of Seurat, who painted a border of broken color around his paintings which mediated between them and the wall. These were his last works and, like Brancusi's, they show a progressive dissolution and activation of their imagery. But these artists were alike in their habit of calculation, their use of extreme stylization, and in the "essential" quality of their images (they both used the word).

Seurat: "Art is harmony."
Brancusi: "Beauty is absolute equity."

Brancusi, it seems, had secrets. He had, for one, a "secret" process for polishing bronze; and the internal structure of the marble *Bird in Space* was unknown till recently. He used every possible hand and motor-driven tool, and he had a wall covered with calipers and other instruments that he called his "arsenal." But the instrument he employed on every occasion was his "eye."

Working with so few elements that the question of relative sizes gains prominence, Brancusi has seemed at times to have subscribed to a mystique of number or to an *a priori* proportional system. Nothing, and surely not the references to number and measurement in this study, can be produced in support of such theses; they would seem, in any case, to be refuted by the many trials and versions in different sizes and proportions. It appears that the proportions in Brancusi's works (as in Mondrian's) were arrived at intuitively. The relation of the dimensions of *Sculpture for the Blind*, no. 164, is a sensible solution to the curious problem Brancusi seems to have undertaken here. The module of *Endless Column* is the only object whose inner proportions may be stated in magically neat terms that have the appearance of a formula. Once these were established, Brancusi had no hesitation in varying the size or number of modules in any column. The proportions of the module of *Endless Column* are clearly a find. In the end we must conclude that Brancusi had, not a faith in number, but in rationality.

The sense of measure arises from the harmonic inner relations of a work. Given his calm of spirit, his health and classic sense, Brancusi produced works whose proportions seem precise, immutable, established under the aspect of eternity.

Measure achieved, absolute size was of minor importance to Brancusi. When questioned about the dimensions of his work, he would reply, in an aphorism difficult to translate, "Measurements are harmful, for they are there, in the things themselves. They can rise up to heaven and come down to earth again without changing proportion."*

Measure assumes an awareness of such imponderable factors as the psychology of imagery, the fitness of size and subject, and those inner and outer relations that we call "scale." In achieving *mesure*, Brancusi's native tact was transmuted into something at once Gallic and technical.

The time of apprehension of this sculpture is instantaneous; shape and image are grasped in a glance, remaining unchanged and ever present. With less speed there develops a realization of the effort and calculation required in its making, succeeded in its turn by a poetic or philosophic reverie induced by the sculptor's image. And certain works—*The Kiss, Bird in Space, Endless Column*†—have implications of time in their subject.

Many works of art give rise to a variety of temporal effects which are usually experienced either exclusively or as enveloping each other, but in the presence of a Brancusi there is a unique and curious sensation of a *friction of durations* as the slower speeds of insight and reverie run counter to the instant of revelation, constantly sustained.

This friction of different times—like the confrontation in his work of object and essence, of weight and lightness, of density and transparency, of order and accident, of the brand-new and the eternal—is another instance of Brancusi having it both ways.

In all the statements attributed to Brancusi the word "space" occurs only once, in the title *Bird in Space;* and in the catalogue of his exhibition at the Brummer Gallery in 1933 he added, beside this title, "Project of Bird which, when enlarged, will fill the sky." If Brancusi could become pre-

* "Les mesures sont nuisibles, car elles sont là, dans les choses. Elles peuvent monter jusqu'au ciel et descendre par terre sans changer de mesure."

† "Time's reverse pendulum"—Brancusi.

cious in his handling of form, there is in his attitude toward space neither preciosity nor obsession. Space constitutes for him so natural a medium, so easy an ambience, that he takes no cognizance of it; he is as confident of his sculpture's existence in the world as he is of his own. As a result the works are, except for very few cases, physically modest, possessed of only the mildest "presence," and unemphatic in their claim for attention. Neither implying nor figuring forth action, their movement is inner; they react to the outer only in their fleeting absorption of reflection, they go beyond their skins only in the light they throw off. Their unique spatial gesture is the creation of an atmosphere of calm. Their tact is perfect: they do not cry out or speak so low as to demand general silence; they are neither haunting not spectral nor threatening; one may pay attention to them or not.

When Brancusi does ask for space he asks for a large amount—"the sky." This is not so much a serious proposal as a clarification of purpose. Yet *Bird in Space* is the only work of Brancusi's that exhibits tension and mirrors that elasticity of the spirit which we know as an exaltation of space.

But basically it is not to real space that he addresses himself, but to the mind, to the intellectual and aesthetic faculties. His sculptures are "occasions for meditation" which he does not mean to disturb. Absence of movement is essential to his purpose, and his atmosphere of calm depends on the real stillness of the sculpture. Time and external movement leave their momentary traces on the reflective surfaces. The stillness of the sculpture only makes more evident the stirring of all else, and especially the play of the consciousness; indeed the sculpture awakens the consciousness by offering its stillness.

Sculpture is the art of that which does not move. This art is of ancient origin, an art of mysteries and dark forces, of death and the tomb. It is one of the accomplishments of Brancusi to have made a modern, inspiring stillness, to have

173

turned its past terrors to sweetness, and its old oppressiveness to freedom and humane play.

In the silence of Brancusi hear Satie.

Several pieces of Brancusi's are contrived to move. *Leda* was mounted on a platform that turned (as was *The Seal* originally) at a very slow speed, and at a late date some smaller works were placed on swivels. The latter device is in the nature of an aid to examination of the work. The former, by its slowness, seems to deepen rather than disturb meditation; it brings into play the slither of light on the surface of *Leda* and the closely related *Seal*, and it *brings back* these two forms which appear at moments to be *going away*. But the fact of movement here, however controlled, is undeniable; it is a logical outgrowth of the reflective surface and points to a problem latent in it—theatricality. Movement belongs to theater. Its occurrence, like that of many other features of the œuvre, is restricted and is relatively late as Brancusi explores one of the limits of sculpture.

If the experience of seeing a sculpture by Brancusi is that of revelation, the after-experience is one of recall. Whatever else it may be, Brancusi's sculpture is memorable, and it is so in two senses of the word. Rodin's sculpture is memorable in only one sense: it is impossible to recall every feature of the form. In Brancusi, the paucity of elements, their clarity and the clarity of their articulation, their repetition (when it occurs), and their differences create a tight system and a total image which inscribe themselves on the memory. The mnemonic is carried to an absolute point since it is possible to see all and remember all with a minimal expenditure of effort; memory is fixed by the ravishing surface and sustained by a parallel memory of the world.

A mnemonic system in art that does not imply the world is an ornamental frieze or fretwork, which is a metaphor of both memory and its opposite, anticipation. In this respect it is worth noting that the *Endless Column* of Tirgu Jiu (a kind of vertical frieze), is sometimes called "Column of Endless Remembrance."

Though Brancusi could discourse, he was given to a habit of aphoristic utterance, and in 1925 permitted the publication of a collection of his sayings which he repeated through the years to numberless listeners. The aphorism is a rationalization of experience, a distillation of wisdom; witty, graspable, memorable, it is statement as object. Brancusi's aphoristic tendency pervades both his verbal and plastic expression, and, more than any design he created, links him to his Oltenian origins. If a literary terminology may be applied to the sculpture, it is not epic or lyric, but gnomic.*

The sculptor does not cast his work in so-called editions. The five metal versions of *Fish* differ from each other significantly in their proportions and drawing. The *Sleeping Muses* show great variation, and of course none of the *Birds* duplicate each other. The two casts of *Pride* are from two casters, as are the three casts of *Head of a Boy*, no. 32. Only the casts of the versions of *Mlle. Pogany* and *White Negress* show no significant variation, although in each case the task of achieving the polished bronze was tantamount to making a new work.

Brancusi prolongs his works in series, and these series are of different kinds. The versions of *Cup* explore *proportions*. *Sleeping Muse* gives rise to a subtly *nuanced* series. *White Negress* and *The Seal* move toward *perfection of the motif*. The *Birds* develop toward the ultimate expression of an *idea*. The versions of *Torment* and *Torso of a Young Man*, and the passage from *Torso of a Young Woman* to the last

* But Hilton Kramer properly notes the "garrulousness" of *King of Kings*, the only work in the œuvre with this characteristic.

175

Torso of a Girl are examples of reduction—different in each case—to *essentiality*. The *Pogany* series is an essay in *purification*. *The Kiss* makes its first appearance as gentle, *"felt" form* and ends as emblematic, *anonymous design*. *The Cock* passes from the state of *intimate object* to that of *public monument*. There are certain themes that are explored twice, as if to test their limits.

But except for these obvious repetitions, Brancusi touches every *idea* only once. That is, while he examines and develops his ideas with an intensity unequaled in sculptural history, he never exploits them by running out a series of different works based on the same structural notion. The structural variety of the heads is a striking example of his changes of approach.

There is only one true column in Brancusi's œuvre; there is only one naturalistic torso, one monumental carving, *King of Kings*, and one monumental sculpture, *The Cock IV*, intended to be cast in metal. The form and content of *The Prodigal Son*, *Timidity*, *The Sorceress*, and *Socrates* are in each case unique in the œuvre. *Little French Girl* is the only carved "full" figure. *The Chief* is the only sculpture that incorporates a piece of metal. *The Kiss* and the *Penguins* are Brancusi's only "group" compositions, the former being the only sculpture that shows an interlace. The surfaces of *The Prayer* and *Stanescu* are unique; the "unfinished" quality of *Sleep* is different from that of *Double Caryatid;* the tenderness of touch in the first *Kiss* is transmuted in time to the almost mechanical hardness of *Boundary Marker*, and in between are the tooled surfaces of the carvings, both in wood and stone, and the reflective surfaces of the bronzes. Sizes vary from the tiny children's heads to the hundred-foot-high *Endless Column*, while these same objects signify the range of imagery.

"It is only of the new one grows tired," said Kierkegaard, "repetition is the seriousness of life." But again Brancusi has it both ways: he repeats his work *and* moves to fresh areas, doing both in unique fashion and seeming to destroy the distinctions between the new and the repeated.

Narrow and limited as the œuvre appears to casual examination, it is surprisingly varied, but is so only on close study. On the other hand, even strongly dissimilar works have hidden connections. *The Prodigal Son* and *Timidity*—both made in 1915—are unique pieces which are yet related to each other by a perfect opposition: one is the sculptor's most open work, the result of a relatively large number of operations on the material, while the other is his most dense work, the result of a single operation on the material. A double impression of variety and unity arises from the fact that Brancusi has the faculty of isolating sculptural problems with scientific neatness while keeping them in constant relation to one another. Eventually, the syntax of structure is explored with programmatic thoroughness.

It was to this intuition that V. G. Paleolog referred in speaking of the "cybernetic" quality of Brancusi's œuvre. For the sculpture is not simply a series of expressions thrown off by an artistic imagination. Brancusi appears rather to separate and specialize the elements of sculpture while making a network of the different strands of his interest. With the passage of time the body of work becomes a sculptural morphology, a systematic study of form whose bit-by-bit analysis is of a modality particular to this century.

It is this quality that causes Hilton Kramer to say (with regret?) that Brancusi's late sculpture results from a "rigorous effort to place the whole of his art beyond the reach of his private experience." For the same reason the early portraits are characterized (with reproach) by Athena Tacha Spear as being in an "impersonal style." Of the latter case we may say that Brancusi was pursuing "truth," and of the former that he was pursuing "form," and that Brancusi conceived both these matters to be outside himself—not personal. Hence his early objectivity with respect to nature; hence his later objectification of form.

Except for *The Prayer,* the *Stanescu, Head of a Girl,* and *The Kiss*—done in sequence—the work of Brancusi, early and late, is styleless. I have observed that the sculptures often need each other, but they do not need the sculptor or his personality. The effacement of self is known to art as the general sign of the classical artist; in Brancusi's case it is his signature. He often dwelt on the thought that "There is a purpose in all things. To get to it one must go beyond oneself."

In a sense Brancusi's whole life was spent in "going beyond." He ran away from Hobitza early, and left his homeland when he was twenty-seven. Even the City of Light did not hold him and he found reason to voyage over the earth, walking, as he said after his visit to Egypt, "on the sands of eternity." His works trancended his experience, and his later versions went beyond the originals. In the end he would say, "I am no longer of this world; I am far from myself, detached from my body. I am among essential things." But by then he had not been making sculpture for some time.

If the scope and nature of artistic and intellectual influence exerted upon Brancusi are largely matters of conjecture, there is no doubt concerning the effects of Brancusi on modern sculpture—from Modigliani and Lehmbruck to the present moment—and on criticism and design. They have been enormous and make a subject too wide-ranging for this study. Here I shall point only to one complicated and interesting situation—the relation between Brancusi and Giacometti—and discuss, however briefly, some of the continuing effects of Brancusi on recent sculpture.

Giacometti said of Brancusi: "He only makes objects." Yet the unusual body of work that brought him his first fame is composed for the most part of object-sculptures or sculptures containing objects. Giacometti spoke of these sculptures as objects, and indeed two are called *Disagreeable Object* and *Object to Be Thrown*. The Brancusian object, existing in a realm of perfection, meditation, and pleasure, has been transmuted into a form now provocative rather than pleasing, psychological rather than philosophical in its purpose, and leading to action rather than contemplation.

Despite this change in artistic intention, there remain certain formal characteristics of the object and a notably Brancusian quality—that of being apprehended at once—and this is no less so in Giacometti's later œuvre. The speed of perception that the one achieves through concision of form, the other achieves through almost skeletal meagerness. Brancusi's impatience with *matter* is exacerbated in Giacometti by a spatial anguish.

Brancusi: (criticizing Michelangelo and plucking the flesh of his arm) "Beefsteak!"

Giacometti: "I cut the fat from space."

There is a sense in which Giacometti is Rodin done over after Brancusi. The sometimes operatic, sometimes suffocating humanism of Rodin is rendered lean and spectral by Giacometti, but only after a formal compression which results in a new object; that is, only after the intervention of Brancusi. This would be dramatically apparent if one were to place in a series three heads or the *Hands* of Rodin, Brancusi, and Giacometti.

Brancusi came of age artistically at a moment when the century was still new, and in the place where its ambitions and self-consciousness were most pronounced. In 1909, with his first adventurous works behind him, he could speak of "the great and pure art of former times." But after the First World War he would say of his starkly formalized heads, "I would rather make them and be wrong than make the Venus de Milo and be right; for she has been done. And she is unendurably old." In 1925, referring to an exhibition of his work in the coming year, he expressed "the hope of being admitted as one belonging to this century." Modernism was

179

for Brancusi an enterprise gleaming with promise and the anticipation of wonders to come. "There still hasn't been any art," he said in 1927; "art is just beginning." And thirty years later, a few months before his death, he declared, of a projected *Endless Column* in steel, "It will be one of the marvels of the world."

The sense of the new, the hopeful, the possible, is Brancusi's first contribution to our modernism. His optimism is frank, uncomplicated, and ultimately purposive, and projects a rare message of joy in which there is no trace of *Angst*.

At the formal level he arouses an awareness of form in its purest sense. Brancusi created works of individual beauty and an œuvre that is intellectually coherent, but beyond these real results he awakens a sense of *form* as a special state of affairs, as a condition unparticularized in any design. The Brancusian universe makes a distinction between form and un-form: the latter has no laws, while the former speaks its reason for being, a reason in itself noble. Form is meaning for Brancusi; it serves in his work as composition serves in other cases. Considerations of form can never again neglect the example of Brancusi; he is the conscience of form in our time.

We may read a recent sculptural tendency to baroque expression as a reaction to Brancusian rigor. It stands in a negative relation to Brancusi, which is how he and his contemporaries stood with respect to Rodin.

His early exploration of the physical properties of polished metal—the mass-dissolving effects of reflectivity, and, in movement, the slither of light—continue to be exploited.

The quasi-mechanical mode of a number of Brancusi's works presages the century's ever-increasing reliance on machine-produced objects, whether artistic or functional. From it stem the recent phenomena of machine-made sculpture, modular sculpture and "primary structures," all related; they elaborate those aspects of Brancusi's thought which remain when his poetry is removed. His intuition of the technological has become a pervasive ingredient of recent sculpture, as has his rationalization of sculptural process.

With Mondrian he was the first to create, however guardedly, an œuvre of systematic formal development, a mode of artistic activity which has recently gained currency. He carries the matter of sculptural logic, unity, economy, and poetry to an absolute point.

His peasant origins and eventual urbanism made Brancusi the natural arena of a struggle between traditional and rational modes of behavior. That struggle is sometimes visible in the difference between sculpture and base. For the most part it is resolved in the joining of opposed forces to each other in the sculpture itself.

Thus the most poignant aspect of his modernity—and the one in need of further assessment—is his effort, in the face of the rationality and absolutism of his art, to preserve—indeed invent—a sweetness, a lyrism, and an intimacy of expression which are no less new. In this difficult countervailing of opposed forces we may read a moral intention: the creation of a modern life and modern style in which intelligence and order are compatible with humor, gentleness, and joy. In Brancusi these qualities are one: his intelligence is sweet and his sweetness is intelligent. In his sculpture the moral values of Hobitza were wedded to the artistic values of Paris—a marriage at once unlikely and fruitful. But how can we overlook, in this strange pairing, the artistic values of Hobitza and the moral values of Paris?

Appendixes

Vitellius, plaster
N. I. Grigorescu Institute
of Art, Bucharest. Courtesy
of Barbu Brezianu, Bucharest.

Ion Gorjan, about 1902.
Photo courtesy Mr. and
Mrs. Stefan Georgescu-
Gorjan, Bucharest.

APPENDIX 3

Jean-Antoine Houdon: **L'Écorché**,
1776. Coll. Edmond Courty,
Chatillon-sous-Bagneux, Seine,
France. From **Houdon**, by H. H.
Arnason, Worcester Art Museum,
1964.

APPENDIX 4

Medardo Rosso: **Ecce Puer**, 1906.
Coll. Mr. and Mrs. Harry L. Winston,
Birmingham, Michigan.

Brancusi: **Monument to Petre Stanescu,** in 1965. Dumbrava Cemetery, Buzau, Rumania.

Brancusi: **The Prayer,** detail, 1907. Muzeul de Arta R. S. R., Bucharest.

Brancusi: **Portrait of Petre Stanescu**, detail, 1907. Dumbrava Cemetery, Buzau, Rumania.

Brancusi in Paris, 1904. Photo courtesy
Biblioteca Academiei, Bucharest.

APPENDIX 8

Ancient Figure, 22½", stone.
Art Institute of Chicago.

Marie Laurencin: **Group of Artists**, 1908.
Baltimore Museum of Art, the Cone Collection.

Marie Laurencin:
Self-portrait, 1906.
Museum of Modern Art, New York.

Elie Nadelman: **Head,** 1906(?).
Joseph H. Hirshhorn Collection,
New York.

Margit Pogany: **Self-portrait,** 1913. Philadelphia Museum of Art.

Margit Pogany in 1910.
Photo courtesy
Andrew Forgas, Melbourne.

Two communications of Miss Margit Pogany, Camberwell, Vict., Australia, reproduced by kind permission of the Museum of Modern Art, New York. The first is dated only by the year and was apparently intended to accompany the *Mlle. Pogany* by Brancusi which she owned and was in the process of selling to the museum; it is typed, and signed by hand.

1952

For several years I studied painting in Paris, as I am an artist. It was there that I met Mr. Brancusi. In 1911 I was living in a boarding house and he used to come there for his meals as he was living nearby. I cannot remember how often we had met when one day he asked me to come to his studio and see some work he had just finished. He seemed very eager to show it, wanting me to come that very day. I went with a friend of mine and he showed us his sculptures. Among them was a head of white marble which attracted me strongly. I felt it was me, although it had none of my features. It was all eyes. I looked at Brancusi and noticed that while he was speaking to my friend, all the time he was slyly observing me. He was awfully pleased that I had recognised myself. (Later he gave me a photograph of the head.) The work he had finished was a sculpture showing the influence of Negro art, something quite novel then. Later it was put up as a headstone for a young Russian woman in the cemetary of Montparnasse and a great many people were shocked by it.

After the first visit I used to see quite a lot of Brancusi. When I left the boarding house and took a studio which I shared with

190

a friend, he often called at our place. I also saw some more of his work and realised he was a real artist, striving hard to find his own self, striving to find the expression for his own conception of art which differed greatly from that of others. He also made me understand that art was not copying nature, as so many artists thought.

I wished very much to have my portrait done by Braneusi and asked whether he would do it. He was greatly pleased by my proposal, would not discuss the financial side, saying anything I should offer would be alright. Knowing that I was to leave Paris shortly he asked me for a few sittings. I sat for him several times. Each time he began and finished a new bust (in clay). Each of these was beautiful and a wonderful likeness, and each time I begged him to keep it and use it for the definite bust—but he only laughed and threw it back into the boxful of clay that stood in the corner of the studio—to my great disappointment. Once I had to sit for my hands but the pose was quite different to that of the present bust, he only wanted to learn them by heart as he already knew my head by heart.

The bust was not yet begun when I left Paris in January 1912. He promised me that I should have it in a few months, but later he wrote he needed much more time for it. It was only in 1913 that he finished the marble and sent it first to an exhibition. Of course few people realised the beauty of it and he was jeered at. I remember when I was once more in Paris, Brancusi showed me a newspaper cutting in which a critic proposed to get in touch with "Mlle. Pogany" and ask her to sue him for libel.

In the autumn of 1913 I got a letter to tell me he had finished the bust in bronze as well as the marble and asked me which I would prefer to have. I left him to choose for me and he sent me the bronze. When it arrived it shone like gold except where it was stained a dull black. Brancusi warned me not to touch it with bare hands as the finger marks would show. For years it kept bright, but when later it got dull I did not mind because I thought it made the modelling more impressive.

Brancusi made a second bust, also both in marble and in bronze. It is the one known by reproductions. I saw a brassy bronze copy of it in his studio a good many years later in 1925. I had not been in Paris for 12 years, owing to the first world war and other reasons. By that time Brancusi had reached, after much suffering, the peak he had striven for and, although not yet known to many, he was already appreciated by the chosen few.

Margit Pogany

After the transfer of the bust to the museum, Miss Pogany wrote

Alfred H. Barr, Jr., its director, a letter dated Aug. 4, 1953, from which the following passages are pertinent:

> I am very glad that you are so interested by the bust that you want some documentary photographs. I am sorry I have not any, as I have left behind all when I left Hungary a few years ago. I cannot get in touch now with those friends who had some of my photos and do not know whether they have them still.
>
> . . . I have got a self portrait made in 1913, some months before I saw the bust by Brancusi. You will note the coincidence of the pose from the enclosed photo. This portrait was a very good likeness and I kept it therefore . . .
>
> Allow me also to rectify some of the data which I probably got wrong when I wrote some time ago.
>
> It was in July 1910 I first visited Mr. Brancusi's studio. I left Paris in January 1911 and our sittings took place in December 1910 and January.

APPENDIX 12

Brancusi:
Pasarea Maiastra, 1910.
Museum of Modern Art,
New York.

Amedeo Modigliani: **Study for Caryatid,** ca. 1915.
Norton Gallery and School of Art, West Palm Beach.

Detail of porch of wooden church, Hobitza, Rumania.

Snapshot by Brancusi sent to H. P. Roché, August 1924, from St. Raphael.
Courtesy Mme. Roché, Sèvres.

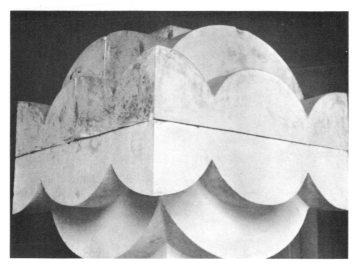

Brancusi: **Model of Temple of Meditation,** ca. 1935.

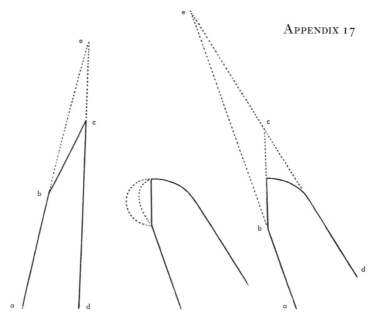

Schematic representation by the author of head of **Bird in Space** and **The Seal.**

The erection of **Endless Column,** Tirgu Jiu, beginning of November 1937; Brancusi walking toward the column. Photo courtesy Stefan Georgescu-Gorjan, Bucharest.

Brancusi: **Flying Turtle,** upright.
Solomon R. Guggenheim Museum, New York.

Jacob Epstein:
Sleeping Child, 1904.

Brancusi: **Sleeping Child,** 1908.
Coll. Mr. and Mrs. Malcolm
Eisenberg, Philadelphia.

APPENDIX 20 *continued*

Jacob Epstein: **Sunflower,** 1910.
Schinman Coll., U.S. Photos
from **Jacob Epstein, sculptor,**
by Richard Buckle,
New York, World, 1963.

Jacob Epstein: **Maternity,** 1911.
Coll. Lady Epstein.

Brancusi: **Caryatid,**
detail, 1915.
Staempfli Gallery,
New York.

Raymond Duchamp-Villon: **The Lovers**, 1913. Tate Gallery, London.

Erik Satie: "Study for a bust of M. Erik Satie, drawn by himself, with a thought: I came too young into a world too old."

From **Despre Erik Satie si Noul Muzicalism,** by V. G. Paleolog, Bucharest, 1945.

The *Birds* of Brancusi.

no. 61.	Pasarea Maiastra	MOMA	1910	white marble
no. 69.	Bird	PMA	1912(?)	" "
no. 70a.	Maiastra	K. Steichen	1912(?)	bronze
no. 70b.	Maiastra	Graham	1912(?)	"
no. 71.	Maiastra	Cowles	1912	pol. bronze
no. 72.	Maiastra	Guggenheim	1912(?)	" "
no. 83.	Bird	MNAM	1915	gray marble
no. 116.	Yellow Bird	Yale	1918	yellow marble
no. 117.	Golden Bird	Chicago	1919	pol. bronze
no. 118.	Golden Bird	Minneapolis	1920	" "
no. 133.	Bird	De Gunzburg	1921(?)	gray marble
no. 146.	Bird in Space	Marx	1923	white marble
no. 150.	Bird in Space	PMA	1924	pol. bronze
no. 154.	Bird in Space	PMA	1925	yellow marble
no. 162.	Bird in Space	Zurich	1925	gray marble
no. 163.	Bird in Space	Meyer	1925	white marble
no. 165.	Bird in Space	Priv. coll.	1926(?)	" "
no. 166.	Bird in Space	E. Steichen	1926	pol. bronze
no. 169.	Bird in Space	Schreiber	1927	" "
no. 170.	Bird in Space	De Rothschild	1927(?)	" "
no. 171.	Bird in Space	MOMA	1928(?)	" "
no. 184a.	Bird in Space	Holkar	1933(?)	" "
no. 185.	Bird in Space	Indore	1933	white marble
no. 186.	Bird in Space	Indore	1933	black marble
no. 196.	Bird in Space	Guggenheim	1940	pol. bronze
no. 197.	Bird in Space	Burden	1941	" "
no. 198.	Bird in Space	MNAM	1941	" "

Dimensions here are recorded to the nearest eighth of an inch. This list includes only those *Birds* executed in a definitive material.

Nos. 70a, 70b, 71, and 72 depend from no. 61; nos. 117 and

		HT.	CIRCUM.	FOOT	FOOT IN %
no. 61.	Pasarea Maiastra	22⅛″	24″		
no. 69.	Bird	23¾″	23″		
no. 70a.	Maiastra	21¾″	23½″		
no. 70b.	Maiastra	22″	23⅞″		
no. 71.	Maiastra	24″	25″		
no. 72.	Maiastra	24⅛″	24⅝″		
no. 83.	Bird	27¾″	20″		
no. 116.	Yellow Bird	36⅝″	21″		
no. 117.	Golden Bird	36½″	21″		
no. 118.	Golden Bird	37¾″	20½″		
no. 133.	Bird	35½″	18¾″		
no. 146.	Bird in Space	50⅝″	18¾″	6¾″	13.19
no. 150.	Bird in Space	50″	17⅞″	6⅝″	13.25
no. 154.	Bird in Space	45¾″	14⅝″	7¾″	16.9
no. 162.	Bird in Space	52¾″	14⅞″	8⅝″	16.4
no. 163.	Bird in Space	71″	18⅜″	10″	13.98
no. 165.	Bird in Space	74⅜″	17⅞″	12⅜″	16.5
no. 166.	Bird in Space	53¼″	15⅜″	9⅝″	17.97
no. 169.	Bird in Space	72½″	18⅜″	11¾″	16.14
no. 170.	Bird in Space	53⅝″	15¾″	9½″	17.7
no. 171.	Bird in Space	54″	15¼″	8¾″	16.25
no. 184a.	Bird in Space	73⅛″	18″	11¾″	16.08
no. 185.	Bird in Space	72½″	17½″	12″	16.56
no. 186.	Bird in Space	76½″	19″	12½″	16.34
no. 196.	Bird in Space	53⅜″	13⅞″	8⅞″	16.6
no. 197.	Bird in Space	72″	17⅜″	11⅞″	16.4
no. 198.	Bird in Space	74¾″	18⅛″	12⅜″	16.55

118, from no. 116; no. 150, from no. 146; nos. 166, 170, 171, and 196, from no. 162; no. 169, probably from no. 163; no. 184a, probably from no. 169; no. 197, from no. 185; and no. 198, from no. 186.

Brancusi: **Endless Column,** sketch over photograph, Tirgu Jiu, end of July 1937.
Courtesy Stefan Georgescu-Gorjan, Bucharest.

A list of associates, students and assistants of Brancusi:

Dr. Dimitrie Gerota. His name appears with that of Brancusi on the
  Écorché, 1902; he probably supervised the work of the
  young sculptor.
Amedeo Modigliani. Started to carve in 1909 under Brancusi's guid-
  ance.
Unidentified helper, possibly a woman. Appears, assisting Brancusi, in a
  watercolor by the sculptor dated 1915; see illus. below.

Brancusi: **Self-portrait at the Anvil,** 1915. Coll. Samuel Staempfli,
Berne. Courtesy Kornfeld & Klipstein, Berne.

Militza Patrascu. Studied with Brancusi, 1919–1923; personal communication, Bucharest, June 1964.
Mrs. Heyworth Mills. Received criticism from Brancusi, 1921–1923;
  communication of M. Duchamp, New York. (Her hus-
  band, who had a kennel, gave Brancusi his dog Polaire.

Romul Ladea. Briefly apprenticed to Brancusi in 1924; catalogue of Ladea exhibition, Muzeul de Arta, Cluj, May 1966, p. 9.

Irène Codreane. Studied with Brancusi in the twenties; personal communication, Paris, Sept. 1964.

Sanda Kessel. Studied with Brancusi in the twenties; Jianou 1963, p. 52, bibl. 46.

Marguerite Cosaceanu. Studied with Brancusi in the twenties; communication of I. Codreane, Brancusi Conference, Bucharest, Oct. 14, 1967.

Isamu Noguchi. Apprenticed to Brancusi, 1927–29; Paul Cummings, *A Dictionary of Contemporary American Artists*, N.Y., St. Martin's, 1966, p. 217.

Jacques Hérold. Worked for Brancusi, spring of 1930 and later; Waldberg 1961, p. 5, bibl. 87.

Joseph Lacasse. Assisted the sculptor, 1933; communication of C. Antonovici, New York, 1964.

Juana Muller. Jianou 1963, p. 52, bibl. 46.

Constantin Antonovici. Assisted Brancusi, 1947–1951; communication of Mr. Antonovici, New York, who has a "certificate" drawn up by Brancusi and testifying to his abilities.

Alexandre Istrati. Assisted Brancusi, 1949; Jianou 1963, p. 60, bibl. 46.

APPENDIX 26

A list of Brancusi's travels outside of France, after his arrival in Paris in 1904:

1909   Bucharest. Early in the year; a letter to F. Storck in Brezianu 1964, p. 391, bibl. 12.

1910   Florence. A brief trip mentioned by the sculptor to P. Dorazio, Rome; communication of Mr. Dorazio, New York, Feb. 19, 1966.

1914   Rumania. May 26–June 17; passport, comunication of B. Brezianu, Bucharest. Installation of the Stanescu monument in Buzau.

1921   Milan. May 25.
       Naples. May 27.
       Rumania. June 3 (Constantza)   Passport, communication
          to June 18 (Halmeu)   of B. Brezianu.
       Prague. June 20.
       Belgium. June 21.
       Corsica. A two-week trip with Raymond Radiguet; Hamnett 1932 p. 196, bibl. 43.

1922   Rumania. Sept. 11–Oct. 7; passport, communication of B. Brezianu. A trip with Miss Eileen Lane that included a visit to Hobitza (Comarnescu 1964, bibl. 20), Craiova (Georgescu-

Gorjan 1965, bibl. 39) and Bucharest (Brezianu 1964, p. 395, bibl. 12).

1925   England. Sept. 30–Oct. 10; passport, communication of B. Brezianu. The sculptor visited London; Giedion-Welcker 1959, p. 25, note 3, bibl. 41, where, however, dated 1924.

1926   New York. ca. Jan. 20–ca. Mar. 24. Visit to attend exhibition at the Wildenstein Galleries; Foster 1926, bibl. 29. Talked to A. Stieglitz, Jan. 29 and Mar. 4; Seligmann 1966, pp. 35, 69, bibl. 80. Passport records embarkation at Le Havre, Jan. 13, and debarkation, Mar. 31; communication of B. Brezianu.

Belgium. May 8–15; passport, communication of B. Brezianu.

New York. Sept. 23–Dec. 3. Visit to attend exhibition at the Brummer Gallery; *NY Times* 1926, bibl. 60. Date of arrival from passport; communication of B. Brezianu. Date of departure from Seligmann 1966, p. 112, bibl. 80.

1930   Rumania. Sept. 26–Oct. 12; passport, communication of B. Brezianu. Visited Bucharest; Brezianu 1964, bibl. 11.

1937   Rumania. Early June–Sept. 2. In Tirgu Jiu "about two months" to work on *Gate of the Kiss* and *Table of Silence;* communication of S. Georgescu-Gorjan, Bucharest. July 26 and "for more than one month" in Petrosani to work on *Endless Column,* and left Bucharest, Sept. 2; Georgescu-Gorjan 1964, pp. 280, 287, bibl. 37.

Rumania. Early November in Tirgu Jiu; Georgescu-Gorjan 1964, p. 291, bibl. 37.

India. November–December. Visit, of about a month, to Indore to discuss "Temple for Meditation"; same as above.

1938   Egypt. January; Giedion-Welcker 1959, p. 35, note 2, bibl. 41.

Holland. "From India I went directly to Holland"; Pandrea 1945. p. 168, bibl. 68.

Rumania. In Tirgu Jiu "at the beginning of the summer" to supervise carving of the *Gate;* "left for Paris on September 20"; Alexandrescu 1965, bibl. 1. Returned "in the autumn"; Hoffman 1939, p. 51, bibl. 44. Visit for inauguration of ensemble. In Bucharest; Brezianu 1964, bibl. 11 and Pandrea 1945, p. 95, bibl. 68.

1939   New York. May–June. Visit to attend "Art in Our Time," May 10–Sept. 10, tenth anniversary exhibition of the Museum of Modern Art. On Long Island, May 14; Giedion-Welcker 1959, p. 206, bibl. 41. At the Art Institute of Chicago, June 3; *Springfield* (Mass.) *Sunday Union and Republican,* June 4, 1939.

The brief trip to Italy, 1921, recorded in the passport, puts in question the trip to Florence, 1910; speaking after the last war, many years after the event, the sculptor may have made a mistake. Other voyages have been suggested: the chronology by Hans Bollinger in Giedion-Welcker 1959, p. 223, bibl. 41, states Brancusi went to New York in 1928; Brancusi, in *The Little Review*, May 1929, p. 20, says, "I find the questionnaire [February?] on arriving from the ends of the earth;" but neither voyage appears in the passport. *A Handbook to the Solomon R. Guggenheim Museum Collection*, N.Y., 1959, p. 190, notes a trip to New York in 1934, but documentation is lacking.

APPENDIX 27

A list of Brancusi's addresses in Paris:

10 Cité Condorcet. On a postcard from Bucharest, dated Nov. 9, 1904, MNAM, Brancusi bequest.

10 Place de la Bourse. On a document of the École des Beaux-Arts, dated July 1, 1905; Brezianu 1964, p. 99, bibl. 8.

16 Place Dauphine. On a letter dated Nov. 23, 1905; Brezianu 1964, p. 385, bibl. 12. In the catalogue of the Société Nationale, Apr. 14, 1907.

54 rue du Montparnasse. Shortly before Apr. 27, 1907; Nicoara 1963, bibl. 62. Inscription on watercolor, 1915 (appendix 25): "dans le petit jardin—rue du Montparnasse."

8 Impasse Ronsin. On a letter dated Oct. 4, 1916; may not be documented. In the catalogue of the Salon des Tuileries, June 1927.

11 Impasse Ronsin. On Oct. 29, 1927, H. S. Ede and H. P. Roché visited Brancusi at this address; diary entry of Mr. Ede, Cambridge, communicated to the author, Feb. 22, 1969.

Notes

page 1   "marvelous events"—Giedion-Welcker 1959, p. 220, bibl. 41.
          "was born"—Much of the information here concerning
              Brancusi's early years is from Brezianu 1965, bibl. 10,
              and Paleolog 1964, bibl. 66.
page 2   "excellent voice"—Comarnescu 1964, bibl. 21.
          "Abbaye de Créteil" and footnote—Robbins 1963-64, bibl.
              75; Duhamel 1947, p. 82, bibl. 29.
page 3   "accompanied Epstein"—Hamnett 1932, p. 45, bibl. 43.
          "carved a poem"—Salmon 1927, p. 56, bibl. 78.
          "began collecting"—May not be documented.
          "military service"—Same as above.
page 4   "in a hospital"—Same as above.
          "Princess X"—Hamnett 1932, p. 124, bibl. 43.
          "to Corsica"—Same as above, p. 196.
          "young woman"—Comarnescu 1964, bibl. 20.
          "game of golf"—Roché 1957, bibl. 77; This Quarter 1925,
              bibl. 84.
          "faces painted"—Hamnett 1932, p. 197, bibl. 43.
          "great little"—Wilson 1923, bibl. 89.
          "builds a temple"—Letter to H. P. Roché, Aug. 6(?), 1924;
              document from Mme. Denise Roché, Sèvres.
          "Festival Dada," "Contre Cubisme . . . ," "Congrès de Paris"
              —Sanouillet, pp. 177 (note 4), 339 and 335, respec-
              tively, bibl. 79.
page 5   "Prix Helena Rubinstein"—Lafranchis 1961, p. 165, bibl. 51.
          "a few lines"—Document from Mme. D. Roché, Sèvres.
          "to New York"—Foster 1926, bibl. 31.
          "gala party"—Communications of L. Bouché, N.Y., D. C.
              Greason, Boston, and C. Howard, London.
          "later that year"—New York Times, Oct. 3, 1926: "He ar-
              rived . . . several weeks ago . . ."; bibl. 60.
          "litigation"—U.S. Customs Court 1927-28, bibl. 85.
          footnote—Document from Mme. D. Roché, Sèvres.
page 6   "Brancusi leads"—Dreyfus 1927, bibl. 28.
          "mes trois baraques"—The Little Review, May 1929, p. 20.
          "twenty-four tons"—New York Times 1933, bibl. 61.
          "to Tirgu Jiu"—Georgescu-Gorjan 1964, bibl. 37.
          "at Indore"—Roché 1957, bibl. 77.
          "enchanted"—Pandrea 1945, p. 165, bibl. 68.

"elephant"—Roché 1957, bibl. 77.

page 7   "polished . . . *Birds*"—Communication of H. Tiwary, Indore, May 24, 1967.

"in Egypt"—Giedion-Welcker 1959, p. 35, bibl. 41.

"last trip"—*Springfield* (Mass.) *Sunday Union and Republican*, June 4, 1939.

page 8   "smoked ceaselessly"—Communication of Miss E. Udriste, Tirgu Jiu, July 1964.

"road to Damascus"—Roché 1957, bibl. 76.

footnote—Communication of O. Chelimsky, Paris, August 1964.

page 11   "portrait . . . lost"—Of Gheorghe Chitsu (1828–1897), Mayor of Craiova, professor of law.

page 15   "calipers"—Georgescu-Gorjan 1965, p. 68, bibl. 39.

"Pursuing researches"—Brezianu 1965, pp. 17–18, bibl. 10.

page 17   "Samfirescu . . . photograph"—Brezianu 1964, p. 86, bibl. 8.

page 19   "almost daily"—Pandrea 1945, p. 160, bibl. 68.

page 20   footnote—Paleolog, Jan. 24, 1965, bibl. 65.

page 24   "assists Rodin"—Nicoara 1963, bibl. 62.

"gets a commission"—Communication of B. Brezianu, Bucharest; unpublished documents.

page 25   "he is ill"—*Brancusi Ill*, drawing by Leon Biju, with inscription by Brancusi dated Feb. 18, 1908; Brezianu 1965, p. 23, bibl. 10. Also, letter to F. Storck—"lately I have been very seriously ill"—dated 1909; Brezianu 1964, p. 391, bibl. 12.

page 33   "was destroyed"—Frachon 1966.

"decides to carve"—Hamnett 1932, pp. 123–124, bibl. 43.

page 35   "Nadelman . . . exhibition"—Lincoln Kirstein, *The Sculpture of Elie Nadelman*, N.Y., Museum of Modern Art, 1948, p. 12.

page 36   footnote: "Tatiana Rachewsky"—Extract of records of decease of the Mairie of the XV$^{me\cdot}$ Arr., Paris; and a communication of the administration of Cimetière Montparnasse, Oct. 10, 1964.

page 38   "Prince Charming"—Pandrea 1945, p. 165, bibl. 68.

page 39   "army officer"—Identified by B. Brezianu, Bucharest; unpublished documents.

page 43   "painted blue"—See no. 70a, "List of the sculptures."

page 44   "photograph, now lost"—Communication of Mrs. G. Farquhar, N.Y., Dec. 5, 1965.

page 47   "great dissappointment"—Pandrea 1945, p. 161, bibl. 68.

page 54   "years of recarving"—Hamnett 1932, p. 124, bibl. 43.

page 56   "withdrawn from Salon"—Same as above.

"Roché remembered"—Document from Mme. D. Roché, Sèvres.

page 66   "furniture music"—Roger Shattuck, *The Banquet Years,*
           N.Y., Harcourt, Brace, 1958, pp. 133-134.
page 67   "Brancusi had difficulty"—Letter; may not be documented.
page 75   "not satisfied"—Communication of Mrs. C. Coggeshall,
           N.Y., who had conversations with the sculptor in
           1948.
page 76   "invents a fable"—Guilbert 1957, bibl. 42.
page 77   "Bucharest journal"—*Contimporanul* 1924, bibl. 23.
           "Roché said"—Document from Mme. D. Roché, Sèvres.
page 79   "levitate"—Pound 1921, bibl. 71.
page 86   "I wanted to show"—Jianou 1963, p. 46, bibl. 46.
           "flash of its spirit"—Hoffman 1939, p. 52, bibl. 44.
page 87   "African woman"—Geist 1964, p. 57, bibl. 34.
page 92   "Pogany visited"—See Pogany memoir, appendix 11.
page 93   "satirize the Pope"—Georgescu-Gorjan 1965, p. 71, bibl. 39.
page 94   "mention it to the editors"—"He is writing a story for the
           Little Review . . . of an adventure he had this past
           summer on the beach down in the Midi with some
           magic sculpture that he had made;" *The Little Re-
           view,* Autumn–Winter 1924–25, pp. 17–18.
page 109   "perhaps I may"—Hoffman 1939, p. 52, bibl. 44.
           footnote—Pound 1950, p. 201, bibl. 72.
page 113   "statement to Roché"—Document from Mme. D. Roché,
           Sèvres.
page 120   "In an early stage"—Alexandrescu 1965, bibl. 1 and Hoff-
           man 1939, p. 69, bibl. 44.
page 122   "Rumanian engineer"—Dates and details of construction of
           Endless Column from Georgescu-Gorjan 1964, bibl.
           37.
page 126   footnote—Hoffman 1939, p. 53, bibl. 44.
page 127   "Now all the things"—Geist 1964, p. 64, bibl. 34.
page 130   "dream of flight"—These observations are much indebted to
           Gaston Bachelard, *L'Air et les songes,* Paris, Corti,
           1943, chap. 1, "Le rêve de vol."
page 137   "I am *The Cock!*"—Paleolog 1966, bibl. 67.
page 141   "Without the discoveries"—To Miss S. Lewis; Portland Art
           Ass'n 1958, bibl. 70.
           "When we are"—*This Quarter* 1925, p. 236, bibl. 84.
           "beginning again"—Quoted by Donald Sutherland, *Ger-
           trude Stein: A biography of her work,* New Haven,
           Yale Univ., 1951, p. 51.
page 142   "portrait of Satie"—Gertrude Stein, *Portraits and Prayers,*
           N.Y., Random House, 1934, p. 27.
page 143   "art is not"—Memoir of M. Pogany, appendix 11.
           "Biblical curse"—Pandrea 1945, p. 173, bibl. 68.
page 144   "I give you"—Zervos 1957, p. 103, bibl. 90.
page 145   "Simplicity"—*This Quarter* 1925, p. 235, bibl. 84.

page 146   "object is not real"—Benjamin Fondane, *Faux traité d'es-thétique*, p. 90; quoted in Gaston Bachelard, *L'Air et les songes*, Paris, Corti, 1943, p. 11.
"I seek"—Guilbert 1957, bibl. 42.
"They are fools"—Same as above.
"Brancusi . . . realist"—Communication of C. Holty, N.Y., June 14, 1966.

page 147   *"Introduction to Metaphysics"*—English translation by T. E. Hulme, London, 1913; first published in *Revue de Métaphysique et de Morale*, Jan. 1903.
"read Bergson"—Brezianu 1966, bibl. 7.
"Plato"—Paleolog 1966, bibl. 67.
"Rabelais, Renan . . ."—Brezianu 1966, bibl. 7.
"small table"—Unpublished photograph; B. Brezianu, Bucharest.

page 148   "Milarepa"—Giedion-Welcker 1959, p. 17, bibl. 41.
"Bacot"—Jacques Bacot, *Le Poète Tibétain Milarépa*, Paris, Bossard, 1925.
"globe of the world"—Photograph in Giedion-Welcker 1959, p. 207, bibl. 41.
"Derain exhibited"—D. H. Kahnweiler, in a letter to the author, Oct. 17, 1963.
"asked . . . Lipchitz"—Barr 1963, p. 71, note 95, bibl. 4.
"the Louvre," "Musée Guimet"—Letter of 1909 to F. Storck; Brezianu 1964, bibl. 12. Also Cutzescu-Storck 1961, bibl. 26.

page 149   *"Piano Lesson"*—The painting, of 1916, is in the collection of the Museum of Modern Art, N.Y.
"Jeannette IV and *V"*—In the collection of the Museum of Modern Art, N.Y.
"against its influence"—Epstein 1940, p. 40, bibl. 30.
"told Epstein"—Same as above, p. 164.
"Epstein . . . *Doves"*—Illus. in Richard Buckle, *Jacob Epstein*, N.Y., World, 1963.
"Temple of Love"—Same as above, p. 18.
"letter of Brancusi's"—May not be documented.
"Socrate . . . goes along"—Roger Shattuck, *The Banquet Years*, N.Y., Harcourt, Brace, 1958, p. 125.
footnote—Severini 1946, p. 163, bibl. 81.

page 151   "Don't look"—Zervos 1957, p. 103, bibl. 90.
"Things are not"—*This Quarter* 1925, p. 236, bibl. 84.
footnote—Sanouillet 1966, p. 528, bibl. 79.

page 152   "Chirico writes"—Chirico 1945, p. 99, bibl. 18.
"state of joy"—Frachon 1966, bibl. 32.
"Who could imagine"—Chelimsky 1958, bibl. 17.

page 153   "It is Leda"—Guilbert 1957, bibl. 42.

page 154   "High polish"—*This Quarter* 1925, p. 235, bibl. 84.

page 156   "My motto"—Pandrea 1945, p. 172, bibl. 68.

"A remarkable text"—Seligmann 1966, p. 69, bibl. 80.

"aesthetes have"—From P. Pandrea, Bucharest; Brancusi 1965, bibl. 6.

"statement of Wagner's"—Quoted in Jean Hytier, *The Poetics of Paul Valéry*, translated by Richard Howard, N.Y., Anchor Books, 1966, p. 49.

"Valéry continues"—Same as above.

page 157   "I have eliminated"—Pandrea 1945, p. 162, bibl. 68.

page 160   "Sensuous beauty"—George Santayana, *The Sense of Beauty*, N.Y., Scribner's, 1898, p. 78.

page 161   "Beauty of materials"—Marcel Iancu, *Contimporanul*, no. 64 (1926).

"portrait of a child"—Communication of D. Stoenescu, N.Y., Aug. 11, 1967.

"Direct carving"—*This Quarter* 1925, p. 235, bibl. 84.

page 164   *"Mais la sculpture"*—Communication of G. Spaventa, N.Y., Mar. 12, 1966.

"darkroom"—Ray 1963, pp. 208-9, bibl. 74.

"bathtub . . . camera"—Communication of Mrs. M. Patrascu, Bucharest, June 1964.

"very demanding"—Communication of Miss C. Scaravaglione, N.Y.

"close-up"—Ionesco 1959, p. 30, bibl. 45.

"bulb and . . . hose"—Lebel 1959, pl. 32, bibl. 52.

"eyeglasses"—Giedion-Welcker 1959, p. 206, pl. 2, bibl. 41.

"trick print"—Zervos 1957, p. 64, bibl. 90.

"pictures of seals"—Musée National d'Art Moderne, Paris.

"large print"—Owned by Miss L. Lord, N.Y.

"what Brauner saw"—Quoted from B. Fondane; Jouffroy 1959, p. 26, bibl. 47.

page 165   "three studies"—The first in the Museum of Modern Art, N.Y.; the other two in the Joseph H. Hirshhorn Coll., N.Y.

"full-size drawings"—Alexandrescu 1965, bibl. 1.

"photograph shows *Caryatid*"—No. 3 in Brummer 1926, bibl. 14.

page 166   "well-planned crime"—Brancusi 1965, bibl. 6.

"three pieces"—Chelimsky 1958, bibl. 17.

"endless"—May not be documented.

"worked very quickly"—Statement of Mlle. I. Codreane, Paris; Jianou 1963, p. 47, bibl. 46.

"A sculptor's toil"—Foster 1926, bibl. 31.

"with other people"—Statement of Mlle. I. Codreane, Paris; Jianou 1963, p. 53, bibl. 46.

page 169   footnote—Cooper 1964, p. 12, bibl. 24.

page 170   "Art is harmony"—John Rewald, *Seurat*, Paris, Albin Michel, 1948, p. 122.

  "absolute equity"—*This Quarter* 1925, p. 236, bibl. 84.

page 171 "secret process"—Communication of C. Antonovici, N.Y., 1964.

  "arsenal"—Liberman 1960, p. 47, bibl. 53.

  "Measurements"—Giedion-Welcker 1959, p. 220, bibl. 41; translated by Maria Jolas and Anne Leroy.

page 172 footnote, "Les mesures"—From French edition of Giedion-Welcker 1959, bibl. 41.

  footnote, "pendulum"—Communication of V. G. Paleolog, Craiova, Nov. 1965.

page 175 "sayings"—Collected by Irène Codreane in *This Quarter* 1925, pp. 235–36, bibl. 19.

  footnote—Kramer 1957, bibl. 48.

page 176 "It is only"—Soren Kierkegaard, *Repetition*, Princeton Univ., 1941, pp. 34, 35.

page 177 "cybernetic"—Geist 1964, p. 56, bibl. 34.

  "rigorous effort"—Kramer 1961, p. 97, bibl. 49.

  "impersonal style"—Spear 1966, p. 45, bibl. 82.

page 178 · "There is a purpose"—Zervos 1957, p. 103, bibl. 90.

  "sands of eternity"—From P. Pandrea, Bucharest; Brancusi 1965, bibl. 6.

  "I am no longer"—Giedion-Welcker 1959, p. 220, bibl. 41.

  "Giacometti said"—To the author, in Paris, Aug. 1950.

page 179 "Beefsteak"—Epstein 1940, p. 41, bibl. 30.

  "great and pure art"—Letter to F. Storck; Brezianu 1964, p. 395, bibl. 12.

  "I would rather"—Wescott 1925, p. 56, bibl. 88.

  "to this century"—*This Quarter* 1925, p. 264, bibl. 84.

page 180 "There still hasn't"—Dreyfus 1927, bibl. 28.

  "It will be"—Letter of Dec. 5, 1956 to B. Hodes, Chicago; Geist 1966, bibl. 35.

List of the sculptures

Abbreviations used in this list:

AIC   Art Institute of Chicago
MAC   Muzeul de Artă, Craiova
MARSR   Muzeul de Arta R. S. R., Bucharest
MNAM   Musée National d'Art Moderne, Paris
MOMA   Museum of Modern Art, N.Y.
PMA   Philadelphia Museum of Art
SRGM   Solomon R. Guggenheim Museum, N.Y.

Single dimensions are of height unless otherwise designated. When three dimensions are given, their order is: height, width, depth.

All caster's cachets include "lost wax," omitted here. No attempt has been made to distinguish between bronze and brass casts from no. 63, below, onward.

1. LAOKOÖN STUDY
lost; clay; 1898

Illus. in This Quarter 1925, bibl. 84, and, captioned "Étude pour le concours d'entrée à l'École des Beaux-Arts de Bucarest," in Zervos 1957, p. 11, bibl. 90.

2. VITELIUS
24"; plaster; 1898
ins: C Brâncuș 1898
MAC

3. MARS BORGHESE *relief*
lost; clay; 1901

Dated and illus. in Brezianu 1964, bibl. 9.

4. ANATOMY STUDY *relief*
lost; clay; 1901

Dated same as above. May have been life-size; Comarnescu 1967, bibl. 22.

5. MALE NUDE *relief*
lost; plaster; 1901

signed

Illus. captioned "Concours du diplôme final de l'École des Beaux-Arts de Bucarest," Zervos 1957, p. 11, bibl. 90.

6. CHARACTER STUDY
lost; plaster; 1902
signed

Dated and illus. in Brezianu 1965, p. 16, bibl. 10.

7. PORTRAIT OF ION GORJAN
20⅜"; plaster; 1902
MARSR; ex Georgescu-Gorjan

Dated in Georgescu-Gorjan 1695, p. 68, bibl. 39. Never exhibited outside of Rumania.

8. ECORCHE
69½"; painted plaster; 1902
a. Medical Institute, Jassy
    ins. with names of Dr. Gerota
        and Brancusi, and date, 1902
b. MAC

ins: Lucrat dupa natura de Prof.
   Dr. D. GEROTA si Brâncuş
   1902
c. Lycèe N. Balcescu, Craiova
   ins: Atitudinea clasicului "Antinous." Anatomia muschi-
   lor superficiali. Lucrare
   dupa natura de Prof. Dr. D.
   GEROTA si Brâncuş [on
   plaque]
No. 8a, communication of B.
Brezianu, Bucharest.

9. GEN. DR. CAROL DAVILA
28"; bronze; 1903
cast: V. V. Rascanu et Comp.,
   Bucuresti 1912
Central Military Hospital, Buch.
Dated in Brezianu 1964, bibl. 11.
Originally kepi had a panache.

10. PORTRAIT OF A
    CONCIERGE
lost; plaster; 1905
Dated and illus. in Brezianu 1964,
bibl. 8.

11. PORTRAIT OF DR.
    ZAHARIE
    SAMFIRESCU
lost; clay; 1905
Dated and illus. same as above.

12. PORTRAIT OF A
    WAITER
lost; plaster; 1905
Dated and illus. same as above.

13. PORTRAIT OF A
    RESTAURANT
    OWNER
lost; patinated plaster(?); 1905
Shown at Société Nationale, Paris,
Apr. 15–June 30, 1906: "1715. Por-
trait de M. G. . . (buste plâtre)."
It is supposed that "M. G. . ."
stands for "Monsieur le Gérant";
the owner of the restaurant was
named Chartier. Illus. in Zervos

1957, bibl. 90.

14. PORTRAIT OF MRS.
    VICTORIA VASCHIDE
lost; clay(?); 1905
Illus. Brezianu 1964, p. 97, bibl. 8.

15. HEAD OF A YOUNG
    WOMAN *relief*
lost; plaster; 1905(?)
Dated by photograph of 1905;
Brezianu 1964, p. 91, bibl. 8.

16. HEAD OF A WOMAN
    relief
lost; plaster; 1905(?)
Dated same as above.

17. PORTRAIT OF A
    WOMAN
lost; plaster; 1905
Dated same as above.

18. PORTRAIT OF A MAN
    WITH A GOATEE
lost; plaster; 1905
Dated same as above.

19. STUDY FOR PRIDE
lost; plaster; 1905
Illus. same as above. Dated by no.
20a, below.

20. PRIDE
12"; bronze; 1905
a. MAC; ex Popp
   cachet: A. A. Hébrard
   ins: C. Brâncuşi 1905
b. Ralph Colin Coll., N.Y.; ex
   Farquhar
   cachet: C. Valsuani
   ins: C BRANCUSI
The plaster shown as No. 220 at
Salon d'Automne, Oct. 6–Nov. 15,
1906.

21. STUDY AFTER HOUDON
lost; clay; 1905
Dated and illus. in Brezianu 1965,

p. 21, bibl. 10. *Identified as after Houdon's* Écorché *in Cummings 1966, bibl. 25.*

22. BUST OF A BOY
13¾"; bronze; 1906
a. ex World House Galleries, N.Y.; ex Pogany
cachet: C. Valsuani
ins: C. Brancusi Paris
b. George Oprescu, Bucharest; ex Popp
ins: Brâncuşi Paris 1906

The plaster shown as No. 219 at the Salon d'Automne, 1906; Brezianu 1964, p. 386, bibl. 8.

23. HEAD OF A BOY
8⅛"; plaster, black patina; 1906
MARSR

The head alone of no. 22, above.

24. PORTRAIT OF G. LUPESCU
lost; plaster; 1906

Shown as No. 218 at Salon d'Automne, 1906, where "Portrait de M. S. Lupesco." Illus. in Brezianu 1965, p. 22, bibl. 10.

25. PORTRAIT OF NICOLAE DARASCU
25¼"; bronze; 1906
cachet: A. A. Hébrard
ins: C Brancuşi
MARSR; ex Simu

Dated in This Quarter *1925. In photograph dated end of 1906; Brezianu 1966, bibl. 13. The bronze shown as No. 1864 at Société Nationale, Apr. 15–June 30, 1908; Niculescu 1966, p. 58, note 24, bibl. 64.*

26. PORTRAIT OF A MAN
lost; clay; 1906

In photograph dated end of 1906; Brezianu 1966, bibl. 13.

27. STUDY OF A BOY
lost; clay; 1906

Dated and illus. same as above.

28. THE REDSKINS
lost; clay(?); 1906

Dated and illus. in Brezianu 1965, p. 22, bibl. 10.

28a. THE ADOLESCENT
lost; plaster; 1906

On postcard dated Aug. 25, 1906; illus. V. G. Paleolog, Tineretea lui Brancusi, *Buch., 1967, pl. 23.*

29. REPOSE
lost; plaster; 1906

On postcard dated Dec. 31, 1906; Brezianu 1964, bibl. 12.

30. TORMENT
bronze; 1906
a. Mrs. S. Fotino-Morar, Buch.
14¼"
cachet: A. A. Hébrard
ins: C Brâncuşi
b. Dr. Jean C. Levaditi, Paris
14"
cachet: C. Valsuani
ins: C. Brancusi

Dated and illus. in Zorach 1926, bibl. 91.

31. TORMENT II
11½"; bronze; 1907
a. Richard Davis, Wayzata, Minn.
cachet: C. Valsuani
ins: C BRANCUSI 1907
b. Coll. N.C., Bucharest
cachet: C. Valsuani
ins: C. BRANCUŞI

32. HEAD OF A BOY
13½"; bronze; 1907
a. MARSR; ex Simu
cachet: C. Valsuani
ins: C BANCUŞI PARIS
b. Muzeul Zambaccian, Bucharest

cachet: illegible, but Valsuani
ins: C. Brâncuşi
c. MAC; ex Popp
   cachet: A. A. Hébrard
   ins: C Brâncuşi

The plaster shown as No. 1819 at Société Nationale, 1907; Nicoara 1966, bibl. 63.

33. PORTRAIT OF A YOUNG WOMAN
lost; plaster; 1907?

Illus. in N.Y. Herald 1918, bibl. 58; Spear 1966, p. 46, bibl. 82.

34. HEAD OF A GIRL
lost; stone; 1907

Illus. in Luceafarul, Mar. 1907; Brezianu 1964, p. 96, bibl. 8.

35. PORTRAIT OF A WOMAN
lost; plaster; 1907(?)

Illus. in This Quarter 1925, bibl. 84, with The Prayer, in plaster.

36. THE PRAYER
43⅞"; bronze; 1907
cachet: C. Valsuani
ins: C BRACUŞI [and on back]
   CRISTE CRSITE
MARSR

Commissioned Apr. 18, 1907; B. Brezianu, unpublished documents. Shown (in plaster?) as no. 717 at Salon des Indépendants, 1910.

37. PORTRAIT OF PETRE STANESCU
30¼"; bronze; 1907
cachet: C. Valsuani
ins: C Brâncuşi
Dumbrava Cemetery, Buzau, Rumania

Dated same as above. Shown in bronze as No. 46 at 14th Tinerimea Artistica, Bucharest, Mar. 30, 1914.

38. HEAD OF A GIRL
lost; stone; 1907

Illus. captioned "Première pierre directe, 190 ." (with year missing) in This Quarter 1925, bibl. 84. Dated to precede no. 39, below.

39. THE KISS
11"; stone; 1907
ins: Brancusi
MAC; ex Popp

"In 1907 he . . . began 'la taille directe' with le Baiser et la sagesse"; This Quarter 1925, p. 264, bibl. 84.

40. THE WISDOM OF THE EARTH
19⅞"; stone; 1907
MARSR; ex Romascu

Dated same as above.

41. DOUBLE CARYATID
29½"; stone; 1908(?)
MOMA

Part of pedestal of no. 61, below.

42. HEAD OF A GIRL
lost; stone; 1908

Dated and illus. in Zorach 1926, p. 143, bibl. 91. Probably final state of no. 34, above.

43. HEAD OF A GIRL
lost; marble; 1908(?)

Photograph labeled "première oeuvre en marbre" by Brancusi; Tacha 1964, bibl. 83.

44. CHILD'S HEAD
lost; marble; 1908(?)
ex Bogdan-Pitesti

Shown as No. 176 at 8th Tinerimea Artistica, Mar. 15–Apr. 15,

1909, and illus. in catalogue.

45. BUST OF A CHILD
lost; white stone; 1906 (?)

Shown as No. 206 in Amsterdam, May 3–25, 1930 and as No. 212 in Brussels, July 20–Aug. 10, in "Exhibition of Modern Rumanian Art". Previously unpublished; from B. Brezianu, Bucharest.

46. SLEEP
10¼" h.; marble; 1908
ins: C Brancusi 1908
MARSR; ex Simu

In Geist 1964, p. 50, bibl. 34, I stated my opinion, shared by others in Bucharest, that the inscribed date is not in the sculptor's hand; the reasons for this opinion are complicated and based on stylistic assumptions which I now reject. The documentary evidence for 1908 is the following: the work is dated "1908" and seems to be a copy of the plaster, Repose, no. 29, above, reproduced on a postcard dated Dec. 31, 1906. Also, since it was bought in Paris from the sculptor by A. Simu in 1909 (see Niculescu 1966, p. 57, note 21, bibl. 64), it seems unlikely that this work, in a style attractive to Brancusi's Rumanian admirers, could have been neglected by them for perhaps two and a half years, and at a time when he was trying to sell his work.

47. SLEEPING CHILD
6¼" l.; bronze; 1908
a. Mr. and Mrs. Malcolm Eisenberg, Philadelphia
   ins: C. Brâncuşi
b. Mme. S.N., Paris; ex Maguy

c. Daniel Bortin, Philadelphia
   ins: C. Brâncuşi 1908

Dated "about 1906" in Giedion-Welcker 1959, p. 63, bibl. 41. The date on no. 47c may be the date of the casting of this copy, which differs from the others in not being hollow on the underside.

48. SLEEPING CHILD
6½" l.; marble; 1908 (?)
MNAM; Brancusi bequest

A copy of no. 47, above.

49. CHILD'S HEAD
9⅞" l.; marble; 1908 (?)
MNAM; Brancusi bequest
Apparently a rejected beginning.

50. SLEEPING CHILD
6⅞" l.; marble; 1908?
ins: C. BRANCUSI
Mme. Yolanda Penteado, Sao Paulo
Inscription from SRGM records.

51. TORSO
9⅞"; marble; 1909
ins: Brancuşi
MAC; ex Popp

Dated in B. Brezianu, "Reportaj in jurul unei camere," Secolul XX, no. 11, 1967, p. 186.

52. NAIADE (?)
11¾"; limestone; 1909?
Apollinaire Coll., Paris

53. STUDY OF RENEE
destroyed; clay; 1909?
Illus. in Brezianu 1966, bibl. 13.

54. WOMAN LOOKING
      INTO A MIRROR
recarved; marble; 1909?

*Illus. in Dreyfus 1923, bibl. 27.
Illus. and dated 1908 in Zorach
1926, bibl. 91.*

55. BARONESS R.F.
dimensions unknown; stone; 1910
Private coll., Bucharest

Dated in This Quarter *1925, bibl.
84.*

56. SLEEPING MUSE
11½" l.; marble; 1910
ins: Brancusi
Joseph H. Hirshhorn Coll., N.Y.;
      ex Davies

Dated by no. 57b, below.

57. SLEEPING MUSE
bronze; 1910
a. AIC; ex Eddy
    11" l.
    cachet: C. Valsuani
    ins: BRNCUSI
b. MNAM
    10⅝" l.
    cachet: C. Valsuani
    ins: C. BRANCUȘI 1910
c. MNAM; ex Frachon
    10¾" l.
    ins: C Brancusi
d. Metropolitan Museum of Art,
    N.Y.; ex Stieglitz
    10¾" l.
    cachet: C. Valsuani
    ins: BRANCUS

58. NARCISSUS
lost; alabaster?; 1910(?)

Dated 1909 in This Quarter *1925,
bibl. 84.*

59. THE KISS
35¼"; stone; 1910
ins: C. BRANCUȘI [on grave-
      stone]
Cimetière Montparnasse, Paris

*Dated by memoir of M. Pogany,
appendix 11. Illus. and dated 1910
with caption, "Now in Montparnasse Cemetery, although not
originally intended as a monument"; Zorach 1926, bibl. 91.*

60. DANAIDE
11⅛", reworked; marble; 1910(?)

*Dated by memoir of M. Pogany,
appendix 11. Shown as No. 3 at
Gallery of the Photo-Secession,
N.Y., Mar. 1914. Illus. in* Amer-
ica & Alfred Stieglitz *1934, pl.
XIIc, bibl. 2. See no. 156, below.*

61. PASAREA MAIASTRA
22⅛"; marble; 1910
MOMA; ex Dreier

*Dated by the sculptor's answer to
Question 9 of an interrogatory:
"I conceived the first idea of
[Bird in Space, no. 166, below] as
long ago as 1910"; U.S. Customs
Court 1927–28, bibl. 85.*

62. PROMETHEUS
7" l.; marble; 1911
ins: C. Brancusi
PMA, Arensberg Coll.; ex Quinn

*Dated and No. 6 in Brummer
1926, bibl. 14. See also no. 63b, below. Inscription from SRGM records.*

63. PROMETHEUS
7" l.; pol. bronze; 1911
a. Joseph H. Hirshhorn Coll.,
    N.Y.; ex De Amaral
    ins: C. Brâncuși 1911
b. Mrs. E. L. Kinney, Washing-
    ton, D.C.
    ins: C. Brâncuși
c. MNAM, Brancusi Studio

64. PORTRAIT OF GEORGE
9¼"; marble; 1911
SRGM; ex Farquhar

Dated by birth of George, Nov.

10, 1910; communication of Mrs. G. Farquhar, N.Y., Dec. 9, 1965.

65. THE KISS
23"; stone; 1911(?)
ins: Brancusi
PMA, Arensberg Coll.; ex Quinn

Inscription from SRGM records. Probably shown as No. 496 at Salon des Indépendants, Mar. 20–May 16, 1912, where listed after Sleeping Muse, 1910, and Prometheus, 1911.

66. A MUSE
17½"; marble; 1912
ins: C BRANCUSI
SRGM; ex Bulova; ex Davies

Dated by exhibition tab for the plaster in the Armory Show, Feb. 1913; Kuhn, bibl. 50.

67. MLLE. POGANY
17½"; marble; 1912
ins: C BRANCUSI
PMA; ex De Schauensee; ex Quinn

Dated same as above. Illus. in America & Alfred Stieglitz 1934, pl. XIIc, bibl. 2.

68. TORSO II
12¼"; marble; 1912
ins: Brancusi 1912
K. Petermann, Stuttgart; ex Davies

Shown as No. 620 in Armory Show, N.Y., Feb. 15–Mar. 15, 1913.

69. BIRD
23¾"; marble; 1912(?)
PMA, Arensberg Coll.

70. MAIASTRA
bronze; 1912(?)

a. Miss Kate R. Steichen, N.Y.
21¾"
cachet: C. Valsuani
b. Mrs. Philip Graham, Washington, D.C.; ex Meyer
22"
cachet: C. Valsuani

71. MAIASTRA
24"; pol. bronze; 1912
ins: C BRANCUSI PARIS 1912
[printed with punches]
John Cowles, Minneapolis; ex Janis

Of this object, exhibited in Bucharest, L. Bachelin, in a review in La Politique, *Apr. 4, 1913, wrote, ". . . le corps est rond comme un oeuf, d'où sort un cou en forme de tuyau, le tout peint en bleu électrique [!]. Ce n'est pas désagréable à voir, on pense à quelque dieu égyptien et, comme tout ce qui est égyptien, cet oiseau mage a du moins l'attrait de l'étrangeté et du mystère;" communication of B. Brezianu, Bucharest.*

72. MAIASTRA
24⅛"; pol. bronze; 1912(?)
Peggy Guggenheim Coll., Venice; ex Poiret

73. DANAIDE
bronze; 1913(?)
a. Mrs. Eugene Meyer, Jr., Mt. Kisco, N.Y.
10⅞"; partly gilded
cachet: C. Valsuani
ins: BRÂNCUSI
b. MNAM, Brancusi Studio
10⅞"; partly gilded
cachet: C. Valsuani
ins: C Brancusi
c. Kunstverein, Winterthur
10⅞"; black patina

cachet: C. Valsuani
ins: C BRANCUSI
d. Tate Gallery, London
11⅛"
ins: C. Brâncuşi
e. PMA; ex White
11"; polished, except hair
ins: C. BRANCUSI
f. Mrs. G. H. Warren, N.Y.
11"; polished
ins: C Brâncusi

Shown as No. 5 at Gallery of the Photo-Secession, N.Y., Mar. 1914. Illus. in America & Alfred Stieglitz 1934, pl. XIIc, bibl. 2. Nos. 73d, 73e and 73f probably cast after 1920.

74. MLLE. POGANY
17¼"; bronze; 1913
a. MOMA; ex Pogany
polished, black patina on hair
cachet: C. Valsuani
ins: C. BRAИCUŞI
b. Mrs. Cecilia Cutzescu-Storck,
Bucharest
ins: C. Brancuşi
c. J. B. Speed Museum, Louisville; ex Degen
polished, black patina on hair
cachet: C. Valsuani
ins: Brancusi
d. William Benenson, N.Y.
polished
cachet: C. Valsuani
ins: Brancusi

Dated by memoir of M. Pogany, appendix 11.

75. THE FIRST STEP
ca. 44", destroyed; wood; 1913
The head alone dated 1913 in Brummer 1926, bibl. 14. Shown as No. 7 at Gallery of the Photo-Secession, N.Y., Mar. 1914. Illus. in America & Alfred Stieglitz 1934, pl. XIIc, bibl. 2. B. Brezianu, Bucharest, has a photo-

graph dated 1912 by the sculptor.

76. HEAD OF FIRST STEP
10⅛"; wood; 1913–14
ins: C. Brancuşi
MNAM, Brancusi Studio
Removed from no. 75, above, after the exhibition cited above.

77. THE FIRST CRY
9⅞"; bronze; 1914(?)
a. ex Jane Wade Ltd., N.Y.; ex Roché
polished bronze
ins: C. Brâncusi
b. Walter A. Bechtler, Zurich
ins: C Brâncuşi
c. C. E. Gamborg, London; ex Duchamp-Villon
ins: C. Brâncuşi

78. SLEEPING MUSE II
11⅜" l.; alabaster; 1914?
ins: C. Brâncuşi
Mrs. H. Gates Lloyd, Haverford,
Pa.; ex Quinn.
Acquired 1922 by Quinn.

79. SLEEPING MUSE II
bronze; 1914?
a. Dr. Heinz Keller, Winterthur
11" l.; polished bronze
ins: C. Brancusi
b. Mr. and Mrs. Frederick Weisman, Beverly Hills, Calif.;
ex Ault.
10½" l.; polished bronze
ins: C. BRÂNCUŞI
c. Mme. Katia Granoff, Paris; ex Badulescu
10⅛" l.
d. Private coll., Bucharest
e. Joseph Pulitzer, Jr. Coll., St. Louis; ex Cassou
10¾"; pol. bronze; 1926(?)

80. THREE PENGUINS
22½" × 21½" × 13¾"; marble;
1914
PMA, Arensberg Coll.; ex Quinn

220

Dated and No. 8 in Brummer 1926, bibl. 14. Acquired 1916 by Quinn.

81. TWO PENGUINS
21¼" × 11⅛" × 12⅛"; marble; 1914
ins: CB
AIC; ex Roché
Dated by Roché.

82. NARCISSUS FOUNTAIN
20½"; plaster cast; 1914(?)
MNAM, Brancusi Studio

Project for a memorial to Spiru Haret (d. 1912), commissioned by Vasile Mortzun, who became Minister of Education in 1914.

83. BIRD
27½"; gray marble; 1915
MNAM, Brancusi Studio

Dated by MNAM records.

84. THE NEWBORN
8⅛" l.; marble; 1915
PMA, Arensberg Coll.; ex Quinn

Dated and No. 5 in Brummer 1926, bibl. 14.

85. STUDY FOR A FIGURE
60½"; plaster; 1915?
MNAM, Brancusi Studio

86. STUDY FOR A HEAD
17¼"; plaster; 1915?
MNAM, Brancusi Studio

87. THE NEWBORN
8⅛" l.; pol. bronze; 1915
a. MOMA
b. Wright Ludington, Santa Barbara, Calif.; ex Force
ins: C. Brancusi

88. TIMIDITY
14⅜"; stone; 1915
MNAM, Brancusi Studio

Dated in Zervos 1957, p. 50, bibl. 90. Pl. 22 in Little Review 1921,

bibl. 54.

89. CARYATID
90⅛"; wood; 1915
New York (?)

Dated by SRGM records from Roché.

90. CARYATID
65⅝"; wood; 1915
Staempfli Gallery, N.Y.; ex Quinn

Dated and No. 3 in Brummer 1926, bibl. 14. Acquired 1916 by Quinn.

91. THE PRODIGAL SON
17½"; oak; 1915
PMA, Arensberg Coll.

Dated and No. 22 in Brummer 1926, bibl. 14.

92. PORTRAIT
ca. 21"; wood; 1915
MNAM, Brancusi Studio

Dated in Giedion-Welcker 1959, pl. 175, bibl. 41. Shown at Brummer Gallery, N.Y., Nov. 17, 1933 to Jan. 13, 1934. Only the central element now exists.

93. PORTRAIT OF MME. L.R.
ca. 37", lost; wood; 1916

Dated in This Quarter 1925, bibl. 84. Pl. 7 in Little Review 1921, bibl. 54; photograph probably of 1919.

94. THE KISS
28⅛"; yellow stone; 1915?
MNAM, Brancusi Studio

95. STUDY FOR COLUMN OF THE KISS
ca. 57", lost; plaster; 1916

Dated in Giedion-Welcker 1937, p. 108, bibl. 40. Pl. 22 in Little Review 1921, bibl. 54.

96. PRINCESS X
22"; marble; 1916

Univ. of Nebraska, Sheldon Memorial Art Gallery; ex Quinn

Acquired 1917 by Quinn.

97. PRINCESS X
23"; pol. bronze; 1916
a. PMA, Arensberg Coll.
b. Arnold and Adele Maremont Coll., Chicago
c. MNAM, Brancusi Studio

Shown as No. 167 at Society of Independent Artists, N.Y., Apr. 10–May 6, 1917, and illus. in catalogue.

98. SCULPTURE FOR THE BLIND
11⅜" l.; marble; 1916?
PMA, Arensberg Coll.; ex Quinn

E. Pound refers to "the egg" (Beginning of the World?) in Pound 1921, p. 5, bibl. 71. "This work [Beginning of the World] came after 'the sculpture for the blind' . . . which was (I think) exhibited at the Independents in New York around 1917"; statement of H. P. Roché, from Mme. Roché, Sèvres.

99. THE SORCERESS
39⅜"; wood; 1916–22(?)
ins: C Brancusi Paris 1916
SRGM

Unfinished in 1922: in photograph with Torso of a Girl, no. 141, below, in Zorach 1926, p. 150, bibl. 91.

100. TORSO OF A YOUNG MAN
19"; maple; 1916(?)
ins: CB [in a circle, three times]
PMA, Arensberg Coll.; ex Stendahl; ex Von Sternberg

Dated by no. 101a, below. But no. 11 and dated 1922 in Brummer

1926, bibl. 14.

101. TORSO OF A YOUNG MAN
polished bronze; 1917
a. Cleveland Museum of Art
18⅜"
ins: C Brancusi PARIS 1917
b. Joseph H. Hirshhorn Coll., N.Y.; ex Roché
18"
ins: C. BRANCUSI PARIS 1924

Differences in height are due to different ways of measuring the mounted figure. Curiously, the "7" in the inscription on no. 101a is uncrossed, as it is on no. 168, below.

102. A MUSE
19¾"; pol. bronze; 1917
Museum of Fine Arts, Houston; ex Quinn

Acquired early in 1918 by Quinn.

103. A MUSE
19½"; pol. bronze; 1917(?)
ins: C. Brâncuşi
Portland Art Museum; ex Lewis

Pl. 12 in Little Review 1921, bibl. 54. Miss S. Lewis acquired the work in 1924 in New York, having first seen it there in 1923; Portland Art Association 1959, bibl. 70.

104. A MUSE
17⅜"; pol. bronze; 1917?
ins: C. BRANCUSI
Herbert and Nannette Rothschild Coll., Ossining, N.Y.

Acquired 1952 by the Rothschilds.

105. ADAM
34⅞"; wood; 1917
SRGM

Dated in Giedion-Welcker 1959,

106. CHIMERA
three sections, 59¾"; oak; 1918
ins: [C. Bran?] cusi
PMA, Arensberg Coll.; ex Quinn

Entered in second exhibition of "Section d'Or," Galerie de la Boétie, but withdrawn by Brancusi; statement of J. Villon in Zervos 1957, p. 82, bibl. 90. Exhibition held March(?) 1920; Cabanne 1963, p. 363, bibl. 16. Work acquired 1922 by Quinn.

107. ARCHITECTURAL PROJECT
37¾"; wood; 1918
MNAM, Brancusi Studio

Dated in Zervos 1957, p. 64, bibl. 90. This photograph, previously unpublished, from B. Brezianu, Bucharest.

108. ENDLESS COLUMN
80" × 10" × 9⅜"; oak; 1918
ins: CB [in a circle]
Mrs. William Sisler, N.Y.; ex Quinn

Dated and No. 3 in Brummer 1926, bibl. 14. Pl. 7 in Little Review 1921, bibl. 54.

109. CUP
6¼" × 10⅞" × 8⅞"; wood; 1918?
MNAM, Brancusi Studio

Pl. 12 in Little Review 1921, bibl. 54; photograph probably of 1918. Brancusi sent Quinn a Cup as a gift, Dec. 1920; letter from the sculptor.

110. CUP II
7½" × 14⅜" × 11⅛"; wood; 1918?
MNAM, Brancusi Studio

Pl. 21 in Little Review 1921, bibl. 54.

111. CUP III
9" × 20⅞" × 17⅜"; wood; 1918–20?
MNAM, Brancusi Studio

112. CUP IV
10¼" × 19¾" × 16½"; wood; before 1925
MNAM, Brancusi Studio

In Steichen photograph, 1925; see frontispiece.

113. LITTLE FRENCH GIRL
49"; oak; 1918?
ins: C. Brâncuşi
SRGM; ex Dreier

Pl. 21 in Little Review 1921, bibl. 54, where unfinished and with Cup II, no. 110, above. Probably shown at the Société Anonyme, N.Y., Apr. 30–June 15, 1920.

114. LITTLE FRENCH GIRL II
ca. 43", destroyed; wood; 1918?
Pl. 7 in Little Review 1921, bibl. 54; photograph probably of 1919.

115. TORSO OF A YOUNG WOMAN
12⅞"; onyx; 1918
ins: C. BRANCUSI
Mme. Denise Roché, Sèvres; ex Quinn

Dated and No. 12 in Brummer 1926, bibl. 14.

116. YELLOW BIRD
36⅜"; yellow marble; 1918
ins: C Brancusi
Yale Univ. Art Gallery; ex Dreier; ex Quinn

Delayed shipment to Quinn in January 1919 because the work broke; letter from sculptor. Acquired 1920 by Quinn.

117. GOLDEN BIRD

223

36½"; pol. bronze; 1919
ins: CB
Arts Club of Chicago; ex Quinn
Dated and No. 20 in Brummer 1926, bibl. 14. Acquired 1920 by Quinn. Pls. 17 and 24 in Little Review *1921, bibl. 54.*

118. GOLDEN BIRD
37¾"; pol. bronze; 1919
ins: C. Brancusi [on base]
Minneapolis Institute of Arts

119. MLLE. POGANY II
17⅜"; veined marble; 1919
ins: C Brâncuşi
Lee A. Ault, N.Y.; ex Quinn
Dated and No. 24 in Brummer 1926, bibl. 14. Acquired 1920 by Quinn. Pls. 6, 9, 10, and 11 in Little Review *1921, bibl. 54.*

120. MLLE. POGANY II
17"; pol. bronze
a. Albright-Knox Art Gallery, Buffalo; ex Quinn
1920
   ins: C. Brâncuşi [and, on base]
1920
b. Norton Gallery, West Palm Beach
1925
   ins: MLLE. POGANY PAR C. Brâncuşi PARIS–1925 [printed with punches except sculptor's name]
c. Miss Katherine Ordway, N.Y.
1925(?)
   ins: C. Brâncuşi

No. 120c acquired from the sculptor ca. 1925.

121. THE NEWBORN II
10¼" l.; marble; 1920(?)
Moderna Museet, Stockholm; ex De Maré

122. THE NEWBORN II
a. MNAM, Brancusi Studio

9¾" l.; stainless steel, on pol. metal disk; 1920(?)
b. MNAM, Brancusi Studio
9¾" l.; pol. bronze, on pol. metal disk; 1920
No. 122b is dated and No. 16 in Brummer 1926, bibl. 14.

123. ENDLESS COLUMN I
161½" × 9¾" × 9¾"; wood; 1920?
MNAM, Brancusi Studio
In two pieces; the larger was shown at Brummer Gallery, N.Y., 1933.

124. ENDLESS COLUMN II
disappeared; wood; 1920?
Like no. 123, above; illus. in Giedion-Welcker 1959, p. 42, bibl. 41.

125. ENDLESS COLUMN III
118" × 11¾" × 11¾"; wood; 1920?
MNAM, Brancusi Studio
Shown at Brummer Gallery, N.Y. 1933.

126. ENDLESS COLUMN IV
ca. 285" × 14½" × 13⅜"; wood; 1920
MNAM, Brancusi Studio
Dimensions above are of original state in E. Steichen's garden in Voulangis. Now 219½" h., in two pieces, the larger of which was shown at Brummer Gallery, N.Y., 1933.

127. KING OF KINGS
118⅛"; oak; 1920(?)
SRGM
Shown at SRGM in 1955 but not dated in catalogue. Does not appear in photographs before 1948 and no observer reports seeing it before then. Motif of crown seems related to ornament on

224

White Negress, *no. 149, below,
and seems to predate it. Also, except for* Socrates, *no. 143, below,
1923, but probably begun earlier,
there is no sculpture after this
point that is pierced.*

128. EXOTIC PLANT
17¾"; wood; 1920
MNAM, Brancusi Studio

Dated in This Quarter *1925, bibl.
84.*

129. VASE
11⅞"; wood; 1920?
MNAM, Brancusi Studio

130. A HAND
12" l.; marble; 1920
ins: C. Brâncuşi à John Quinn
      Paris 1920 [and]
      BRANCUSI a ME HARE
      NEW-YORK 1926
Fogg Art Museum, Cambridge

131. LEDA
21" h.; marble; 1920
AIC; ex Dreier

Pl. 14 in Little Review *1921, bibl.
54.*

132. BEGINNING OF THE
      WORLD
12" l.; marble, on pol. metal disk;
      1920(?)
ins: CB [in a circle]
James Clark, Dallas; ex Roché

*E. Pound discusses "the egg" in
Pound 1921, p. 5, bibl. 71. Roché,
in statement quoted at no. 98,
above, says this work came from
Quinn and dates it 1924; but
Quinn died in 1924 and his last
acquisition from the sculptor was
in 1923.*

133. BIRD
35½"; gray marble; 1921(?)
ins: C BRANCUSI

Alain de Gunzburg, Paris; ex
Y. Penteado

134. ADAM AND EVE
94¼"; *Eve alone,* 46"; oak, chestnut, limestone; 1921
ins: CB [three times]
SRGM; ex Quinn

*Dated in Brummer 1926, bibl. 14.
Acquired 1922 by Quinn.*

135. THE KISS
14⅛"; brown stone; 1921?
MNAM, Brancusi Studio

Illus. in This Quarter *1925, bibl.
84.*

136. THE KISS
23¼"; gray stone with iron rings;
      1921?
MNAM, Brancusi Studio

Illus. in This Quarter *1925, bibl.
84, in photograph probably made
in 1925.*

137. SLEEPING CHILD
7½" l.; white stone; 1921?
MNAM, Brancusi Studio

138. SLEEPING CHILD
7⅞" l.; black stone; 1921?
MNAM, Brancusi Studio

139. TORSO OF A GIRL
12⅞"; onyx; 1922
ins: CB [in a circle]
Private coll., U.S.

140. TORSO OF A GIRL II
13"; onyx; 1922
PMA, Gallatin Coll.; ex Quinn

*Dated and No. 21 in Brummer
1926, bibl. 14. Acquired 1922 by
Quinn.*

141. FISH
5" × 16⅞" × 1 3/16"; veined
      marble, on circular mirror;
      1922
PMA, Arensberg Coll.; ex Quinn

225

Acquired 1923 by Quinn.

142. STUDY FOR BIRD IN
SPACE
44¼"; plaster, marble; 1922 (?)

Illus. with Adam and Eve, *1921,
acquired 1922 by Quinn, in M.M.
1923, p. 28, bibl. 57, in photograph
probably taken 1922.* In MNAM.

143. SOCRATES
51¼"; wood; 1923
MOMA

Dated in This Quarter *1925, bibl.
84; probably begun much earlier.
The footing, which split, was
carved anew by C. Antonovici,
N.Y.; see appendix 25.*

144. TORSO OF A YOUNG
MAN
16⅞"; wood; 1923
ins: 15 C. Brancus PARIS 1923
MNAM, Brancusi Studio
*Listed as No. 15 in Brummer
1933, bibl. 15.*

145. HEAD
12"; wood; 1923
Mme. Yolanda Penteado, Sao
Paulo

*Probably separated 1923 from
Little French Girl II, no. 110,
above, which is entire in photograph taken 1922; see no. 142.*

146. BIRD IN SPACE
50⅛"; marble; 1923
Marx-Schoenborn Coll., N.Y.; ex
Quinn

*Dated and No. 26 in Brummer
1926, bibl. 14. Acquired 1923 by
Quinn.*

147. FISH
5" x 16⅝" x 1⅛"; pol. bronze;
1924
ins: N.1 C. BRÂNCUŞI–PARIS
–1924 [printed with punches]

James W. Alsdorf, Winnetka,
Ill.; ex H. Rodman

148. BEGINNING OF THE
WORLD
11¼" l.; pol. bronze, on pol.
metal disk; 1924?
MNAM, Brancusi Studio

149. WHITE NEGRESS
15"; veined marble; 1924
PMA, Arensberg Coll.

Illus. in This Quarter *(Spring)
1925, bibl. 84.*

150. BIRD IN SPACE
50"; pol. bronze; 1924
ins: C. Brancusi
PMA, Arensberg Coll.

*Dated after no. 146, above, from
which it derives and which was
sent to Quinn in Dec. 1923. Inscription from Arensberg 1954,
bibl. 3, where also, the work is
listed as from the Quinn Collection; but it does not appear on
any Quinn list.*

151. THE COCK
36⅛"; walnut; 1924
ins: A AUDREY CHADWICK.
C. BRANCUŞI PARIS
MOMA

*Dated and No. 28 in Brummer
1926, bibl. 14.*

152. THE COCK I
100¾" × 11¾" × 22½"; plaster;
1924
MNAM, Brancusi Studio

Illus. in This Quarter *1925, bibl.
84.*

153. THE COCK II
131⅞" × 17¾" × 31½"; plaster;
1924–33
MNAM, Brancusi Studio

154. BIRD IN SPACE
45¾"; yellow marble; 1925

226

ins: C. Brancusi
PMA, Arensberg Coll.; ex Stendahl

Dated and No. 37 in Brummer 1926, bibl. 14. Inscription from Arensberg 1954, bibl. 3.

155. TORSO OF A GIRL III
10⅜" × 8⅝" × 6½"; marble; 1925
MNAM, Brancusi Studio

Dated by MNAM.

156. HEAD OF A WOMAN
11⅛"; marble; 1925
ins: 53B C. Brancusi PARIS 1925
Mr. and Mrs. Isadore Levin, Detroit

Surely Danaïde, no. 60, above, recarved. Inscription from SRGM records. "53B" refers to Brummer 1933, bibl. 15, where "52. Study—(marble)."

157. EILEEN
11¼"; white stone; 1925?
MNAM, Brancusi Studio

In 1948 the sculptor told Mrs. C. Coggeshall, N.Y., that this work was a portrait of his friend, Eileen.

158. LEDA
21" h.; pol. bronze on pol. metal disk; 1925
cast by Alexis Rudier
MNAM, Brancusi Studio

Dated and No. 4 at "Contemporary French Art," Moscow, May-June 1928. Shown as No. 303 at Salon des Tuileries, June 1927.

159. THE CHIEF
20"; wood and iron; 1925
ins: C Brancusi PARIS
Mrs. Phyllis Lambert, N.Y.

Illus. in unfinished state dated 1924 in This Quarter *1925, bibl.*

84. Dated 1925 and No. 25 in Brummer 1926, bibl. 14.

160. PORTRAIT OF NANCY CUNARD
20⅜"; wood; 1925
Mrs. Marcel Duchamp, N.Y.

Dated by inscription on plaster version at MNAM, "1925–1928;" communication of Mrs. M. Duchamp. This plaster, 22¼" h., is itself the study for the bronze, no. 181, below.

161. LITTLE BIRD
16¼" × 8½" × 11¾"; colored marble; 1925
ins: C. BRANCUSI PARIS 1925
R. Sturgis Ingersoll, Penllyn, Pa.

Inscription from SRGM records. Shown as No. 252 at Salon des Tuileries, June 1926. Described in Zorach *(March) 1926, bibl. 91.*

162. BIRD IN SPACE
52¾"; gray marble; 1925
Kunsthaus, Zurich

Dated in Giedion-Welcker 1937, p. 131, bibl. 40.

163. BIRD IN SPACE
71"; marble; 1925
Mrs. Eugene Meyer, Jr., Mt. Kisco, N.Y.

Dated and No. 30 in Brummer 1926, bibl. 14. Illus. in Zorach (March) 1926, bibl. 91; also in frontispiece.

164. SCULPTURE FOR THE BLIND
6⅞" × 12¾" × 9½"; onyx; 1925
MNAM, Brancusi Studio

The Salon des Indépendants, Mar. 20–May 2, 1926, lists a single work by Brancusi: "450 Muse Endormie (sculpture pour aveu-

gles) (*albâtre*)." *But Brancusi was traveling Jan. 13 to Mar. 31, 1926 (see appendix 26); hence dating of 1925. Brummer 1933, bibl. 15, lists: "50. Sculpture for the Blind —(alabaster)." In unfinished state, on table in frontispiece.*

165. BIRD IN SPACE
74⅜"; marble; 1926(?)
Private coll., N.Y.; ex Ault

166. BIRD IN SPACE
53¼"; pol. bronze; 1926
ins: BRANCUSI PARIS 1926
Mrs. Edward Steichen, Conn.

Inscription from SRGM records. Dated 1925 and No. 33 in Brummer 1926, bibl. 14. The Bird of the U.S. Customs trial, 1927–28.

167. BLOND NEGRESS
15⅛"; pol. bronze; 1926
a. Arnold and Adele Maremont Coll., Chicago; ex Gourgault
b. San Francisco Museum of Art; ex Haas; ex Meyer
   ins: Brancusi Paris 1926
c. Duisburg Museum; ex
   O. Penteado
   ins: C. BRANCUSI PARIS 1926

168. FISH
pol. bronze, on pol. metal disk
a. Mrs. Samuel Bronfman, Montreal; ex Maitland
   5½" h., 16⅛" l.; 1926
   ins: C. BRANCUSI PARIS 1926 [on disk]
b. E. John Power, London; ex Ault
   5" h., 16" l.; 1926?
c. Sidney Janis Gallery, N.Y.
   5" × 16½" × 1 3/16"; 1926?
d. Museum of Fine Arts, Boston; ex Ede
   4½" h., 16½" l.; 1926?

169. BIRD IN SPACE

72½"; pol. bronze; 1927
ins: C. BRANCUSI 1927
Taft B. Schreiber, Beverly Hills, Calif.; ex Rubinstein

170. BIRD IN SPACE
53¾"; pol. bronze; 1927(?)
Philippe de Rothschild, Pauillac

The sculptor stated that he was working on the first replica of no. 166, above, in an interrogatory held on Nov. 21, 1927; U.S. Customs Court 1927–28, bibl. 85.

171. BIRD IN SPACE
54"; pol. bronze; 1928(?)
MOMA

Presumably in "Contemporary French Art," State Museum of New Western Art, Moscow, May–June 1928, which lists: "3. Bird in Space. Polished bronze. Ht. 137 cm. Signed: C. Brancusi."

172. LITTLE BIRD
15⅝"; pol. bronze; 1928
ins: C. Brancusi PARIS 1928
William Burden, N.Y.; gift to MOMA

173. WHITE NEGRESS II
15⅞"; marble; 1928
ins: C. Brancusi 1928 [on cylinder]
AIC; ex Rubinstein

174. LARGE LITTLE BIRD
25¼" × 11¾" × 15⅛"; colored marble; 1929
MNAM, Brancusi Studio

Shown at "2ᵐᵉ Exposition Internationale de la Sculpture," Galerie Georges Bernheim, Apr. 1929.

175. PORTRAIT OF MRS. EUGENE MEYER, JR.
52⅛"; with bases, 90⅞"; black marble; 1930
Mrs. Eugene Meyer, Jr., Mt. Kisco, N.Y.

Dated by Mrs. Meyer: the sculpture completed a year after her portrait by Despiau, 1929. Salon des Tuileries, June 1933, lists: "345 Mme Eugène Meyer, Jeune, s." No. 2 in Brummer 1933, bibl. 15.

176. STUDY FOR PORTRAIT OF MRS. MEYER
32⅞"; wood; 1916-30(?)
ins: 17 C Brancusi PARIS 1916
MNAM, Brancusi Studio

In unfinished state in This Quarter 1925, bibl. 84. Also in frontispiece here, behind sculptor's head. In 1948 the sculptor told Mrs. C. Coggeshall, N.Y., that the work was completed after no. 175, above.

177. FISH
21⅛" h., 71¼" l.; blue-gray marble; 1930
ins: C. Brancusi Paris 1930
MOMA

178. NOCTURNAL ANIMAL
9¾" × 27¼" × 7"; wood; 1930?
MNAM, Brancusi Studio

179. PLASTER FORM
14⅜" × 27⅛" × 13½"; plaster; 1930
ins: 20B C. Brancusi Paris 1930
MNAM; Brancusi bequest

Shown at Brummer Gallery, N.Y., Nov. 1933. Brummer 1933, bibl. 15, lists: "20. Plaster form." Previously unpublished.

180. MLLE. POGANY III
17¾"; marble; 1931
ins: C. Brancusi Paris 1931
PMA, Arensberg Coll.

Inscription from Arensberg 1954, bibl. 3.

181. PORTRAIT OF NANCY CUNARD
21¾"; pol. bronze; 1932
ins: C. Brancusi [and again] PAR C Brancusi 1932 PARIS 1928
Frederick Stafford Coll., N.Y.

No. 26 in Brummer 1933, bibl. 15.

182. BLOND NEGRESS II
15⅞"; pol. bronze; 1933
a. MOMA; ex Goodwin
  ins: C. Brâncusi 39B Paris F 1933 [on cylinder]
b. H. L. Winston, Birmingham, Mich.
  ins: C Brancusi [and] Brancusi

On no. 182a, "39B" refers to No. 39 in Brummer 1933, bibl. 15.

183. MLLE. POGANY III
17½"; pol. bronze; 1933
a. MNAM, Brancusi Studio
b. Mrs. J. Wintersteen, Chestnut Hill, Pa.
  ins: BRANCUSI PARIS 1933

184. COLUMN OF THE KISS
118"; plaster; before 1933
MNAM, Brancusi Studio

No. 3 in Brummer 1933, bibl. 15.

185. BIRD IN SPACE
72½"; marble; 1933
Maharani Usha Devi, Indore

Acquired 1933 by Maharajah of Indore; Roché 1957, bibl. 77.

186. BIRD IN SPACE
76½"; black marble; 1933
Maharani Usha Devi, Indore

187. THE COCK
40⅝" × 4¾" × 11¾"; pol. bronze; 1935
ins: C. Brancusi 1935
MNAM

Inscription from SRGM records.

229

188. THE SEAL
42¾" × 44⅞" × 13"; marble; 1936
SRGM
Dated in Giedion-Welcker 1937, p. 104, bibl. 40.

189. STUDY FOR ENDLESS COLUMN
237½" × 24" × 24"; plaster; 1936(?)
MNAM, Brancusi Studio
Presumed study for monumental Endless Column, no. 195, below.

190. MODEL FOR COLUMN OF GATE
13¼" × 6½" × 6½"; stone; 1937(?)
MNAM, Brancusi Studio
Dated by no. 191, below.

191. MODEL FOR GATE OF THE KISS
ca. 20⅞" h.; plaster; 1937(?)

Brancusi gave Malvina Hoffman a photograph of the model in the fall of 1938; Hoffman 1939, bibl. 44. In private coll., Bucharest.

192. TABLE
31½" h., 68⅞" diam.; stone; 1938
Tirgu Jiu, Rumania
Dated by no. 193, below.

193. TABLE OF SILENCE
table: 31½" h., 84⅞" diam.;
stools: 21⅛" h., 17¾" diam.; diam. of installation, ca. 18' 3"; stone; 1938
Public Park, Tirgu Jiu, Rumania
Dated by A. Balintescu, "Contributii documentare referitoare la Constantin Brancusi," Muzeul de Arta, Craiova, 1967.

194. GATE OF THE KISS
17' 3½" × 21' 7⅛" × 6' ½";
stone; 1938
Public Park, Tirgu Jiu, Rumania
Dated by Alexandrescu 1965, bibl. 1.

195. ENDLESS COLUMN
96' 2⅞" × 35⅜" × 35⅜"; cast iron; 1937
Tirgu Jiu, Rumania
Dated in Georgescu-Gorjan 1964, bibl. 37.

196. BIRD IN SPACE
53⅜"; pol. bronze; 1940
Peggy Guggenheim Coll., Venice
Dated by statement of Miss Guggenheim; Zervos 1957, p. 89, bibl. 90.

197. BIRD IN SPACE
ca. 72", now less; pol. bronze; 1941(?)
William Burden, N.Y., gift to MOMA; ex Senior
A version of no. 185, 1933, above. Now leans far back off the vertical (and is therefore shorter than originally) as the result of an accident in shipment.

198. BIRD IN SPACE
74¾"; pol. bronze; 1941
MNAM, Brancusi Studio
A version of no. 186, 1933, above. Dated by statement of Mme. C. Giedion-Welcker; Zervos 1957, p. 88, bibl. 90.

199. THE SEAL II
43¾" h., 13⅜" d.; blue-gray marble; 1943
MNAM
Dated by MNAM.

200. THE TURTLE
9¾" × 22¾" × 20"; plaster; 1943
MNAM

230

The original wood, badly damaged and now restored, illus. in View, *1946, p. 17, bibl. 86.*

201. FLYING TURTLE
the object: 12½″ × 36⅜″ × 27½″
as mounted: 17⅞″ h., but varies; marble; 1940–45(?)
SRGM
Dated "after 1943" by SRGM.

202. BOUNDARY MARKER
62¾″ × 16″ × 11⅞″; stone; 1945
MNAM, Brancusi Studio
Dated in André Salmon article on the sculptor in Bénézit 1949, p.

102, bibl. 5.

203. THE COCK III
133⅛″ × 17¾″ × 32½″; plaster; after 1933
MNAM, Brancusi Studio
No. 48 in Brummer 1933, bibl. 15, but reworked later.

204. THE COCK IV
191″ × 23⅜″ × 39⅜″; plaster; 1949
MNAM, Brancusi Studio
Dated by C. Antonovici, N.Y., who assisted the sculptor; see appendix 25.

ADDENDA TO THE LIST OF THE SCULPTURES

Plaster casts:
MNAM has about sixty plaster casts not listed above. *The Kiss,* no. 40, Mrs. Cecilia Cutzescu-Storck; *Prometheus,* no. 62, Mrs. Zoe Cuclin; *Torment,* no. 31, Mrs. Zoe Dumitrescu-Busulenga; *Torment II,* no. 32, Mrs. Lucia Brandl, *Model for Column of the Gate,* varies slightly from no. 190, MARSR; in Bucharest. *The Kiss,* no. 40, Kunsthalle, Hamburg. *Prometheus,* cement cast, with touches of gilding, of no. 62, J. C. Moore; *Model for Column of Gate,* no. 190, and three abstract elements, Alexandre Istrati; *The Kiss,* no. 135 slightly reworked, 1950, Dr. P. Atanasiu; in Paris. *Torso,* no. 51, Harold Diamond; *A Muse,* two copies of no. 66, SRGM; *Sleeping Muse,* a version of no. 56, Reader's Digest Coll.; *The Kiss,* no. 40, Mrs. J. D. Rockefeller, and another copy, ex Farquhar, sold at auction, Apr. 5, 1967; in New York.

Lost works of which no photographs exist:
Portrait of Gheorghe Chitsu (1828–1897), wood; two *Medallions* and several other unidentifiable objects in bibl. 15; *Portrait of Dan,* patinated plaster, early 1930's, ex Dan Stoenescu, New York. Over twenty imprecisely titled objects in early exhibitions have not been identified.

Objects of doubtful status:
Ancient Figure, 22½″, stone, AIC; Brancusi, upon seeing a photograph of it in an album of his exhibition at SRGM in 1955, told James Johnson Sweeney, then director of the museum, that the

231

work was not his. *The Kiss*, 12½", stone, Mrs. James Laughlin, Norfolk, Conn.; unfortunately I have not been able to examine this work. *Vitelius*, bronze, MAC; a cast made by the state in 1964 from the original plaster. *The Prayer*, cast stone, Dumbrava Cemetery, Buzau, Rumania; made by the state to replace the bronze now in MARSR. *The Prayer*, bronze, Belu Cemetery, Bucharest; made by the state in 1963. *Mlle. Pogany*, two bronze casts of no. 74b, Bucharest; certainly not worked on by Brancusi. In Geist 1964, p. 70, bibl. 33, I reproduced a doubtful work in order to lay it open for discussion; it remains doubtful.

PHOTOGRAPH CREDITS
References are to the number of the work here and the appendixes.

Oliver Baker, N.Y.—132
C. Brancusi—5?, 8, 13, 33–35, 38, 41–44, 54–56, 58, 93, 95, 107, 109, 114, 142, 189, 191; apps. 15, 16
Lee Brian, Palm Beach—app. 13
Rudolph Burckhardt, N.Y.—68
Eliot Elisofon, N.Y.—103
Florea B. Florescu, Bucharest—194, 195
S. Geist—25, 32, 36, 37, 59, 61, 63, 79, 82, 83, 85, 86, 94, 98, 104, 105, 110–112, 122, 129, 135–138, 143, 144, 146–148, 150, 152, 153, 155, 157, 164, 166, 169, 171, 174, 178, 180, 182, 183, 188, 190, 192, 193, 198, 200–204; apps. 5, 14
Dan Grigorescu, Bucharest—app. 6
Robert E. Mates, N.Y.—66, 77, 89, 96, 99, 113, 115, 127, 134, 201; app. 19
Allen Mewbourn, Houston—102
Emil Misilim, Buzau—app. 4a
B. Moosbrugger, Zurich—88, 162
R. V. Pandya, Indore City—185, 186
John D. Schiff, N.Y.—73, 78, 90, 108, 119, 130, 167; app. 10
Edward Steichen, West Redding, Conn.—126, 161, 163
Soichi Sunami, N.Y.—87, 92, 101, 123, 128, 158, 160, 172, 175, 176, 179, 184; app. 20
Steve Szabo, Washington, D.C.—70b
Taylor and Dull, N.Y.—173
Charles Uht, N.Y.—165, 197

The Institutul de Istoria Artei, Bucharest, is the source of 2–4, 6, 9–12, 14–21, 23, 24, 26–29, 39, 40, 46, 51, 53; app. 7. Zervos 1957, bibl. 90, is the source of 50, 70a, 133, 145. Other photographs supplied by the owners of the works, without designation of photographers.

Bibliography

1. Alexandrescu, Ion. "Marturiile unui cioplitor," *Ramuri,* Craiova, Mar. 23, 1965.
2. *America & Alfred Stieglitz.* A collective portrait; several editors. N.Y., Doubleday, 1934.
3. Arensberg, Louise and Walter. *The Arensberg Collection,* Philadelphia Museum of Art, 1954.
4. Barr, Margaret Scolari. *Medardo Rosso.* N.Y., Museum of Modern Art, 1963.
5. Bénézit, E. *Dictionnaire des Peintres, Sculpteurs, Dessinateurs et Graveurs.* Paris, Gründ, 1949, Vol. 2.
6. Brancusi, Constantin. "Aphorisms," *Rumanian Literature,* XIX/1 (1965).
7. Brezianu, Barbu. "Relatiile lui Brancusi cu cultura vremii sale," an unpublished paper read at the centenary of the Rumanian Academy, Sept. 23, 1966.
8. —————. "Les Débuts de Brancusi," *Revue Roumaine d'Histoire de l'Art,* I/1 (1964), pp. 85–100.
9. —————. "Inceputurile lui Brancusi," *Secolul XX,* 3 (1964), pp. 145–69. (A version of the above.)
10. —————. "The Beginnings of Brancusi," *Art Journal,* XXV/1 (1965), pp. 15–25. (A version of the above.)
11. —————. "O statue de Brincusi," *Gazeta Literara,* Bucharest, Apr. 9, 1964.
12. —————."Pages inédites de la correspondance de Brancusi," *Revue Roumaine d'Histoire de l'Art,* I/2 (1964), pp. 385–400.
13. —————. "Iconografie brancusiana," *Tribuna,* Cluj, Feb. 24, 1966.
14. Brummer Gallery, N.Y. Catalogue of Brancusi exhibition, Nov. 17–Dec. 15, 1926.
15. —————. Catalogue of Brancusi exhibition, Nov. 17, 1933–Jan. 13, 1934.
16. Cabanne, Pierre. *L'Epopée du cubisme.* Paris, La Table Ronde, 1963.
17. Chelimsky, Oscar. "A Memoir of Brancusi," *Arts,* N.Y., 32/9 (June 1958), pp. 19–21.
18. Chirico, Giorgio de. *Memorie della Mia Vita.* Rome, Astrolabio, 1945.

19. Codreane, Irène. Aphorisms of Brancusi, *This Quarter*, 1/1, 1925, pp. 235–6.

20. Comarnescu, Petru. "Marturii despre Brancusi," *Gazeta Literara*, Bucharest, Aug. 6, 1964.

21. ──────────. "Desene de Brancusi din timpul studiilor in tara," *Tribuna*, Cluj, Oct. 20, 1964.

22. ──────────. "Fotografiile brancusiene din ultimele numere ale 'Tribunei,'" *Tribuna*, Cluj, May 11, 1967.

23. *Contimporanul*, no. 49 (1924).

24. Cooper, Douglas, "Portrait of a Genius But," *New York Review of Books*, Sept. 16, 1965. (A review of two books on Giacometti.)

25. Cummings, Fred J. A letter concerning an article by B. Brezianu (bibl. 8); *Art Journal*, XXV/3 (1966), p. 266.

26. Cutzescu-Storck, Cecilia. Extracts from an unpublished autobiography, *O Viata cu Pensula si Paleta in Mine*, 1961.

27. Dreyfus, Albert: "Brancusi," *Der Querschnitt*, III/3–4 (1923).

28. ──────────. "Brancusi," *Cahiers d'Art*, 2/2 (1927), pp. 69–75.

29. Duhamel, Georges. *Lumières sur ma vie*. Paris, Hartmann, 1947, vol. 3.

30. Epstein, Jacob. *Let There Be Sculpture*. N.Y., Putnam, 1940.

31. Foster, Jeanne Robert. Article on Brancusi, *New York Herald-Tribune*, Feb. 21, 1926.

32. Frachon, Renée Irana. An unpublished memoir, 1967.

33. Geist, Sidney. "Brancusi Catalogued?" *Arts*, N.Y., 38/4 (Jan. 1964), pp. 66–73. (A review of bibl. 46.)

34. ──────────. "Looking for Brancusi," *Arts*, N.Y., 39/1 (Oct. 1964), pp. 48–57.

35. ──────────. "O coloana la sfirsit," *Tribuna*, Cluj, Feb. 24, 1966.

36. ──────────. "Numai ochi," *Contemporanul*, Bucharest, Sept. 9, 1966.

37. Georgescu-Gorjan, Stefan. "The Genesis of the 'Column without End,'" *Revue Roumaine d'Histoire de l'Art*. I/2 (1964), pp. 279–93.

38. ──────────. "Biografia si perspectivele Coloanei infinite," *Ramuri*, Craiova, Dec. 30, 1964.

39. ──────────. "Marturii despre Brancusi," *Studii si Cercetari de Istoria Artei*, XII/1 (1965), pp. 65–74.

40. Giedion-Welcker, Carola. *Moderne Plastik*. Zurich, 1937.

41. ──────────. *Brancusi*, N.Y., Braziller, 1959.

42. Guilbert, Claire Gilles. "Propos de Brancusi," *Prisme des Arts*, 12 (1957), pp. 5–7.

43. Hamnett, Nina. *Laughing Torso*. N.Y., Long and Smith, 1932.

44. Hoffman, Malvina. *Sculpture Inside and Out*. N.Y., Norton, 1939.

45. Ionesco, Eugène. "Témoignages sur Brancusi," *Cahiers du Musée de Poche*, 3 (Dec. 1959), pp. 25–39.

46. Jianou, Ionel. *Brancusi*. N.Y., Tudor, 1963.

47. Jouffroy, Alain. *Brauner*. Paris, Ed. de Poche, 1959.
48. Kramer, Hilton. "Month in Review," *Arts*, N.Y., 31/10 (Sept. 1957), pp. 51-4.
49. ——————. "Reflections on Lachaise," *Arts Yearbook 4*, N.Y., 1961, pp. 97-100.
50. Kuhn, Walt. The Walt Kuhn Papers, Archives of American Art, Detroit. (Documents of the Armory Show on microfilm.)
51. Lafranchis, Jean. *Marcoussis*. Paris, Ed. du Temps, 1961.
52. Lebel, Robert. *Marcel Duchamp*. N.Y., Grove, 1959.
53. Liberman, Alexander. *The Artist in his Studio*. N.Y., Viking, 1960.
54. *The Little Review*, Brancusi number, Autumn 1921. (24 plates and an article by E. Pound, bibl. 71.)
55. ——————. May 1929.
56. *Luceafarul*, No. 49 (Nov. 1924).
57. M. M. "Constantin Brancusi: A Summary of Many Conversations," *The Arts*, IV/1 (July 1923).
58. *New York Herald*, Sept. 29, 1918.
59. *New York Herald-Tribune*, Feb. 28, 1926.
60. *New York Times*, Oct. 3, 1926.
61. ——————. Nov. 18, 1933.
62. Nicoara, Mircea. "Marturii despre Brancusi," *Tribuna*, Oradea, Nov. 21, 1963.
63. ——————. "Insemnari," *Familia*, Bucharest, Feb. 1966.
64. Niculescu, Remus. "Bourdelle et Anastase Simu," *Revue Roumaine d'Histoire de l'Art*, III (1966), pp. 39-87.
65. Paleolog, V.G. *C. Brancusi*. Bucharest, 1947. (In French.)
66. ——————. A series of occasional articles on Brancusi in *Inainte*, Craiova, beginning June 21, 1964, and continuing to the present.
67. ——————. " 'Cocosul' lui Brancusi," *Arta Plastica*, 4 (1966), p. 11.
68. Pandrea, Petre. *Portrete si controverse*. Bucharest, 1945, Vol. 1. (Pp. 95-173 on Brancusi.)
69. Patrascu, Militza. "Brancus," *Contimporanul*, no. 52 (Jan. 1925).
70. Portland Art Association. Sixty-seventh Annual Report, 1959, p. 2.
71. Pound, Ezra. "Brancusi," *The Little Review*, Autumn 1921, pp. 3-7.
72. ——————. *The Letters of Ezra Pound, 1907-1941*. Edited by D. D. Paige. N.Y., Harcourt, Brace, 1950.
73. Quinn, John. Catalogue of the John Quinn Collection. Huntington, N.Y., Pidgeon Hill Press, 1926. (Published posthumously.)
74. Ray, Man. *Self Portrait*. Boston, Little, Brown, 1963.
75. Robbins, Daniel. "From Symbolism to Cubism," *The Art Journal*, XXIII/2 (1963-64), pp. 111-116.
76. Roché, Henri Pierre. "L'Enterrement de Brancusi," *Hommage de*

la *Sculpture à Brancusi*, Paris, Ed. de Beaune, 1957, pp. 26–9.

77. —————. "Souvenirs sur Brancusi," *L'Oeil*, 29 (May 1957), pp. 12–7.
78. Salmon, André. *Henri Rousseau*. Paris, Crès, 1927.
79. Sanouillet, Michel. *Dada à Paris*. Paris, Pauvert, 1966.
80. Seligmann, Herbert J. *Alfred Stieglitz Talking*. New Haven, Yale Univ. Library, 1966.
81. Severini, Gino. *Tutta la vita di un pittore*. Cernusco sul Naviglio, Garzanti, 1946.
82. Spear, Athena Tacha. "A Contribution to Brancusi Chronology," *The Art Bulletin*, XLVIII/1 (Mar. 1966), pp. 45–54.
83. Tacha, Athena C. A review of *Brancusi* by I. Jianou (bibl. 46); *The Art Bulletin*, XLVI/2 (June 1964), pp. 260–6.
84. *This Quarter*, Spring 1925. (With an Art Supplement including 4 portraits of Brancusi, 5 drawings, 36 plates of works, aphorisms of Brancusi collected by Irène Codreane, and a tale, "Histoire de Brigands," written by Brancusi.)
85. U.S. Customs Court 3rd Div., Protest 209109-G. The record of the trial in New York, 1927–28.
86. *View*, VI/2–3 (Mar.–Apr. 1946), p. 17.
87. Waldberg, Patrick. *Jacques Hérold*. Chicago, Copley Foundation, 1961.
88. Wescott, Glenway. "Picasso, Matisse, Brancusi and Arthur Lee." *Vanity Fair*, June 1925.
89. Wilson, Angus. "A Visit to Brancusi's," *New York Times*, Aug. 19, 1923.
90. Zervos, Christian. *Constantin Brancusi*. Paris, Cahiers d'Art, 1957.
91. Zorach, William. "The Sculpture of Constantin Brancusi," *The Arts*, IX/3 (Mar. 1926), pp. 143–50.

The Rumanian articles in this bibliography, and others not listed, are deposited in the library of the Museum of Modern Art, New York. Correspondence of a documentary nature is deposited in the library of the Solomon R. Guggenheim Museum.

Index

Works by Brancusi are indexed by title; works by other artists are listed under their names. Page numbers in italics refer to illustrations. The bibliography, references to the bibliography, and addenda to the list of the sculptures are not indexed.

Abbaye de Créteil, 2, 141.
the absolute, 147, 155, 156, 157,181.
Adam, no. 105, *60*, 61, 79, 158.
Adam and Eve, no. 134, *78*, 79, 84, 94, 105, 142, 149, 158.
The Adolescent, no. 28a, *22*, 22.
African art, 45, 52, 149, 152, 190.
Agero, 150n.
ambiguity, 32, 42, 61, 76, 92.
Amsterdam, exhibition, 217.
Anatomy Study, no. 4, 12, *13*.
Ancient Figure, 30, *187*.
anti-Rodinism, 142–143.
Antonovici, Constantin, 204, 212, 226, 231.
the aphorism, 175.
Apollinaire, Guillaume, 3, 32, 149, 152; collection: *Naiade* (?), *32*.
Archipenko, Alexander, 140, 150, 150n.
Architectural Project, no. 107, *62*, *63*, 75, 145, 158, 164.
Arcos, René, 2n.
Arensberg, Louise and Walter C., 6; collection: *39* (no. 62), *40*, *42* (no. 69), *46* (no. 80), *48* (no. 84), *52*, *56*, *58*, *62* (no. 106), *82* (no. 141), *87*, *88*, *90* (no. 154), *109*. See Philadelphia Museum of Art.
Armory Show, 3, 169, 219.
Arnason, H. A., 184.

Arp, Jean, 144.
artistic evolution, 139.
Ault, Lee, collection: *Mlle. Pogany*, 70 (no. 119).
axis, 104, 152.

Bachelard, Gaston, 209, 210.
Bachelin, L., 219.
Bacot, Jacques, 148, 210.
Baltimore Museum of Art, the Cone Collection: Laurencin, *Group of Artists*, *188*.
Baroness R. F., no. 55, *33*, 33, 35.
Barr, Alfred H., Jr., 192.
Barzun, Henri-Martin, 2n.
Beginning of the World, no. 132, 77, *77*, 81, 92, 141, 162, 170.
Beginning of the World, no. 148, *86*, 86.
Bell, Clive, 2.
Bergson, Henri, 147.
Biju, Leon, 208.
biography, 156.
Bird, no. 69, *42*, 42, 47, 58.
Bird, no. 83, *47*, 47, 68, 169.
Bird, no. 133, *78*, 79, 85, 128.
Bird, William, 109n.
Bird in Space, no. 146, *85*, 85, 88, 89, 94, 95, 98, 103, 104, 116, 117, 129, 130, 132, 133, 150, 151, 155, 160, 172, 173; schematic drawing of, *195*.
Bird in Space, no. 150, *88*, 88, 89,

91, 101.
Bird in Space, no. 154, *90*, 91, 95, 130, 159, 163.
Bird in Space, no. 162, *95*, 95, 98, 99, 127, 128, 129.
Bird in Space, no. 163, 95, *96*, 99, 162.
Bird in Space, no. 165, 96, *97*, 113, 171.
Bird in Space, no. 166, *98*, 98, 99, 101, 127, 128.
Bird in Space, no. 169, 99, *100*.
Bird in Space, no. 170, 99, *100*, 127.
Bird in Space, no. 171, 99, *100*, 127.
Bird in Space, no. 185, 6, 7, 113, *114*, 128.
Bird in Space, no. 186, 6, 7, 113, *114*, 128.
Bird in Space, no. 196, *127*, 127.
Bird in Space, no. 197, *128*, 128.
Bird in Space, no. 198, 128, *129*.
Blond Negress, no. 167, *98*, 98, 102.
Blond Negress, no. 182, *110*, 111, 175.
Boccioni, Umberto, 66, 149, 150n.
Bollinger, Hans, 205.
Bouché, Louis, 207.
Boundary Marker, no. 202, 133, *134*, 176.
Brancusi, Constantin, assistants, 166, 203; portraits of, frontispiece, *187;* snapshot by, *194;* studios in Paris, frontispiece, *18, 167, 206; travels, 167, 178, 204; watercolor by, *203*.
Brancusi, Constantin, exhibitions: see Amsterdam; Armory Show; Brummer Gallery; Brussels; Bucharest; Gallery of the Photo-Secession; Galleries, Paris; London; Moscow; Prague; Salons, Paris; Société Anonyme; Society of Independent Artists; Wildenstein Galleries.
Brancusi, Constantin, quotations

from, 1, 2, 5, 5n, 6, 8, 21n, 38, 56, 57, 86, 109, 115, 126, 127, 129, 137, 141, 143, 144, 145, 146, 151, 152, 153, 154, 155, 156, 157, 160, 161, 164, 166, 168, 171, 178, 179, 180, 205.
Braque, Georges, 4, 149.
Brauner, Victor, 164.
Breton, André, 5, 151n.
Breuer, Marcel, 169n.
Brezianu, Barbu, 183, 204, 205, 208, 210, 214, 216, 217, 219, 223, 230.
Bronfman, Mrs. Samuel, collection: *Fish, 99* (no. 168a).
Brummer Gallery, exhibitions in, (1926) 5, 205; (1933) 6, *72, 112*, 113, 135, 172, 221, 224, 229.
Brussels, exhibition, 217.
Bucharest, exhibitions, 3; Tinerimea Artistica (1909), 216, (1914) 216.
Bucharest, Muzeul de Arta R. S. R., 7; see works illustrated *14* (no. 7), *20* (no. 23), *21* (no. 25), *23* (no. 32), *25, 29, 31* (no. 46).
Bucharest, Central Military Hospital, *Gen. Dr. Carol Davila, 16*.
Buckle, Richard, 198, 210.
Buffalo, Albright-Knox Art Gallery: *Mlle. Pogany*, 70 (no. 120).
Burden, William, collection: *Bird in Space, 128; Little Bird, 101*.
Bust of a Boy, no. 22, *20*, 20.
Bust of a Child, no. 45, *31*, 31.
Buzau, Rumania, 25; *Monument to Petre Stanescu, 185*.

Cambridge, Fogg Art Museum: *A Hand*, 76.
Caryatid, no. 89, 49, *50*, 142.
Caryatid, no. 90, *50*, 51, 66, 105, 149, 165, *198*.
Cendrars, Blaise, 3.

Character Study, no. 6, 13, *13*.
Chartier, restaurant owner, 214.
Chelimsky, Oscar, 208.
Chicago, Art Institute of Chicago, 7, 205; see works illustrated *35*, *46*, (no. 81), 77 (no. 131), *102*.
Chicago, Arts Club of Chicago: *Golden Bird, 69* (no. 117).
The Chief, no. 159, *93*, 93, 94, 104, 165, 176.
Child's Head, no. 44, *31*, 31.
Child's Head, no. 49, 32, 155.
Chimera, no. 106, 61, *62*, 83, 106.
Chirico, Giorgio de, 152.
Chitsu, Gheorghe, 208.
Clark, James, collection: *Beginning of the World*, 77 (no. 132).
Cleveland Museum of Art: *Torso of a Young Man, 59* (no. 101).
The Cock, no. 151, 88, *89*, 93, 94, 104, 106, 115, 131, 137, 159, 160, 176.
The Cock, no. 152, 89, *90*, 165.
The Cock, no. 153, 89, *90*.
The Cock, no. 187, *115*, 115.
The Cock, no. 203, *134*, 135.
The Cock, no. 204, 135, *136*, 161, 176.
Cocteau, Jean 3.
Codreane, Irène, 204, 211.
Coggeshall, Mrs. Calvert, 209, 227, 229.
Column of the Kiss, no. 184, 111, *112*, 121.
contingency, 157–158.
Cooper, Douglas, 169n.
Cosaceanu, Marguerite, 204.
Courty, Edmond, collection: Houdon, *L'Ecorché, 184.*
Cowles, John, collection: *Maiastra, 43* (no. 71).
Craiova, 1; Muzeul de Arta, see works illustrated *12* (no. 2), *19* (no. 20), *28* (no. 39), *32* (no. 51).
Csaky, Joseph, 140.

cubism, 3, 5, 52, 54, 101, 146, 149, 217.
Cummings, Paul, 204.
Cunard, Nancy, 93n; portraits, *94, 110.*
Cup, no. 109, *64*, 65, 73, 76, 79, 150, 160, 162, 175.
Cup, no. 110, *65*, 65.
Cup, no. 111, *65*, 65.
Cup, no. 112, *65*, 65.

Dada, 4, 5, 150.
Danaïde, no. 60, *37*, 37, 39, 41, 45, 54, 92, 142.
Danaïde, no. 73, *44*, 44.
Darascu, Nicolae, 21; portrait, *21*.
Davila, Gen. Dr. Carol, 15; portrait, *16*.
Davis, Richard S., collection: *Torment, 23.*
Derain, André, 140, 148.
Despiau, Charles, 140, 229.
direct carving, 161.
Donne, John, 80.
Dorazio, Piero, 204.
Double Caryatid, no. 41, *30*, 30, 31, 38, 44, 170, 176.
dream, 130, 150.
Dreier, Katherine S., 6.
Duchamp, Marcel, 164, 203.
Duchamp, Mrs. Marcel, 227; collection: *Portrait of Nancy Cunard, 94.*
Duchamp-Villon, Raymond, 140, 150, 150n; *The Lovers, 199.*
Duhamel, Georges, 2n.

economy, 57, 64, 154.
Ecorché, no. 8, *14*, 15, 203.
Eileen, no. 157, *92*, 92, 111, 145, 162.
Eisenberg, Mr. and Mrs. Malcolm, collection: *Sleeping Child, 31.*
Endless Column, no. 108, *64*, 64, 67, 150, 160, 163, 169, 170, 171, 172, 180.
Endless Column, no. 123, 71, *72*, 119.

Endless Column, no. 124, 73, 118.
Endless Column, no. 125, 71, 72.
Endless Column, no. 126, 71, 71,
    72, 75, 104, 159, 165.
Endless Column, no. 195, 6, 117,
    122–127, 123, 164, 175, 176, 205;
    erection of, 196.
Epstein, Jacob, 3, 5, 109n, 149;
    Maternity, 198; Sleeping Child,
    197; Sunflower, 198.
Epstein, Lady, collection: Epstein,
    Maternity, 198.
equilibrium, 57, 83, 105, 162–164.
essence, 144, 145, 146, 152, 170.
Exotic Plant, no. 128, 74, 75, 104.

Fabre d'Olivet, Antoine, 148.
Farquhar, George, 39, 44; portrait,
    39.
Farquhar, Mrs. George, 208, 219.
the Fauves, 142.
The First Step, no. 75, 44, 44, 52,
    59, 165.
The First Cry, no. 77, 45, 45, 48,
    55, 149, 152.
Fish, no. 141, 82, 82, 86, 91, 93, 98,
    106, 133, 163, 165, 170, 175.
Fish, no. 147, 86, 86.
Fish, no. 168a, 98, 99.
Fish, no. 168b, 98, 99.
Fish, no. 177, 106, 106, 108, 116,
    155, 165.
Flaubert, Gustave, 141.
Flying Turtle, no. 201, 7, 132, 133,
    155, 164, 165, 197.
Fondane, Benjamin, 146, 210, 211.
Forgas, Andrew, 190.
form, 180.
Foster, Jeanne Robert, 4.
Fotino-Morar, Mrs. Stanca, col-
    lection: Torment, 22.
Frachon, Baroness Renée Irana,
    33; portraits, 33 (nos. 53, 55),
    34.
Freundlich, Otto, 140.
futurism, 52, 149.

Gallatin, A. E., collection: Torso
    of a Girl, 82 (no. 140). See
    Philadelphia Museum of Art.
Gallery of the Photo-Secession,
    3, 169, 217, 218, 220.
Galleries, Paris: Galerie de la
    Boétie, 223; Galerie Georges
    Bernheim, 228.
Gargallo, Pablo, 140.
Gate of the Kiss, no. 194, 119, 121,
    123–127, 135, 143, 157, 165, 205,
    206.
Gaudier-Brzeska, Henri, 109n.
Gauguin, Paul, 142, 148.
Gen. Dr. Carol Davila, no. 9, 15,
    16.
Genghis Khan, 75.
geometry, 145, 153.
Georgeseu-Gorjan, Stefan, 122,
    183, 196, 202, 205, 230.
Gerota, Dr. Dimitrie, 15, 203.
Giacometti, Alberto, 178–179.
Gide, André, 147.
Giedion-Welckev, Carola, 230.
Gleizes, Albert, 2n.
Golden Bird, no. 117, 69, 69, 83.
Golden Bird, no. 118, 69, 69.
González, Julio, 3, 140.
Gorjan, Ion, 13; photograph of,
    183; portrait, 14.
Graham, Mrs. Philip, collection:
    Maiastra, 43 (no. 70b).
Greason, Donald C., 207.
Guggenheim, Miss Peggy, 230;
    collection: Bird in Space, 127;
    Maiastra, 43 (no. 72).
Gunzburg, Alain de, collection:
    Bird, 78.

A Hand, no. 130, 76, 142, 179.
Haret, Spiru, 47, 221.
Harvey, Anne, 5.
Head, no. 145, 85, 85.
Head of a Boy, no. 23, 20, 20.
Head of a Boy, no. 32, 23, 23, 175.
Head of First Step, no. 76, 45, 45.
Head of a Girl, no. 34, 24, 24, 30.

Head of a Girl, no. 38, *28*, 28, 37.
Head of a Girl, no. 42, *30*, 30, 40, 58.
Head of a Girl, no. 43, *31*, 31.
Head of a Woman, no. 16, *18*, 18.
Head of a Woman, no. 156, *92*, 92.
Head of a Young Woman, no. 15, *18*, 18.
Hérold, Jacques, 204.
Hirshhorn, Joseph H., 211; collection: *Prometheus, 39* (no. 63); *Sleeping Muse, 34;* Nadelman, *Head, 189.*
Hodes, Barnet, 212.
Hoffman, Malvina, 126n, 230.
Holkar, Maharajah, of Indore, 6, 113, 115, 201, 229.
Holty, Carl, 210.
Homer, 147.
Houdon, Jean–Antoine, *L'Ecorché*, 19, *184.*
Houston, Museum of Fine Arts: *A Muse, 59.*
Howard, Charles, 207.
Howard, Richard, 211.
Hulme, T. E., 210.
Hytier, Jean, 211.

Iancu, Marcel, 211.
illusion, 67, 87.
immediacy, 144, 146, 179.
influences, 148–151, 178.
Ingersoll, R. Sturgis, collection: *Little Bird, 94.*
intuition, 146.
Istrati, Alexandre, 204.
Istrati, Panaït, 147.

Jacob, Max, 3.
Jolas, Maria, 212.
joy, 143, 151–152, 180, 181.

Kahnweiler, D. H., 210.
Keller, Dr. Heinz, collection: *Sleeping Muse, 45* (no. 79).
Kessel, Sanda, 204.
Kierkegaard, Soren, 176, 212.

King of Kings, no. 127, 73, 74, 83, 84, 87, 104, 162, 175, 176.
Kirstein, Lincoln, 208.
The Kiss, no. 39, *28*, 28, 36, 37, 38, 46, 80, 131, 142, 155, 158, 162, 163, 172, 176.
The Kiss, no. 59, 8, *36*, 36, 37, 121, 133, 143, 148.
The Kiss, no. 65, *40*, 40, 54, 169.
The Kiss, no. 94, *54*, 54, 80.
The Kiss, no. 135, *80*, 80, 81, 92, 164.
The Kiss, no. 136, 80, *81*, 81, 92.
Kramer, Hilton, 175n, 177.

Lacasse, Joseph, 204.
Ladea, Romul, 204.
Lambert, Mrs. Phyllis, collection: *The Chief, 93.*
Lane, Eileen, 87, 204; portrait, *92.*
Laokoön Study, no. 1, *11*, 13, 22, 23.
Large Little Bird, no. 174, 102, *103.*
Laurencin, Marie, 32; *Group of Artists*, 32, *188; Self-portrait, 188.*
Laurens, Henri, 5, 140.
Leda, no. 131, 76, 77, 87, 104, 116, 117, 163, 174.
Leda, no. 158, 92, *93.*
Léger, Fernand, 3, 149.
Lehmbruck, Wilhelm, 140, 178.
Levin, Mr. and Mrs. Isadore, collection: *Head of a Woman*, *92.*
Lewis, Sally, 209.
Lewis, Wyndham, 109n.
Linard, Lucien, 2n.
Lipchitz, Jacques, 3, 140, 148.
Little Bird, no. 161, *94*, 94, 101, 103, 104.
Little Bird, no. 172, *101*, 101.
Little French Girl, no. 113, *66*, 66, 83, 176.
Little French Girl, no. 114, *66*, 67, 85.

The Little Review, 4, 94, 205, 209.
Lloyd, Mrs. H. Gates, collection:
  Sleeping Muse, 45 (no. 78).
London, exhibition, 3.
London, Tate Gallery, collection:
  Duchamp-Villon, The Lovers,
  199.
Lord, Lois, 211.

Mlle. Pogany, no. 67, 41, 41, 44,
  46, 54, 70, 76, 87, 104, 145, 148,
  152, 155, 162.
Mlle. Pogany, no. 74, 44, 44, 175.
Mlle. Pogany, no. 119, 69, 70, 109.
Mlle. Pogany, no. 120, 70, 70, 175.
Mlle. Pogany, no. 180, 109, 109.
Mlle. Pogany, no. 183, 110, 111,
  175.
Maiastra, no. 70a, 43, 43, 168.
Maiastra, no. 70b, 43, 43.
Maiastra, no. 71, 43, 43.
Maiastra, no. 72, 43, 43.
Male Nude, no. 5, 12, 13.
Manet, Edouard, 22.
Maremont, Arnold and Adele,
  collection: Blond Negress, 98.
Mars Borghese, no. 3, 12, 13.
Marx-Schoenborn Collection:
  Bird in Space, 85.
materials, 158–161.
Matisse, Henri, 3, 140, 149.
meaning, 145.
memory, 142, 161, 174.
Mercereau, Alexandre, 2n, 3.
Mercié, Antonin, 2, 24.
mesure, 124, 140, 171–172.
Meyer, Mrs. Eugene, Jr., 105n,
  229; collection: Bird in Space,
  96; Danaïde, 44; Portrait of
  Mrs. Eugene Meyer, Jr., 104;
  portraits, 104, 105.
Michelangelo, 152, 159, 179.
Milarepa, 7, 148.
Milian, Claudia, 230.
Mills, Mrs. Heyworth, 203.
Minneapolis Institute of Arts:
  Golden Bird, 69 (no. 118).

Model for Column of Gate, no.
  190, 119, 119.
Model for Gate of the Kiss, no.
  191, 119, 119.
modernism, 143, 160, 179.
Modigliani, Amedeo, 3, 28, 49,
  140, 148, 178, 203; Study for
  Caryatid, 193.
Mondrian, Piet, 139, 146, 171, 181.
the monoform, 87, 152.
Moore, Henry, 144.
Mortzun, Vasile, 221.
Moscow, exhibition, 227, 228.
movement, 80, 163, 173, 174.
Muller, Juana, 204.
A Muse, no. 66, 40, 41, 42, 48, 76,
  142, 152, 155.
A Muse, no. 102, 59, 59.
A Muse, no. 103, 59, 60.
A Muse, no. 104, 60, 61.

Nadelman, Elie, 35, 140, 148;
  Head, 189.
Naiade (?), no. 52, 32, 32.
Narcissus, no. 58, 35, 37, 39, 54.
Narcissus Fountain, no. 82, 47, 47,
  55, 108, 131, 150.
Nebraska, University of, collection: Princess X, 54.
necessity, 169.
New Haven, Yale University Art
  Gallery: Yellow Bird, 68.
New York, Museum of Modern
  Art, 7, 49, 205, 206, 210, 211,
  236; see works illustrated 30,
  38, 44 (no. 74), 49 (no. 87),
  84, 89, 100 (no. 171), 106, 110
  (no. 182); Laurencin, Self-
  portrait, 188.
New York, Solomon R. Guggenheim Museum, 7, 206, 215, 218,
  219, 221, 224, 227, 228, 229, 231,
  236; see works illustrated 39
  (no. 64), 41 (no. 66), 57, 60
  (no. 105), 66 (no. 113), 74 (no.
  127), 78 (no. 134), 117, 133.

The Newborn, no. 84, *48,* 48, 52,
  66, 81, 104, 152, 155.
The Newborn, no. 87, 48, *49,* 55.
The Newborn, no. 121, 70, 70.
The Newborn, no. 122, *71,* 71.
Nocturnal Animal, no. 178, *107,*
  107, 108, 132, 163.
Noguchi, Isamu, 204.
number, 171.

the object, 35, 38, 45, 59, 65, 76,
  145, 146, 178.
objectivity, 177–178.
Olivier, Fernande, 32.
orientation, spatial, 82, 132.
Orloff, Chana, 140.

Pach, Walter, 3.
Paleolog, Vasile G., 7, 177, 199,
  212, 215.
Pandrea, Petre, 211, 212.
Paris, Cimetière Montparnasse,
  The Kiss, 36.
Paris, Musée Guimet, 148.
Paris, Musée du Louvre, 13, 148.
Paris, Musée du Luxembourg, 148.
Paris, Musée National d'Art Moderne, 63, 167, 211, 221, 227,
  230; see works illustrated *45*
  (no. 76), *47* (nos. 82, 83), *48*
  (no. 85), *49* (nos. 86, 88), *53*
  (no. 92), *54* (no. 94), *64* (no.
  109), *65, 71, 72,* 74 (no. 128),
  75, 80, 81 (nos. 136–138), *85*
  (no. 144), *86* (no. 148), *90*
  (nos. 152, 153), *91, 92* (no.
  157), *93* (no. 158), *96* (no.
  164), *103, 105, 107, 108, 110*
  (no. 183), *112, 115, 118, 119*
  (no. 190), *129, 131, 132, 134,*
  136.
Pasarea Maiastra, no. 61, 37, *38,*
  43, 44, 45, 47, 58, 128, 160, 162,
  168, 169, 170, 175, *192.*
Patrascu, Militza, 127, 164, 203,
  211.
the pedestal, 168–170.

Penguin Club, 5.
Penteado, Mme. Yolanda, collection: *Head, 85; Sleeping Child,*
  32.
perfection, 155–156.
Petermann, K., collection: *Torso,*
  42.
Philadelphia Museum of Art, see
  works illustrated *39* (no. 62),
  40, 41 (no. 67), *42* (no. 69),
  46 (no. 80), *48* (no. 84), *52,*
  56, 58, 62 (no. 106), *82, 87,*
  88, 90 (no. 154), *109;* Pogany,
  Self-portrait, 189.
photography, 164–165.
Picabia, Francis, 151n.
Picasso, Pablo, 3, 4n, 8, 32, 66,
  140, 149.
Plaster Form, no. 179, *108,* 108,
  132, 163.
Plato, 37, 84, 147.
Pogany, Margit, 37, 41, 42, 92;
  memoir by, 190–192; photograph of, *190;* portraits, 37, *41,*
  70, *109; Self-portrait, 189.*
Poincaré, Henri, 148.
polish, 154–155, 157, 160, 163, 180.
Popp, Victor N., 3.
Portland (Ore.) Art Museum:
  A Muse, 60 (no. 103).
Portrait, no. 92, 52, *53,* 79.
Portrait of a Concierge, no. 10,
  16, 17.
*Portrait of Dr. Zaharie Samfi-
  rescu,* no. 11, *16,* 17.
Portrait of George, no. 64, *39,* 39,
  46, 59, 152.
Portrait of G. Lupescu, no. 24, *20,*
  20.
Portrait of Ion Gorjan, no. 7, 13,
  14.
Portrait of Mme. L. R., no. 93,
  53, 53, 58, 63, 66, 79, 83, 84,
  106.
Portrait of a Man, no. 26, *21,* 21.
Portrait of a Man with a Goatee,
  no. 18, *18,* 18.

Portrait of Mrs. Eugene Meyer, Jr., no. 175, 103, *104*, 107, 145, 155, 160, 163.
Portrait of Mrs. Victoria Vaschide, no. 14, *16*, 17.
Portrait of Nancy Cunard, no. 160, 93, *94*, 103, 104, 105, 111, 145.
Portrait of Nancy Cunard, no. 181, *110*, 111.
Portrait of Nicolae Darascu, no. 25, 20, *21*, 22, 139.
Portrait of Petre Stanescu, no. 37, 27, 27, 139, 169; detail of, *186*.
Portrait of a Restaurant Owner, no. 13, *16*, 17.
Portrait of a Waiter, no. 12, *16*, 17.
Portrait of a Woman, no. 17, *18*, 18.
Portrait of a Woman, no. 35, *24*, 24, 27.
Portrait of a Young Woman, no. 33, *24*, 24.
Pound, Ezra, 4, 79, 109n.
Power, E. John, collection: *Fish*, *99* (no. 168b).
Prague, exhibition, 3, 217.
The Prayer, no. 36, 2, 8, *25*, 25, 27, 32, 33, 47, 58, 67, 89, 140, 142, 162, 169; detail of, *185*.
presence, 173.
Pride, no. 20, 18, *19*, 22, 175.
primitivism, 140, 141, 142.
Princess X, no. 96, *54*, 54.
Princess X, no. 97, *55*, *56*.
The Prodigal Son, no. 91, *52*, 52, 58, 104, 142, 149, 152, 176.
Prometheus, no. 62, 38, *39*, 152.
Prometheus, no. 63, *39*, 39, 55.
proportion—see *mesure*.

Quinn, John, 3, 4, 5, 6, 169, 219, 220, 221, 222, 224, 225, 226.

Rabelais, 147.
Rachewsky, Tatiana, 36n.

Radiguet, Raymond, 4, 204.
rationality, rationalization, 56, 143, 144, 145, 181.
Ray, Man, 164.
The Redskins, no. 28, *22*, 22, 141.
reductiveness, 86, 141.
Reich, Wilhelm, 162.
Renan, Ernest, 147.
Repose, no. 29, *22*, 22, 31.
revelation 147, 161.
Rewald, John, 211.
Reynolds, Mary, 164.
Roché, Mme. Denise, 194, 207, 208, 222; collection: *Torso of a Young Woman*, 67.
Roché, Henri Pierre, 4, 8, 56, 77, 113, 194, 221, 222.
Rodin, Auguste, 2, 5, 24, 25, 31, 32, 49, 76, 139, 140, 141, 142, 143, 148, 154, 174, 179.
Rosenberg, Mme. Léonce, 53.
Rosso, Medardo, 23, 148; *Ecce Puer*, 23, *184*.
Rothschild, Herbert and Nannette, collection: *A Muse*, *60* (no. 104).
Rothschild, Philippe de, collection: *Bird in Space*, *100* (no. 170).
Rousseau, Henri, 3, 142.
Rubinstein, Helena, Prix, 5.
Rumanian art and folklore, 38, 125, 148, 149, *193*.

Salmon, André, 231.
Salons, Paris, (1906) 2, 23, 148, 214, 215; (1907) 22, 25, 206, 214, 215, 216; (1908) 215; (1910) 216; (1912) 219; (1913) 150, 219; (1919) 150; (1920) 4, 56; (1926) 227; (1927) 206, 227; (1928) 206; (1933) 229.
Santayana, George, 160, 211.
Satie, Erik, 4, 5, 66, 84, 141, 142, 150, 174; *Self-portrait*, *199*.
Scaravaglione, Concetta, 211.
Schinman Collection: Epstein,

Sunflower, *198.*
Schreiber, Taft B., collection:
    Bird in Space, 100 (no. 169).
Sculpture for the Blind, no. 98,
    56, 56, 77, 79, 87, 162.
Sculpture for the Blind, no. 164,
    96, 96, 171.
The Seal, no. 188, 115, *117,* 130,
    155, 163, 174, 175; schematic
    drawing of, *195.*
The Seal, no. 199, 130, *131.*
Section d'Or, 223.
series, 91, 175–176.
Seurat, Georges, 170.
Severini, Gino, 150n.
Shattuck, Roger, 150, 209, 210.
simplicity, 141, 143, 145.
Simu, Anastase, 217.
Sisler, Mrs. William, collection:
    Endless Column, 64.
Sleep, no. 46, *31,* 31, 142, 176.
Sleeping Child, no. 47, *31,* 31, 81,
    197.
Sleeping Child, no. 48, 31.
Sleeping Child, no. 50, *32,* 32.
Sleeping Child, no. 137, *81,* 81.
Sleeping Child, no. 138, *81,* 81.
Sleeping Muse, no. 56, *34,* 34, 39,
    40, 142, 145, 152, 162, 175.
Sleeping Muse, no. 57, *35,* 35, 175.
Sleeping Muse, no. 78, *45,* 45.
Sleeping Muse, no. 79, *45,* 45.
Société Anonyme, 6, 223.
Society of Independent Artists,
    222.
Socrates, 84.
Socrates, no. 143, 83, *84,* 105, 106,
    150, 176.
The Sorceress, no. 99, *57,* 57, 58,
    63, 83, 89, 106, 152, 159, 165,
    169, 176.
space, 172–173.
Spaventa, George, 211.
Spear, Mrs. Athena Tacha, 177.
Staempfli, Samuel, collection:
    Self-portrait at the Anvil,
    watercolor, *203.*

Staempfli Gallery: *Caryatid, 50*
    (no. 90).
Stafford, Frederick, collection:
    Portrait of Nancy Cunard,
    110.
Stanescu, Petre, 25; monument,
    185; portrait, *27;* portrait, de-
    tail, *186.*
Steichen, Edward, 71, 159, 219,
    223, 224, 229.
Steichen, Mrs. Edward, collec-
    tion: *Bird in Space, 98.*
Steichen, Kate R., collection:
    Maiastra, 43 (no. 70a).
Stein, Gertrude, 4n, 141, 209.
Stieglitz, Alfred, 3, 52, 156, 205.
Stockholm, Moderna Museet:
    The Newborn, 70 (no. 121).
Stoenescu, Dan, 211.
Storck, Frederic, 204, 208, 210,
    212.
the studio, 167.
Study for Bird in Space, no. 142,
    83, 83, 85.
Study of a Boy, no. 27, *21,* 21, 22.
Study for Column of the Kiss,
    no. 95, *54,* 54, 113, 121.
Study for Endless Column, no.
    189, 117, *118.*
Study for a Figure, no. 85, *48,*
    48, 66.
Study for a Head, no. 86, 48, *49.*
Study after Houdon, no. 21, *19,*
    19.
Study for Portrait of Mrs. Meyer,
    no. 176, *105,* 105, 160, 165.
Study for Pride, no. 19, *18,* 18,
    19, 29.
Study of Renée, no. 53, *33,* 33.
surface, 25, 27, 176.
surrealism, 150.
Sutherland, Donald, 209.
Sweeney, James Johnson, 231.
symmetry, 92, 104, 106, 116.

Table, no. 192, *124,* 124.
Table of Silence, no. 193, 119, *120,*

245

123–127, 158, 205, 206.
tact, 139, 173.
tactility, 56, 77, 161–162.
"Temple of Love," 108, 109n, 113, 119, 149.
"Temple of Meditation," 113, 119, *195*, 205.
This Quarter, 4.
Three Penquins, no. 80, *46*, 46, 54, 149, 152, 176.
time, 141, 142, 172, 173.
Timidity, no. 88, *49*, 49, 106, 176.
Tirgu Jiu, Rumania, 1, 6, 117, 119, 124, 127, 145, 158, 164, 170, 175, *202*, 205, 206; see works illustrated *120, 121, 123, 124*.
Tiwary, H., 208.
Torment, no. 30, *22*, 22, 24, 139, 175.
Torment, no. 31, *23*, 23.
Torso, no. 51, *32*, 32, 67, 159.
Torso, no. 68, *42*, 42, 67.
Torso of a Girl, no. 139, *81*, 81, 87, 94, 131, 162, 176.
Torso of a Girl, no. 140, *82*, 82.
Torso of a Girl, no. 155, *91*, 91.
Torso of a Young Man, no. 100, *58*, 58, 104, 131, 145, 159, 175.
Torso of a Young Man, no. 101, *59*, 59, 61.
Torso of a Young Man, no. 144, 84, *85*, 92.
Torso of a Young Woman, no. 115, *67*, 67, 81, 169, 175.
the transatlantic review, 4.
transcendance, 178.
The Turtle, no. 200, 7, 131, *132*, 159.
Two Penguins, no. 81, *46*, 46, 54, 149, 152, 176.
Tzara, Tristan, 5.

Udriste, Elena, 208.
unity, 152.
Usha Devi, Maharani, collection: *Bird in Space*, nos. 185, 186, *114*.

U. S. Customs Office, 5.

Valéry, Paul, 156.
variety, 176–177.
Vaschide, Mrs. Victoria, 24; portrait, *24*.
Vase, no. 129, *75*, 75.
Vildrac, Charles, 2n.
Villon, Jacques, 223.
Vitelius, no. 2, 11, *12*, 15.
Vitellius, Emperor, 11; portraits, *12*, *183*.

ex Wade, Jane, Ltd.: *The First Cry*, *45*.
Wagner, Richard, 141, 156.
West Palm Beach, Norton Gallery and School of Art, collection: Modigliani, *Study for Caryatid*, *193*.
White Negress, no. 149, *87*, 87, 93, 98, 102, 104, 145, 155, 162, 175.
White Negress, no. 173, *102*, 102.
Wilde, Oscar, memorial, 3.
Wildenstein Galleries, 5, 205.
Winston, Mr. and Mrs. Harry L., collection: Rosso, *Ecce Puer*, *184*.
The Wisdom of the Earth, no. 40, *29*, 29, 36, 37, 148, 155, 158, 162.
Woman Looking into a Mirror, no. 54, *33*, 33, 34, 47, 54.
work habits, 166, 171, 191.
ex World House Galleries: *Bust of a Boy*, *20*.

Yellow Bird, no. 116, *68*, 68, 79, 150, 163.

Zadkine, Ossip, 140.
Zarate, Ortiz de, 3.
Zorach, William, 5.
Zurich, Kunsthaus: *Bird in Space*, *95*.

Addendum

As this book was going to press the author learned of the location of *Bird in Space*, no. 184a, which had long disappeared from view. The photograph and the information below were kindly supplied by Lorenz Eitner, chairman of the Department of Art and Architecture of Stanford University, Stanford, California, where the work was on display. Its measurements have been integrated with the tables in Appendix 23.

184a. Bird in Space
73 1/16"; polished bronze; before 1933
Richard Holkar, Dallas, Texas; ex Maharaja Holkar of Indore

Erratum

Bust of a Child, no. 45 in this list and in the text, page 31, is not in its correct position. It should be between nos. 23 and 31.

This book is set in Janson,
the display type is Folio.
Composed and printed
by Connecticut Printers,
Hartford, Conn.
Technique by Ray Fudjinski.
Designed by the author.